Empire and Pilgrimage in Conrad and Joyce

The Florida James Joyce Series

UNIVERSITY PRESS OF FLORIDA

Florida A&M University, Tallahassee
Florida Atlantic University, Boca Raton
Florida Gulf Coast University, Ft. Myers
Florida International University, Miami
Florida State University, Tallahassee
New College of Florida, Sarasota
University of Central Florida, Orlando
University of Florida, Gainesville
University of North Florida, Jacksonville
University of South Florida, Tampa
University of West Florida, Pensacola

EMPIRE AND PILGRIMAGE IN CONRAD AND JOYCE

Agata Szczeszak-Brewer

Foreword by Sebastian D. G. Knowles

University Press of Florida
Gainesville · Tallahassee · Tampa · Boca Raton
Pensacola · Orlando · Miami · Jacksonville · Ft. Myers · Sarasota

22 21 20 19 18 17   6 5 4 3 2 1

First cloth printing, 2011
First paperback printing, 2017

LIBRARY OF CONGRESS CATALOGING-IN-PUBLICATION DATA
Szczeszak-Brewer, Agata.
Empire and pilgrimage in Conrad and Joyce / Agata Szczeszak-Brewer ;
foreword by Sebastian D. G. Knowles.
p. cm.—(The Florida James Joyce series)
Includes bibliographical references and index.
ISBN 978-0-8130-3539-0 (cloth: alk. paper)
ISBN 978-0-8130-5464-3 (pbk.)
1. Joyce, James, 1882–1941—Criticism and interpretation. 2. Conrad, Joseph,
1857–1924—Criticism and interpretation. 3. Imperialism in literature.
4. Pilgrims and pilgrimages in literature. I. Title.
PR6019.O9Z825 2010
823.'912—dc22
2010020782

The University Press of Florida is the scholarly publishing agency for the State
University System of Florida, comprising Florida A&M University, Florida
Atlantic University, Florida Gulf Coast University, Florida International
University, Florida State University, New College of Florida, University of
Central Florida, University of Florida, University of North Florida, University
of South Florida, and University of West Florida.

University Press of Florida
15 Northwest 15th Street
Gainesville, FL 32611-2079
http://upress.ufl.edu

In memory of Izabela and Wincenty Stelmaczonek

Contents

Foreword

Conrad and Joyce: I like to think of them as Corley and Lenehan in "Two Mandarins," an imaginary short story from a lost collection called *Modernists* (which also features D. H. Lawrence as Bob Doran, W. B. Yeats as Little Chandler, and T. S. Eliot as Gabriel Conroy). In that story, the two unlikely companions wander through the turn-of-the-century universe, maddeningly unclear in their discourse and intentions, searching for a transcendence to which they are both pathologically averse. It is Agata Szczeszak-Brewer's great achievement that she can see through her authors' smokescreens, can tolerate their paradoxes and hypocrisies, and can flick them into focus with a clear and dispassionate eye. Szczeszak-Brewer marches them up the hill, through a subtle and sympathetic reading of Conrad's teleological and hegemonic ambitions, and marches them down again, through a freewheeling engagement with Joyce's subversive attitudes to the colonialist enterprise. The resulting dyad gives us Conrad and Joyce as a combined Penelope figure, first weaving (Joseph Conrad, conquering the day) and then unweaving (James Joyce, unconquering the night). By considering the characters in Joyce and Conrad's work together, we now see that Don John Conmee and Inspector Heat are cut from the same cloth, as are, from a more variegated bolt, the Harlequin and Buck Mulligan. Dedalus has a marked resemblance to Decoud; Leopold Bloom and Nostromo share, in their stealth and circularity, the habits of the *flâneur*. We now understand how "The Dead" shares a swooning uncertainty with *Lord Jim*, and why the most important thing about the first part of *Ulysses* is that it ends, as *Heart of Darkness* begins, with a ship.

Above all, Szczeszak-Brewer has provided depth and balance for the outward odysseys of all the journeyers in Joyce and Conrad, and by extension, of all the pilgrims in modernism from Rachel Vinrace to the fisherman of "What the Thunder Said": each outward journey now has its inward counterpart, a voyage in every way the equal of the journey in the world. The act of colonialization has been internalized, with deep and useful results. Conrad and Joyce, through the work of this important study, have been shown to be two things of opposite natures depending on one another, as the imagined on the real. To be able to bring such opposites together requires art as well as scholarship: *Empire and Pilgrimage in Conrad and Joyce* is a work of both clarity and grace.

Sebastian D. G. Knowles
Series Editor

Acknowledgments

I am deeply indebted to Thomas Jackson Rice, my mentor and friend, for invaluable insight, motivation, and an example of exceptional scholarship. Sebastian Knowles gave me useful suggestions and asked challenging questions, as did Georgia Johnston and the anonymous reviewer of the manuscript. I am also grateful to other people who have been generous readers and commented on all or some parts of the manuscript: Kevin Dettmar, Meili Steele, Kevin Lewis, Ed Madden, Jeanne Garane, Julia Levin, Sarah Allen, Warren Rosenberg, Crystal Benedicks, Robert Royalty, and David Blix. My thanks go to Wiesław Krajka for scholarly guidance when this project was in its infancy and to my mother, Maria Szczeszak, for my first lessons in English.

I wish to thank several organizations and fellowships for their generous support of my research. The National Endowment for the Humanities awarded me a stipend to participate in the summer 2007 seminar on *Ulysses* at Trinity College, Dublin. I would like to thank the seminar's participants for inspiration and encouragement. My thanks also go to the Wabash College Dean's Office, the English Department, and the college's Faculty Development Fund as well as its Byron K. Trippet research fund. I also received support from the Newberry Library in Chicago, the National Library of Ireland, and Trinity College Library, and travel grants from the International James Joyce Foundation and the Joseph Conrad Society of America. The Rotary Foundation Scholarship for International Ambassadorial Scholars provided very generous funding for the first two years of my research.

Chapter 5 is an expanded and revised version of "Conrad, Joyce, and the Development of Urban Psychological Cartographies," an essay published in *Beyond the Roots: The Evolution of Conrad's Ideology and Art,* edited by Wiesław Krajka (New York: Columbia University Press, 2005).

Portions of chapter 6 appeared in "Teleology without a Telos? Constitutive Absence in James Joyce's Pilgrimage" in *Displacing the Center: Pilgrimage in a Mobile World*, edited by Simon Coleman and John Eade, special issue of *Mobilities* 2 (November 2007): 347–62. I wish to thank the editors of these volumes for their kind permissions to reprint sections of my articles in this book.

Above all, I would like to thank my husband, Josh Brewer, for his unconditional love, scholarly advice, and enormous patience, and my son, Kuba, for putting all my worries about commas and square brackets into perspective.

Introduction

Cartographers and Pilgrims

Mapping the Void

Colonial conquest has always relied on territorial representations—map-making and charting of new itineraries—but also on skillful interpretation of gathered data. In order to claim, appropriate, and exploit new land, European powers sent out explorers, land surveyors, and other "readers" of foreign landscapes who had to tame the real into the symbolic, the representational. Literary criticism employs similar tactics. Frank Budgen comments on his familiarity with James Joyce's *Work in Progress* by emphasizing that Joyce records his thoughts "as one who has visited a foreign country not yet on Baedeker's list—not as an authoritative guide but as a traveller with sufficient sensibility, sufficient power of observation to record an impression that may encourage the adventurous to risk a more extended visit to the same shores" (284). Joseph Conrad and James Joyce were themselves fascinated with maps, one by blank, unexplored spaces on them, the other by the possibility of re-creating cityscapes in fiction. One writes about the color-coded map of the British Empire, with its ever-present red ink marking the conquered territory; the other composes the "Wandering Rocks" chapter "with compass and slide rule, a surveyor with theodolite and measuring chain or, more Ulyssean perhaps, a ship's officer taking the sun, reading the log and calculating current drift and leeway" (Budgen 121), tracing "in red ink the paths of Earl Dudley and Father Conmee" (122).

Can one and should one superimpose the trajectories of Joyce's characters in colonial Dublin upon a map of imperial conquests in Africa? Can one compare King Leopold's insatiable quest for rubber and ivory in the Congo and the European missionary zeal in Africa to Dublin's erratic, solemn, anxious, drunken, limping walkers? After all, the Congo and other non-European colonized spaces are linguistically and ethnically different from the "second city of the British Empire," a city under the panoptic control of the towering Nelson, an imposing reminder of the walkers' subaltern status. Joyce's red-inked paths of Lord Dudley and Father Conmee, "Christ and Caesar . . . not in conflict—only in opposition" (Budgen 121) might echo to a certain extent Conrad's portrayal of the imperial fervor as inextricable from a self-congratulatory missionary project of one kind or another. What does this possible crisscrossing of different paths, goals, and narratives tell us about humanity or—in a narrower sense—about, say, one character's need for fulfillment in a place demarcated by impermeable borders, colors on the map representing colonial possessions, and ethnic allegiances? After all, Eavan Boland has already told us that "the science of cartography is limited" because

the line which says woodland and cries hunger
and gives out among sweet pine and cypress,
and finds no horizon

will not be there. (25–28)

Although most think of cartography as a science of image-making, rendering the Earth on a flat surface, it is—as the etymology of the word suggests—also an act of map writing. In Greek, *chartis* means "a map," and *graphein* is "to write." Could we then assume that writing about an infamous Belgian colony, an imaginary republic in Central America, or an island struggling to emerge from centuries of British oppression—the *map writing* of the psychology and teleology of both the colonizer and the colonized—is doomed to failure as well? Boland's famine roads witnessed suffering beyond cartographic representation, but the poet is here to remind us about that which goes unnoticed in traditional spatial images. So is Conrad, with his disturbing account of groves of death filled with emaciated bodies of Congolese slaves, unmarked on any official maps of the empire, and so is Joyce, who calls to life the ghosts of church- and colonial oppression—an interpellative power absent from cartographic representations of Ireland.

Empire and Pilgrimage investigates the ways in which two male modernist expatriates, a generation apart, respond to various pressures within this endeavor to chart spaces of power and oppression, and—not entirely incidentally—within modernism. Conrad and Joyce explore the motives and results of colonial domination and the paths chosen by those who are—willingly or not—implicated in the enterprise. Inherent in spatial and temporal representations of their late-colonial modernist pathfinders, or pilgrims, are tensions between the sacred and the profane, order and chaos, hierarchical dualisms and linear movement. What happens when Conrad and Joyce, following seemingly incongruous aesthetic and thematic interests, grapple with the same questions of paralyzing grand narratives, hegemonic practices, and an individual's quest for unencumbered self-definition and expression? How do they approach the issues of political coercion and individual freedom in their "map writing" of the empire and its subjects' trajectories within it?

Anthropologists tell us that archaic societies organized space around one focal site, the sacred center. Whether a pillar or temple, it was the *omphalos*, the navel of the universe and the only *real* place. The sacred center was static. It organized space, providing a landmark for travelers and seekers; or—as Michel de Certeau reminds us—it was a way to guard the real space against the bewitched Other (*Practice* 36). In Jewish and Christian ideologies of the ancient world, the sacred center acquired new metaphorical meanings: it was Yahweh, the Temple, Jesus, even the Apocalypse itself; and thus in Judeo-Christian traditions, it acquired a teleology. But what happens when this center no longer provides meaning? What or who organizes our conception of space, order, telos?

Both Conrad and Joyce, situated within the colonial and late-colonial milieu, rejected formal religion and yet remained supersaturated with it. Although this book recognizes numerous parallels between these authors' political and religious formations, the main focus of this study is the way in which Conrad and Joyce expose and often complicate numerous dichotomies in the official discourse constructed and owned by the Western hegemonic establishment, including the distinction between the sacred and the profane. They expose the appropriation of conveniently divisive categories in the imperial practice, and recognize the danger of transforming dismantled discourse of oppression into other prescriptive narratives, such as revolutions and mythologies of fledgling nations.

A part of my inquiry concerns the inherent relationship between imperialism and the atavistic drive toward the sacred: a connection present in
Conrad's and Joyce's fiction pointing to and often subverting traditional,
arbitrary binaries. This dichotomy comes from a conviction that the West
is the epistemic and epistemological center of the world. The cosmogonic
myth is a way to explain re-ordering of "chaos" according to familiar laws
of the "center." Such an axiom is expedient in producing and maintaining
prejudice against and fear of the other. We see this false assumption at
work in Kurtz's projects, first to "enlighten" the people of the Congo, and
then to exterminate them, but also in Mr Gould's worship of "material
interests" (*Nostromo* 170) and Jim's proud self-creation in Patusan. Joyce
reveals the same hypocrisy, if more subtly, in Lord Dudley's cavalcade or
Haines's anthropological interest in Irish folklore, but he further compli-
cates and destabilizes the contrived dichotomy of the sacred and the profane, the colonizer and the colonized, self and other. Stephen's desire to fly
by the nets of the sacred is not at all a simple need to free himself from colonial oppression; the citizen's chauvinistic rant mirrors the imperial rhetoric he is fighting against; Bloom's unsettling presence in Catholic Dublin
upsets simple categories of nation, race, and even gender. Both Conrad
and Joyce, unlike many Anglophone authors before them, react against
narrow and biased definitions of nation, the sacred, and other categories
that created societies split along the lines of race and/or ethnicity.

Such a fragmented world is not hospitable to those who search for self-
definition or a private center, regardless of their status within the imperial enterprise. The narrators and characters in Conrad's and Joyce's texts
attempt to negotiate the realm of the profane, traditionally associated
with alterity, disorder, incompletion, and inarticulation, through literal
and metaphorical forms of pilgrimage. This book will grapple with the
possibility of a successful teleological project in Conrad's and Joyce's fiction. What are the conditions for self-definition in a colonial setting? Do
Conrad and Joyce offer any alternatives to the world of rigid demarcations? Why are so many of their characters, including Marlow, Stephen,
and Bloom, eager to embrace uncertainty and nebulous boundaries? Is
this a successful strategy in transgressing the official discourse?

Conrad's and Joyce's educations must have exposed them to a variety
of cosmogonic myths; the contents of their private libraries attest to this.
In the beginning was the word. The great water. Chaos. Void. Then the
ordering process began, often resulting in a clear separation of the sacred

and the profane. One way to reach the sacred was through pilgrimage, movement toward the center, something young Józef and James certainly learned in their Catholic households, if not at school. What their texts imply is that both cosmogony and pilgrimage are means of acquiring control over space. Colonial reenactments of the cosmogonic myth strive to achieve this control through racial or racist spatialization, that is, through the division between the "proper" white and the "improper" black. Pilgrimage, however, may become an endeavor to define one's self irrespective of that compartmentalizing enterprise and to transform the traditionally understood categories of "proper" and "improper," sacred and profane. The characters in Conrad's and Joyce's fiction are not traditional walkers. They take on new, often subversive roles that mirror Zygmunt Bauman's modern and postmodern traveler types: the stroller, the vagabond, the tourist, and the player. Are they successful in their transgression of communal coercion and colonial, patriarchal limitations, the invisible lines erased from conventional maps?

The displacement and fragmentation typical of the colonial milieu necessitate profound changes in the pilgrim's tactics. To define oneself in the hegemonic matrix, one has to employ makeshift maneuvers to either challenge or evade inflexible boundaries. This book also engages in a broader argument concerning power relations and the mostly metaphorically understood quest. In Conrad, individual and collective "pilgrimaging" is a continually unaccomplished desire for a relief from the profane world of uncertainty, alienation, and subordination. It is also a way to affirm one's power. And yet it is Marlow who insists that truth does not lie in precise definitions, not "inside of a kernel but outside, enveloping the tale which brought it out only as a glow brings out a haze, in the likeness of one of these misty halos that sometimes are made visible by the spectral illumination of moonshine" (*Heart of Darkness* 48). Joyce also portrays pilgrim figures whose quest departs from the traditional forms of breaking out from the realm of the profane—his strollers, vagabonds, tourists, and players navigate their ways through the colonial setting. What price do Conrad's and Joyce's characters pay for traveling in the fragmented milieu? How do they react to the frustrating mobility of the telos?

David Adams notes in his *Colonial Odysseys* that modernist narratives of literal and figurative passage are "often distracted from geopolitical phenomena they seem to represent" (2) since they displace the self onto an imaginary, exotic plane. Adams claims that the emphasis of such narratives is on the redemptive voyage out (following Woolf's title), and that the desired redemption comes from what Blumenberg calls reoccupation (72). Focusing mainly on Conrad and rather marginally on Woolf, this very fine study nevertheless opens up a series of questions. Although modernist narratives never depict a triumphant homecoming, aren't their characters constantly aware of "home," in a political as much as private sense? Don't they travel *in* as much as out, *toward* as much as away from? Is the modernist "melancholy drive toward death" (4) also true about Stephen in *Portrait*, even when he prepares to separate himself from his nation, the perilous dyad severed?[1]

Although the subject of Adams's book is the reemergence of the odyssey narrative within modernist British texts (Conrad's and Woolf's primarily), the god-shaped void at the core of his argument denotes the absence of a markedly Christian God. It seems to me that the foundation of this not exclusively modernist or even modern anxiety is the need for the sacred in general, a desire that predates and generates worship, doctrine, and ritual, a desire that creates myth and (re)imagines gods. Was the void generated or suddenly rediscovered in modernism? Though I would not disclaim the upsetting effects of the Industrial Revolution, the Great War, various scientific discoveries undermining the teachings of the Church, and other traumatic experiences, I believe that modernists rediscovered rather than generated the void. The void wasn't produced entirely by the crisis of Christian faith. That void is as old as humanity, but it is through the eyes of modernists that we finally see the futility of scrambling to fill it in, despite the commonly proclaimed ordering drive of modernist art.

Escaping the Nets

Conrad and Joyce were particularly given to exposing the pointlessness and even dangers of attempts to reach the sacred, which in their milieux was often synonymous as much with Christian God as with the nationalist ethos. Aiding my discussion of these key issues are intersections between Conrad and Joyce's personal and aesthetic rebellion and rejection of traditional means of national identification. Their experimentation with narrative voice, points of view, and functions of language in general is, in many ways, anti-teleological. Conrad's Marlow is not interested in making his experiences comprehensible for his audience, nor does he trust in his and others' ability to investigate and discover the ultimate, clear, and digestible truth about himself, to reach narrative understanding of his own identity, history, and culture. Similarly, the multiple voices of *Ulysses* as well as the eruption of sound, the multilayered meaning, and defamiliarization of reality in *Finnegans Wake* point to Joyce's renunciation of the linear system and formal depiction leading to a climactic moment of self-understanding. And yet, de-centered, anti-mimetic narratives aside, both Conrad and Joyce grapple with the possibility and danger of human consciousness determined by collective identity, with an erasure of individual autonomy, and with complicated concepts of fate, chance, agency, and political responsibility of an individual.

It is worth noting, then, that Conrad's and Joyce's literary careers flourished after their emigration and, perhaps incidentally, after their renunciation of the Catholic religion, an act less vocal but equally daring in Conrad's case. Joyce openly admitted his inability to create freely amid the restraints of his country, his church, and his family; he called himself a "vagabond" (*Selected Letters* 26), and referred to his situation as that of "voluntary exile" (56). Though Conrad was never so vociferous in his rejection of Poland and the Catholic Church, he nevertheless fled his nation, family, and finally the Church. Thus self-exile furnished both authors with a sense of dejection and ostracism, which, in turn, provided inspiration and the necessary distance from the familiar, detachment which many creative writers consider as invaluable in the process of capturing complexities of fictional settings. Both turned away from organized religion in order to make their personal pilgrimages possible.

The writers' choice to escape the bondage of their native lands was influenced, to a great extent, by the oppression within their respective countries. There are important, though usually neglected, affinities between Polish and Irish cultures, histories, and mentalities, shaped by the overwhelming necessity to fight against or survive under colonization by their powerful neighbors. These affinities are helpful in my attempt to understand Conrad's and Joyce's aesthetic and thematic choices, their attitudes toward the Church and nationalism, the humiliating "progress" of imperialism, and one's search for self-definition in a setting hostile to ambiguity and difference.

The environments in which Conrad's and Joyce's personalities, preferences, and literary tastes were molded were highly unstable. For generations, Poland and Ireland had incessantly fought for their independence and political rights; both nations were torn by unsuccessful attempts to resist their oppressors (Russia, Prussia, and Austria on the one hand, and England on the other) and by inner conflicts and indecisions (e.g., whether to seek independence through peaceful negotiations or through armed resistance). In Poland and Ireland, pacifism inspired by Catholic spiritual ideals, as well as by the more material search for personal gain, clashed with forces advocating bloodshed, dismissed by many observers as pointless. The constant tension and anxiety within Conrad's and Joyce's milieux undoubtedly influenced their fiction's concern with the juxtaposition between the paralysis of the oppressed and an atmosphere of escalating violence: gratuitous, genocidal, or resulting from personal follies and bravado.

Having grown up in such politically uncertain environments, where one of very few constants was the Catholic Church with its strict rituals, both Conrad and Joyce fled from their native countries. Both had felt constrained and smothered by these conflicts; both regarded their exile as self-imposed; both were harshly criticized for their emigration by their compatriots, often very unfairly. Wiesław Krajka observes that Conrad's emigration was an affront to Polish nationalists because "[when] Poland was partitioned by Russia, Prussia and Austria between 1795–1918 . . . nationalism was a kind of shrine for all the values and ideals [the Poles] cherished, so that [their] identity might remain undestroyed by hostile foreign and domestic oppressors" (*Conrad and Poland* 44). Irish nationalism professed almost identical principles. These were often the basis of attacks on Joyce's apparent lack of respect for the national cause.

Joyce himself focuses on this affinity between the historical and political paradigm of the Irish and the Slavonic nations in his lecture "Ireland, Island of Saints and Sages." A compelling discussion of this work is offered by Caroline Hyland in her article "Równoległe Biografie" (Parallel Biographies), in which she compares Poland and Ireland in terms of their long heritage of suppression and unsuccessful upheavals, the messianic nature of their literature and political thought, as well as the undeniable role of the Catholic Church in their political, social, and cultural lives, and finally in terms of their geography, as she remarks that both Ireland and Poland lie on the margins of Europe (*Wokół Jamesa Joyce'a* 31–40). Although Joyce sympathized with the plight of the suppressed Slavonic nations, Conrad did not support the Irish cause in turn. On the contrary, Conrad revealed little compassion and understanding for Irish aspirations; Zdzisław Najder calls his ill will toward the Easter Rising "a sad paradox in a son of the conquered nation" (2: 209).[2] We could speculate whether Conrad would have been pleased by Ottoline Morrell's impression after her first meeting with the writer, when she observed that he displayed many features typical of the Irish (Najder 2: 173).

What probably directed Conrad's sympathies away from, or even against, the Irish cause was his Anglomania. After all, he settled in England, having fallen in love with the sound of the English language, as he recalls in *Personal Record* (Author's Note x). But in his stories he disrupts the continuity and coherence of English and questions the assumed correspondences between the signified and the signifier or reality and narrative. Similarly, Joyce subverts the basic functions of English in *Ulysses* and especially in *Finnegans Wake*, playing with it and contorting it to unrecognizable shapes and meanings. Modernist narratives in general often abolish the subject-object binary; their circularity and ambiguity represent a bold anti-Hegelian rejection of dialectical progress and imply an inherently political, emancipatory drive in the development of modernist aesthetics. However, Conrad and Joyce, just as other authors, became innovators of form and subject matter not because of some powerful and impersonal force sweeping across the continent and its literary circles, but primarily because they were shaped by very concrete circumstances: mainly colonial injustice and nationalist resistance. That one writer was infatuated with the sound of English and thought of it as liberatory (at least in terms of his creative skills) and the other had a very ambivalent attitude toward English as the language of literary expression and political oppression prompts questions about different ways in which their characters strive for self-identification, often through and in logos.

When Adolf Nowaczyński called the Irish the Poles "of the Western world" ("Teatr irlandzki" 63), he recognized the connection between the plight of both countries and expressed support for Irish Home Rule and, finally, full independence for Ireland.[3] In fact, Nowaczyński mocked the English for viewing Poland as "a modified paraphrase of Ireland, linked in a painful, burdensome, and inseparable alliance with the 'England' of Russia" ("Polska w literaturze" 60). He saw in the Irish theater a potent aesthetic and political influence upon Polish culture: "The Irish stage becomes an arena, a cathedral, a pulpit, a minaret of the muezzin, a confessional of the nation, and a spiritual parliament of the people who do not yet have a political parliament" ("Teatr irlandzki" 64). He also observed that "all these texts can be translated into Polish; change only the names, move them to us, and they will become lives taken directly from the Polish psyche" (64).[4]

Ireland and Poland have been among the strongholds of the Roman Catholic Church, with the majority of the population practicing the Catholic religion. The colonization of both countries was not triggered solely by plans of land acquisition, but also by deeply rooted stigma attached to the nations loyal to the sovereignty of the pope on the continent transformed and "enlightened" by the Reformation. True, Conrad and Joyce were averse to their nations' loyalty to the pope. They point to the bigotry and parochialism of the people blindly following the teachings of the Catholic Church and abandoning intellectual independence. Both authors, however, display (rather unconsciously) a deeply ingrained attachment to the Church in their employment of liturgical symbols and parables and, in Conrad's case, in a socially conservative worldview. Both also seem to recognize that skin color and ethnicity were the common markers of bestiality. But while most scholars are familiar with the offensive caricatures of Africans and Irish Catholics printed in popular magazines such as *Punch*, I need to stress that the Irish were not the only European ethnic group ridiculed for its adherence to the backward Catholic ways. Prussian newspapers and magazines routinely referred to subjugated Poles as pigs and rabbits or disorderly, unstoppable, grotesque drunks. Although Christianity in general haunted the colonial enterprises of the Spanish/Portuguese (Catholic) and English/Dutch (Protestant) empires equally, Catholicism in particular had often been linked not only to incompetence and ignorance, as in the case of the colonized Irish and Poles, but also to cannibalism and vampirism. Walter Walsh attacked the Roman Catholic Church as a vampire in 1897 (O'Malley 130), and before him, Robert Wilberforce's 1847 tract told us that the "evil spirit comes to us in the garb and under the name of ritualism—a mild force of Romanism,—seeking to attract us to its service by a gorgeous ceremonial and a dazzling spectacle" (O'Malley 131). Resistance to this recurring image, I'd like to claim, might have influenced Conrad's and Joyce's subversion of the traditional model of the monstrous colonized vs. saintly colonizer, in which the Catholic-Protestant dichotomy was partially inscribed.

Subject to ethnic prejudice, positioned in a dangerous proximity to powerful neighbors ready for expansion, and torn by internal conflicts, Poland and Ireland were relatively easy targets for dominant European countries which, after invading their "backward" neighbors, embarked on a long process of assimilation. Ireland became gradually anglicized and even more impoverished; the imperial powers governing the partitioned Poland inflicted their own measures to eradicate intellectuals considered a threat to the status quo, to limit or outlaw education in the native language of the colonized people—the law of *Kulturkampf* being an example of such restrictive regulations[5]—and to forbid the Poles from acquiring land and properties, which led to their destitution. The English achieved the same results through their confiscation of the property from the native Irish. The repressive laws implemented by the colonizers placed both ethnic groups under extremely discriminatory legislation at the turn of the century.[6]

In the face of overwhelming oppression, the people of Ireland and Poland embraced largely thwarted and tragically unsuccessful active resistance (which Conrad's father pursued until his premature death), clandestine debates and arrangements, and peaceful negotiation. "In the absence of a national state, Polish national consciousness drew on four fundamental sources of inspiration—Church, Language, History, and Race," says Norman Davies (*God's Playground* 18). These rudimentary elements were also crucial in maintaining the Irish collective identity. After all, their overpowering presence and importance in the daily life of the Irish repelled Joyce and contributed to his decision to flee his native country. Joyce distances himself from his contemporaries, refusing to take an active role in their nationalistic and often chauvinist agendas infused with religious rhetoric, and remaining aloof in the presence of both Irish patriots and English oppressors. Similarly, Conrad's decision to leave Poland, apart from his unquenchable thirst for adventure and the unknown (which he recalls in *Personal Record*), stemmed from his aversion to religious orthodoxy, his impatience with ineffective planning and execution of insurrection, and his distaste for the hypocrisy inherent in all extreme nationalist movements, including those in Poland. Thus, through his exile and the choice of a literary career in a foreign language, he escaped the same confines that inhibited Joyce: his family, his fatherland, and his church.

Conrad and Joyce spent their most formative years, then, in territories geographically remote from each other but linked through similar political struggles, as well as religious affiliations and influences. These countries were also joined by similar aesthetic responses to oppression, especially in literary portrayals of the nations' endangered existence.

John A. Merchant, in his observations on the cultural kinship between the Young Poland and the Celtic Revival, points to a renewed interest in folk culture in both countries, including the growing popularity of the motifs of the supernatural and the legendary used to address questions of national identity (46). Joyce's employment of the quest motif from the ancient myth of Odysseus and Conrad's description of the perilous journey to the underworld in *Heart of Darkness* point to these writers' saturation with the political exploitation of mythology and legends for the purpose of raising contemporary national consciousness. Because of the repressive censorship in the subjugated countries and the messianic nature of both Polish and Irish nationalisms, politics often blended with religion and myth when young Józef's and James's aesthetic sensibilities were being shaped. Instead of blindly assimilating the messianic zeal, both authors expose and often ridicule official colonial and nationalist discourse conveniently relying on such dogmatic parallelism. They write about foreign invasion and occupation (but also blind patriotism of parochial zealots) as inextricable from the search for the sacred and ultimately futile. They also map their characters' passages within these artificial demarcations of the sacred, the nation, and the colony. Some of these characters consciously search for identity detached from rigid boundaries of the sacred order and the profane disorder.

Mapping *Profane Pilgrimage*

The first section of this book focuses on the concepts of cosmogony and officially constructed dichotomies of race, while the second describes the motif of pilgrimage as a way to circumvent panoptic control and established limitations within the British Empire. The first part discusses division and appropriation; the second investigates the characters' paths and movements in their attempts to define themselves in the fragmented (or "cosmicized") environment, and sometimes to transgress the arbitrarily set boundaries between the subaltern and the powerful.[7] Finally, it explores the possibility of a teleological project in these modernist narratives of quest and contingency.

What makes the demarcations between self and other uncertain and blurred? Since the division between the sacred cosmos and the profane chaos (that is, between the virtuous self and the evil other) entered popular consciousness through a variety of media in hegemonic nations, the link between the desire to reach the sacred and the demonization and appropriation of the other is traceable to the European colonies which Conrad and Joyce knew intimately and described in their fiction. Conrad enacts what Michel de Certeau calls *"writing that conquers"* (*The Writing of History* xxv) by presenting the Congo of *Heart of Darkness* and the Costaguana of *Nostromo* as nebulous, bewildering, and chaotic territories. However, he also criticizes European and American imperial practices. Thus he endorses *and* undercuts stock stereotypes serving colonial purposes, revealing, nevertheless, the duplicity and single-mindedness inherent in the drive toward the "sacred" order. Like Conrad, Joyce discerns the prevailing dichotomy between chaos and cosmos in the governing colonial structure, and like Conrad, he exposes its intrinsic rigidity and chauvinism. The colonizers' esprit de corps engenders both sectionalism and arrogation of superiority. Joyce's critique of the British and Roman Catholic oppression of his nation conducted under the veneer of sacred motives leads to his attempt to transgress the prescriptive categories of the sacred and the profane through ridicule, cunning subversion, and the carnivalesque.

Two terms, "the center" and "telos," appear in many texts on myth and pilgrimage in relation to the search for the sacred. Though the first term is often associated with stasis, a focal point in space, and the second with movement, both center and telos are fixed points toward which pilgrims, adventurers, or thinkers progress. In the first section of this book, I explain the connection between chaos and cosmos, and the profane "othered" margin and the sacred "civilized" center. This polarized worldview, constructed by the hegemonic power in order to gain and maintain control, fabricates the center as the place of being, while the margin remains a place of non-being. In pilgrimage, the quest to reach self-recognition occurs from the margin towards the center. The telos of this progress is, then, the center, unless the social and colonial hierarchies are abolished.

Through a multidisciplinary investigation of the relationship between imperialism, the sacred, and pilgrimage, this book explores the (im)possibility of trespassing and maneuvering between the boundaries of racial/racist spatialization in Conrad's and Joyce's texts. The myth producing chromatic binarisms (that is, essentialist divisions based on skin color) and masquerading, for instance, as an ultimately beneficial exchange between cultures, produces modern forms of prehistoric Manichaeism.[8] This dual theology locks the subaltern in an immobile position within the confines of Western "civilization," but also restricts the colonizer to a limited space of his own creation, the cosmos or center. This study examines Conrad's and Joyce's response to the superimposed dichotomy of colonialism and their reactions to the challenge of transforming the profane world of alterity and fragmentation.

I

COSMOGONY

1

Cosmogony and Colonialism

Charting Non-Places

"Reality is not dialectical, colonialism is."
Hardt and Negri, *Empire*

Maps, color-coded or not, simplify reality, impose an established symbolic order, and reduce historical and cultural significance to abstract spatial markers. European colonial powers found this taming of fragmented land acquisitions into a coherent picture helpful in expanding and maintaining their control. Filling in "blank" spaces with missionaries, soldiers, and traders was an act of creation. At first glance, cosmogony, a theory of the origin of the universe, seems to belong solely to the realm of ancient mythologies or to a scientific inquiry about the beginning of all matter. With the advance of scientific theories on the creation of the cosmos—involving such areas as quantum physics, astronomy, or geodynamics—as well as anthropological and theological approaches to the question of the beginning of the world, there is a tendency to treat those areas of research as hermetic, highly specialized, and self-contained branches of knowledge. However, ordering the unknown, one of the driving forces behind colonization, points to atavistic residues in the way colonizers (often through pro-imperial texts in the nineteenth and twentieth centuries) justify the cause, direction, and intent of their enterprise. The ideology of imperialism is an altered form of primordial and even more recent religious convictions and myths rooted in patriarchy and irrational fear of the other. The first myths and legends of archaic civilizations offering ontological explanations might provide a unique insight into the anxieties, paradoxes, and search for meaning present in Conrad's and Joyce's fiction. Both writers operate in a moment of ontogenetic and epistemological uncertainty—triggered by successive wars, by ongoing revelations about systems of oppression and discrimination, and by rebellious voices of independent thinkers such as Nietzsche and his followers—that cannot be effectively addressed by religious or political leaders. It would be a mistake, however, to think that this insecurity is a marker of modernism only. Change has an unsettling effect on people of all ages; genocide and large-scale warfare did not suddenly emerge as an ordering tactic with the dawn of the twentieth century; dissent within political and religious systems is not a new phenomenon, either. Critics who point to the tragedy of the god-shaped hole as uniquely modern and/or modernist ignore the struggle of Byron's Manfred, Marlowe's Faustus, Shakespeare's Hamlet, and Homer's Odysseus. The existential torment often goes hand-in-hand with an unfulfilled need for order, predictable patterns, *nostos*. It is the way in which modernist writers cope with that void which is unique, not the problem itself.

In an attempt to reveal and explain the mechanism of political and military dominance, as well as fear of the other, Conrad's and Joyce's political writing and fiction point to a connection between the driving forces behind colonization and the primitive theories of cosmogony and to atavistic residues in the official colonial discourse. But these authors also subvert numerous concepts essential to these systems. Underlying my argument, which connects chromatism with the myth of cosmogony, is the assumption that the dichotomy of the margin and the center originates much earlier than first colonial exploits or the beginnings of national consciousness; such uncompromising distinctions between self and other exist in the first myths of creation. They are, therefore, inextricable from another juxtaposition of essential categories: the profane and the sacred. Conrad and Joyce expose and often undermine these traditional dichotomies entrenched in the colonial enterprise.

Chaos, Cosmos, and Colonialism

To discuss the connection between ancient cosmogonies and modern ethics, and to analyze imperial ideology as a residue of archaic cosmogonic systems underlying the ethno- and logocentric drive to contain the world, we need to recognize and define two fundamental elements in the process of creation: chaos and cosmos. A good starting point is Mircea Eliade's analysis of belief systems of traditional societies based on the original act of creation performed by a divine power which set the pattern for all other formative or generative steps. This reenactment of the divine act of creation, which always had to follow the original pattern set arbitrarily by gods, was a vital element in the myth of the eternal return, which gave the reality of archaic societies ultimate validity and allowed them to participate through ritual in the sacred time, in a non-durational existence. Like Marlow's "idea—something you can set up, and bow down before, and offer sacrifice to" (*Heart of Darkness* 51), this pursuit of the sacred, of an immanent deity (gods, self-congratulatory benevolence, or mammon) redeems in the eyes of the conquerors any inhumanity and ignorant pride that accompany the ordering of the universe.

Cosmogony, in crude terms, is a transformation of chaos into cosmos. The simple dichotomy between those two entities explains the archaic societies' fear of the unknown and the unprecedented and their drive to consecrate (and before that, obviously, to invade) the unknown land. Eliade claims that these traditional societies were collectively aware of the essential difference between "their inhabited territory and the unknown and indeterminate space that surrounds it." This "other world" is "a foreign, chaotic space, peopled by ghosts, demons, 'foreigners'" (*The Sacred and the Profane* 29). The unknown participates in "the undifferentiated, formless modality of pre-Creation" (*The Myth of the Eternal Return* 9).

The qualities of cosmos and chaos correspond to the characteristics traditionally and conveniently assigned to the colonizing and the colonized. This formlessness and the "fluid and larval modality of chaos" (*Sacred* 31) justified the apparent necessity for appropriation of territories and peoples in the eyes of the constructors of *gārhapatya* in Vedic India, the Spanish and Portuguese conquistadores discovering and taking possession of new lands in the name of Jesus, or the English navigators taking "possession of conquered countries in the name of the king of England, new Cosmocrator" (*Myth* 11). Thus colonization of an apparently uncultivated territory was equivalent to an act of Creation. Consciously or not, archaic societies reenacted the ritual of cosmogony in order to approach the sacred. For instance, as Eliade tells us, when the Scandinavian colonists invaded Iceland, they considered this act "neither as an original undertaking nor as human and profane work. For them, their labor was only repetition of a primordial act, the transformation of chaos into cosmos by the divine act of creation." Therefore, "when they tilled the desert soil, they were in fact repeating the act of the gods who had organized chaos by giving it a structure, forms, and norms" (*Sacred* 31). The official justification of invading foreign lands as an act of spreading God-given freedom (e.g., liberation from "uncivilized" behavior, from eternal damnation) often appears in the messianic character of modern nationalism.[1]

The (re)construction of order is therefore present in both imperialist and liberationist ideologies, especially those incorporating religious allegiances as essential to their collective identities. The same polarity of qualities distinguishing the "civilized" (same) from the "savage" (other) appears in both imperial propaganda and in nationalistic discourse within the colonized societies. The concepts equivalent to those of cosmos and chaos motivate contemporary ruses and strategies employed by those assuming control. Michel de Certeau, for example, indicates in *The Practice of Everyday Life* the strategic rationalization of power acquisition as "an effort to delimit one's own place in a world bewitched by the invisible powers of the Other" (36). Similar themes of bewitchment and the irresistible pull of the exotic are at the basis of Edward Said's study of the Western conceptualization of the Orient and contrasting qualities conceived by Europeans in order to create a category of cultures that would be compliant and conquerable. The West imagined itself as the epistemic center of the world, the *axis mundi* of humanity. Benedict Anderson observes that all the powerful "classical communities conceived of themselves as cosmically central, through the medium of a sacred language linked to a superterrestrial order of power" (13), and that "the literati were adepts, strategic strata in a cosmological hierarchy of which the apex was divine. The fundamental conceptions about 'social groups' were centripetal and hierarchical, rather than boundary-oriented and horizontal" (15). Similarly, in *Reflections on Exile*, Said emphasizes that "successful nationalisms consign truth exclusively to themselves and relegate falsehood and inferiority to outsiders (as in the rhetoric of capitalist versus communist, or the European versus the Asiatic)" (176–77). The sacred center thus defines cosmos and recognizes where chaos begins. This need to delineate one's own cosmos and chart the unknown territory of chaos preceded the development of cartography and modern warfare. In order to fill the nebulous unknown with meaning, one had to occupy it and reimagine it through a totalizing circumscribing of space. The British Ordnance Survey maps—including the one of Ireland, which Bloom looks at in "Ithaca"— and the European colonial drive in general participate in the self-assigned and self-righteous mission to bestow ontological certainty upon chaos. As Ngũgĩ wa Thiong'o reminds us in *Moving the Centre*, "Hegelian Africa was a European myth" (4).

De Certeau tackles the same issue in *Heterologies*, where he says that "there never is anything 'natural' or 'inevitable' or to be taken for granted in the setting up of center and periphery. It is always the result of specific and discernible operations: rhetorical ones in texts, power ones in the broader social area" (xi).[2] This negative identification, the construction of self through recognition of what one is not, has consistently functioned among archaic and modern societies. As Michael Hardt and Antonio Negri indicate, "because the difference of the Other is absolute, it can be inverted in a second moment as the foundation of the Self. In other words, the evil, barbarity, and licentiousness of the colonized Other are what make possible the goodness, civility, and propriety of the European Self" (127).

Even the most recent attempts to define one's consciousness regardless of the long-established and arbitrary characterization of the other—such as the subaltern studies project, in its attempt to reclaim Indian historiography through identification of peasant consciousness—have often been undermined and discredited by scholars and thinkers. Gayatri Chakravorty Spivak decides to address the subaltern studies "against the grain," and rejects this "positivistic project" (10) of isolating peasant consciousness from the colonial experience, of looking for a raw, dehistoricized form of the subaltern.[3] The same form of negative identification is the premise of the cosmos-chaos dichotomy. The colonizers cannot define their "cosmos" without constructing the space of the other, or "chaos." They perceive and perform their collective identities through the inverted gaze of the subaltern, the subject characterized by its lack, whose geographical location is, officially, nowhere or in the nebulous space of chaos.

Mapping Alterity

The need to occupy and transform unknown territories as an act of communication with the sacred or, perhaps more appropriately, of imitating and acting as the divine power and reaping the benefits of this privileged position, is still a driving factor in the colonial enterprise, even if it exists beyond the collective and individual awareness of more advanced societies. Similar motives have appeared in various attempts to justify European greed for new land and the atrocities committed in interaction with and exploitation of the native peoples. The colonizers communicate these motives using more contemporary terms; they replace *cosmos, chaos,* and *divinity* with words more familiar to the nineteenth- and twentieth-century public: *civilization, savagery, mission.* The unshakeable faith in "civilization," in the model of existence accepted and exercised in the colonizing country, prompts European powers to take up "the White Man's burden," the "toil of serf and sweeper," and to guide the "silent, sullen peoples" and "fluttered folk and wild" "toward the light" (Kipling 1152). This divine mission requires sacrifice. It is a dangerous and honorable quest to transform an "other world" into "our world"; the invaded land becomes, to use Eliade's words, "a foreign, chaotic space peopled by ghosts, demons, 'foreigners,'" a place that needs to be organized, mapped, "cosmicized" (*Sacred* 29). The aggression is therefore justified as an attempt to transfigure the "larval state" of underdeveloped, raw, and unsophisticated territories, to enlighten the "half-devil and half-child" of a native (Kipling 1152), to face "'backward populations' or 'lower breeds'" who will never "be capable of governing themselves without supervision" (Arendt 130–31), and hence allegedly to impose the rules and norms existing in the invading country. In order to exploit the ideology of "lack" (the void of "chaos"), those in power fabricate the native as deficient in ethics, intelligence, or physiognomy. The subaltern must remain diametrically other so that the "cosmicizing" process could last indefinitely and those in power could sustain their self-definition and self-appreciation through such negative identification.

Nineteenth-century cartoons in *Punch* and other publications featuring such polarizing conceptualizations of the other, whether the indigenous people of the Congo or Ireland, justified the "cosmicizing" process introduced into the allegedly disordered and degenerate territory. Numerous posters, pictures, and pamphlets depict native inhabitants of both Africa and Ireland (and sometimes the Americas) as less than human, simianized, degenerate, lacking. Like Eliade's foreigners, they are random elements of chaotic space that should be ordered by instruction, classification, and "civilized" laws. This dehumanizing Manichaeism produces an image of the subaltern as a negation of ethical values. As Hardt and Negri affirm in *Empire*, "colonial identity functions first of all through a

Manichean logic of exclusion" (124), but the alterity ascribed to the colonized is "not given, but produced" (125) to facilitate acquisition and justification of power.

This manufactured and exaggerated alterity appears in Aidan O'Sullivan's interesting study of the crannogs as places of resistance in early modern Ireland. The Irish, like the Iroquois, were to be civilized, their primitive landscape contained and managed. O'Sullivan's study offers valuable comments on the role of cartography in the English colonial enterprise and the pictorial representation of the polarizing division between "order" and "disorder" that lies at the roots of imperial military exploitation. Just as Africa and the Americas were considered chaotic and lawless spaces at the end of the sixteenth century, the north and west of Ireland remained "terra incognita, from which stories came of great lakes (the north-west is actually largely lake-bound), mysterious off-shore islands (mostly nonexistent!) and a mountainous interior (the Irish midlands are entirely low-lying)" (91). These fantastic tales prompted by ignorance and ethnocentric pride revealed an urgent need for maps of the conquered and to-be-conquered territories. These maps "aimed to transform the native Gaelic oral knowledge of the landscape into a cartographic knowledge, which could then be used for political ends" (91). Thus even the initial process of map making was symptomatic of the great "cosmicizing" fever of the powerful European countries. The perceived fragmentariness of the empire had to be ordered into a totalizing representation of British possessions. In some of the early maps (drawn by Bartlett), "the subjective viewer is provided with *a bird's-eye view* of an objective landscape, which is framed within *the cartographer's chosen boundaries*" (91). Therefore, the maps present the Irish framed within the colonial order as chaos effectively controlled.

Richard Bartlett's maps were "full of political meaning, intended as they were to symbolize the Irish defeat and provide cartographic proof of the overthrow of the old Gaelic order" (O'Sullivan 91). The English saw the Gaelic crannogs in particular as "a metaphor for the displacement of the old Gaelic social order and its replacement, through English and Scottish conquest and plantation, with an entirely new way of life." The native Irish population viewed cartography as dangerous; they realized the potential importance of these maps in the English conquest. When Bartlett came to what is now known as west Ulster, "the inhabitants took off his head, because they would not have their country discovered" (O'Sullivan 95).

Racializing Chaos

What was designed to justify this ordering process—whether undertaken by the military, the cartographers, or the legislators—was the invading power's self-righteous concern about the damnation of the heathen and primitive inhabitants of the island and the ostensible drive to teach them productivity and responsibility. The aforementioned cartoons indicate a large-scale project in the British press to portray the Irish as a parasitical nation of sloth and irresponsibility. Although the initiators and participants of the Celtic Revival embraced the idea of racial genius of the Irish, the formerly established discourse of racial difference between the Anglo-Saxon colonizers and the Gaelic inhabitants served as justification for the land-grabbing aggressors. Numerous English texts dating from the late fifteenth century onward compare the Irish physiognomy, habits, and culture to those of Native Americans and African tribes, all three groups apparently linked by their shared savagery. Some even juxtapose selected Irish faces to those of monkeys or patients suffering from syphilis, capitalizing perhaps on the general tendency to speak of the other in terms of contamination, disease, and corruption.[4] Steve Garner traces the ethnocentric attitudes of the colonizers in Ireland throughout centuries of invasion and subjugation of its population, from the process of racializing the Irish in the Early Middle Ages to contemporary nationalist struggle. Expressions like "wild people" (78), "careless and bestial" (77) "wild places" (78), "dark and impenetrable forests," "threatening places among which a savage and implacable enemy fleetingly appears and disappears" (79)—used by Spenser, Smith, Campion, and others[5]—so evocative of Marlow's description of African interior, were an integral part of the hegemonic discourse of the English colonizers whose posited objective was to bring the entire nation (or "race") into God-given civility. The Anglicization of Ireland depended to a certain degree upon official and covert juxtapositions of the barbaric land and people, especially those in the west of the island, with the Protestant, enlightened English cityscapes, an image instrumental in creating the perception of the enormous sacrifice of the English in transforming the profane chaos into sacred cosmos.[6]

Arthur Conan Doyle compares the expropriations of the Europeans in Africa to those of the Normans in England and the English colonizers in Ireland. In *The Crime of the Congo*, published at the beginning of the twentieth century, he accuses the Roman Catholic Church—except the

Jesuits, who have "always had a most noble record in its treatment of native races" (98)—of turning a blind eye to the human rights violations in the Congo and on the atrocities committed in the name of "a curious and mysterious creation . . . the *Domaine de la Couronne*" (99). The ignorance of and acquiescence to the brutality of colonization of both Ireland and the Congo stem from, in part, the European collective imagination of the native people inhabiting the invaded territories, successfully manufactured through enforced stereotypes, inventions, and strategies of fear.

Similar to the fear-inducing description of the Irish that highlighted biological and cultural difference, early travelogues and adventure stories set in Africa also emphasized the distinction between the "cosmos" of European civilization and the "chaos" of "the Dark Continent" (Johnston vi) that needed to be appropriated and transformed. H. H. Johnston's *The River Congo*, first published in 1884, is a classic example of a fantastically distorted exposition of travelers' observations filtered through xenophobia and racism. Not surprisingly, Johnston favors tribes characterized by a lighter skin color that allegedly are less "debased" and "degraded" (274). The natives of the Congo region, according to Johnston, give off an "offensive smell" (271) and are immoral, "indolent, fickle, and sensual" (274), "particularly obscene," and "corrupt" (276). Although "gentle and effeminate" (275), when the natives' "passions are excited, . . . by fear of witchcraft or a wish to revenge grave injuries, they can become very demons of fanatical rage" (274). Such nomenclature—the constant association of the native tribes in the Congo with demons, devils, or evil spirits—points to the atavistic need of continuous assertions of one's divinely privileged position in construction of societal hierarchies. In the struggle between the sacred and the profane, only one side has the moral high ground. Thus the appropriation of the land in the Congo, says Johnston, has met with "the approval of the natives, who have so long served under their new masters abroad that they will take kindly to their dominion at home" (272). The "cosmicization" of the native tribes in Africa is a form of commanding benevolence on the part of the European colonizers.

Likewise, T. Alexander Barns travels "in pitch darkness," with a dim light of "a lamp held by a little Belgian" (17) through the African interior— a trip he describes in *The Wonderland of the Eastern Congo: The Region of the Snow-Crowned Volcanoes, the Pygmies, the Giant Gorilla, and the Okapi*. He and his companions stay in places where "drums are to be heard beating at all hours of the day and even at night" (168). They "penetrate an unknown region" (170) populated by "the untamed element" (175), "the semi-human Congo savage (without such a thing as pity in his composition or language)" (171); they travel among "the human hyæna" (177), or "degraded savages" (170), "smelly devils with low types of countenance and nasty ways" (28), who practice "the execrable burial murders . . . and their accompanying cannibal orgies" (171) and "other diabolical customs" (171), "so bizarre as to be almost past belief" (171). Above the chaos of Africa, however, lurks "the indomitable spirit of the Anglo-Saxon" (15). The boundary between the profane and the sacred could not have been charted any more emphatically.

It is not astonishing, then, that imperial England, despite its overwhelming aversion to Catholicism, produced Catechetical, question-and-answer textbooks and guides for the citizens who never set foot on the African continent, but who were curious about the people that their armies or the armies of their European neighbors "civilized." Among such texts is W.F.P. Burton's *How They Live in Congoland: An Account of the Character and Customs of This Most Interesting Race and Efforts to Win Them for Christ*, with a front-page drawing of a naked African man reaching in desperation from darkness toward a source of diffused light and pleading: "Come and save us." Here the Eliadean devils and foreigners inhabiting chaos become mischievous but lovable children, "the black folk that we love," "our black chums" (3), who, thanks to their European saviors, turn from the profane path of tribal dances and polygamy to acknowledge the ordering power of Jesus. With unabashed prejudice and condescension, Burton advocates colonization of their minds and customs. After centuries of terrible plights that the natives of the Congo had endured, "suddenly a wonderful thing happened. The white men arrived, with their guns and their boats. . . . The poor natives were so overjoyed that they threw themselves at the feet of their rescuers, crying out: 'O great gods, do not leave us. Stay with us always, and keep us in safety'" (123).

This binary system of qualifications helps justify the colonizing enterprise. Without it, we enter into a region of ambiguous motives, personal gains, and insatiable ambition. On the one hand, contemporary cartography, travelogues, and fiction present uncultivated regions populated by monsters or half-humans; on the other hand, we read accounts of those who claim their task to be ordering, "civilizing," and converting the other into the familiar (though not the same). Historical and cultural significance of the invaded territory disappears in cartographic spatial simplification that aids the panoptic control over colonies. As Gaston Bachelard says in *The Poetics of Space*, the profound metaphysics of the dialectics of the outside and inside, which philosophers explain in terms of being and non-being, is based on inherent geometry which "confers spatiality upon thought" (212).

Cosmogony is, then, less a genealogical than an ontological issue. It is a way to explain a power hierarchy in society, sanctioned by the sacred, even if the very understanding of what is sacred shifts from culture to culture. From supernatural omnipotence to hard cash, the sacred is the normative and formative organizational principle. However, an important question arises: What is behind this social vindication of cosmogonical myth? The drive for power, as well as the fear and appropriation of the other, seem to be not the *result* but the *cause* of the myth; the very existence of the myth appears to be a consequence of that drive.[7] The system of binaries that enhances the constructed picture of the civilized and savage worlds is an excellent tool that helps to point back at the perennial struggle between the sacred and the profane and therefore to justify new forms of that conflict.

Conrad and Joyce are insightful observers of the underlying mechanisms of political and military aggression and self-righteous endeavor to classify, normalize, and instruct the other. Their texts, exposing and then often subverting binaries sanctioned by hegemony, comment on and undermine the traditionally understood struggle between the sacred and the profane, between cosmos and chaos. The "ordering" process of the unknown or dangerous territory, justified by centuries of myths and indoctrination, becomes a symptom of paralysis or regression. This critique of the forms of behavior and thought associated with modern Christianity (and much older religious systems) is an underlying feature of modernism and its discontent with theological explanations of the fragmented world.

False Gods of Imperialism in Conrad

Imperialist propaganda in politics, media, arts, and hence in the European collective unconscious was extremely effective in conveniently embedding racist and ethnocentric views in the public discourse mainly because it successfully induced fear of the other and, at the same time, evoked a sense of moral and intellectual superiority and entitlement in European society. Peter Forbath thus begins his prologue in *The River Congo*, published in 1977, long after Conrad's *Heart of Darkness*, and before he could be aware of the heated debate initiated, in part, by Chinua Achebe's claim that Conrad was a "bloody racist": "Congo: two sudden syllables beat on the imagination like the beat of a jungle drum, calling up nightmare visions of primeval darkness, unfathomable mystery, dreadful savagery. No other word has quite that power; no other symbol stands more vividly for the myth and magic of Africa than the fabulous river those two barbaric syllables name" (ix). Mr Forbath never mentions what kind of visions and phonetic associations the two syllables of his own last name might bring to life, but in a Conradesque fashion, his book describes the African river as repository of nightmarish reveries intensified by the feverish drumbeat and prehistoric darkness. The name itself, claims Forbath, is "barbaric" and is therefore an apt signifier.

Conrad's Congo, with its heat, savagery, "unspeakable rites," and overpowering incompetence, resembles his Costaguana, the imaginary country in Central America, a place tormented by waves of revolutions and weakened by a general ineptitude of its citizens.[1] Both lands suffer invasion by foreign powers: the Belgians (or Europeans in general) in *Heart of Darkness* and "An Outpost of Progress"; Spanish colonizers and Italian immigrants, followed by the English aided with American money in *Nostromo*. Their appearance is, in many cases, detrimental to the development of self-reliance and community building in the occupied territories.

The mechanisms of Belgian colonization resembled those of the British conquest, even though Joseph Conrad apparently was not willing to admit this. Some critics emphasize Conrad's Anglophilia as a reason for his favoring the British political decisions and actions over Belgian barbarity. Peter Edgerly Firchow remarks that "with certain notable exceptions, Conrad is consistently less well disposed toward German, Russian, Dutch, Belgian, Arab, North American, or Irish characters than he is toward English, Scottish, Malay, or French ones" (*Envisioning Africa* 6). As Conrad's biographers noted, the writer's childhood experience in a country divided between three European powers (and specifically in the territory that was occupied by Russia) shaped to a certain extent his sympathies and dislikes on the world political scene. Conrad portrays both "quixotic fools" convinced of the civilizing (or cosmicizing) mission they are about to perform, as well as those individuals who have no illusion as to the character of the colonizing work in Africa or Central America. But, above all, his characters' expectations and reactions to the dichotomy between the "civilized" and "savage" and finally their disillusionment and abandonment of their previous preconceptions about the civilizing mission indicate how close to the traditional vision of cosmos and chaos those preconceptions were and how accurately the official motives for the exploitation of Africa and her people correspond to the archaic myth of cosmogony.

Marlow's Chaos and "Writing That Conquers"

Marlow's encounter with the colonized land and peoples provokes the "fascination of the abomination" of the exotic, godforsaken land (*Heart of Darkness* 50); he feels both enchantment and abhorrence. Just as the archaic man stood before chaos, mesmerized and fearful, Conrad's characters approach the unknown and unexplored land with destabilizing awe. The formlessness of chaos is translated into the shapeless, raw image of Africa, which is equally unknown and indeterminate.

Marlow's inability to describe and comprehend images stretching before his eyes becomes apparent in his use of dreamlike language and his constant repetition of words indicating incomplete perception. Any territory outside the center, beyond the "cradle of civilization," manifests "the mystery of an unknown earth" (17), "senseless delusion" (30), "oppressive wonder" (31), and "insoluble mystery" (33). It is a land of a "mysterious sound" (34), "unreal" (46), a place of "absurdity, surprise, and bewilderment" (50), of "implacable force" and "inscrutable intention" (60), generating dreams, narcotic-like visions, and reveries, populated by "phantoms" (62). Although its narrator is unnamed, a similar voice in "An Outpost of Progress" describes the station as surrounded by "the river, the forests, the impenetrable bush that seemed to cut off the station from the rest of the world" ("Outpost" 4), by the "vast and dark country" (4). Kayerts and Carlier lose their contexts in this new, "chaotic" space, their identities slowly erased in the strange wilderness of Africa, in its fluid and larval state, where even "the brilliant sunshine disclosed nothing intelligible. Things appeared and disappeared before their eyes in an unconnected and aimless kind of way. The river seemed to come from nowhere and flow nowhither. It flowed through a void" (7). They dwell in the "impenetrable forest" (17) and fancy that the earth somehow became "bigger and very empty" (16). Notably, Marlow refers in *Heart of Darkness* to "the empty immensity of earth, sky, and water" (61–62), the monotonous landscape—"Paths, paths, everywhere; a stamped-in network of paths spreading over the empty land, through long grass, through burnt grass, through thickets . . . and a solitude, a solitude, nobody, not a hut" (70)—and, consequently, to his desire to "be out of chaos" (68). Here the emptiness of the landscape that is threatening but also full of generative potential clashes with confusing excess—of paths, flora, the sky.

The frequency of such expressions as "impalpable," "inconceivable" (115), "improbable, inexplicable," or "bewildering" (126) is the basis of F. R. Leavis's criticism of Conrad's "adjectival insistence" (Leavis 179), that is, the writer's tendency to mystify and occlude his picture of Africa.[2] However, this recurrent image of monotony, impenetrability, and formlessness, and this dreamlike atmosphere enveloping the account of the trip into the unknown establish a sharp contrast between the normal and the abnormal, the civilized and the primitive, cosmos and chaos. It is impossible to belong to both worlds at the same time—traditional societies inhabit the center, and only after conquering and ordering the periphery according to the rules of the center (that is, after cosmicizing the periphery) can they discern all the shapes and comprehend the environment.

Conrad indicates that Marlow is incapable of discerning distinct shapes and contours not because they do not exist, but because he encounters obstacles blurring his vision. Marlow often admits that he has to deal with "the blinding sunshine" (65), or "a white fog, very warm and clammy, and more blinding than the night" (101). At times, he is able to discern "vague forms . . . leaping, gliding, distinct, incomplete, evanescent" (111). He compares himself, in his attempts to maneuver the steamboat, to "a blindfolded man set to drive a van over a bad road" (94)—an association he derives from the other, familiar world, in order to render his bewilderment and disorientation in the new, unknown environment.[3]

Similarly, "a heavy . . . mist penetrating, enveloping, and silent" (22) descends upon Kayerts and Carlier of "Outpost." They live "like blind men in a large room, aware only of what came in contact with them (and of that only imperfectly), but unable to see the general aspect of things" (7). Kayerts feels "as if he had taken a dose of opium" (21), and he suspects himself of "dreaming," of having "a horrible illusion" (19). Bewitched by Africa, they lose clarity of vision and cannot comprehend the foreign milieu. The implied dichotomy here is that of the real European metropolis and the unreal periphery which should not be granted any ontological or ontogenetic status, let alone political autonomy. In both *Heart of Darkness* and "Outpost," fog, mist, and hallucinatory visions induced by the weather and the environment are symbols of clouded perception and biased opinions; however, they also indicate a virtual inability to form a clear judgment, a handicap defined as intrinsic to Africa. Conrad, while acknowledging the narrow-mindedness of the characters' perception, seems to indicate that one of the reasons for this limited vision is Africa itself—its climate, forbidding paths, frantic drumbeat, and overabundant flora. Africa's blankness, darkness, and formlessness imply non-being, the uncreated space upon which something must be formed. When Michel de Certeau talks about "a colonization of the body by the discourse of power" and "*writing that conquers*" (*The Writing of History* xxv), he insists that it "will use the New World as if it were a blank, 'savage' page on which Western desire will be written. It will transform the space of the other into a field of expansion for a system of production" (xxv–xxvi). Conrad's Congo lends itself to this new construction because of its void suggested through the characters' and the narrators' inability to see.

Since Marlow belongs to the world of cosmos, he suspects the unexplored space, chaos, to be governed by devilish, irrational, and unpredictable forces. His cultural pride, a form of idolatry, blocks his intellect. He often blames his inability to act, or see, on some kind of charm or madness. Neither space nor time has its limits here, in the fluidity of chaos. Emptiness, silence, disorientation, and the eerie suspicion of some unnatural force exercising its evil power over the unknown land make

Marlow think that he is navigating in a space without rules, without all the landmarks that make orientation in cosmos possible. He notices white men who have "the appearance of being held [on the shore] captive by a spell" (61), the land of "the lurking death" and "the hidden evil" (58); even his sleep "seemed unnatural, like a state of trance" (67). When the adventure comes to an end, and Marlow finds himself back in "the sepulchral city" (114), in the world of "commonplace individuals going about their business in the assurance of perfect safety" (114), he admits that the whole enterprise acquired some unreal shape. Marlow is not even certain whether Kurtz really existed: "Sometimes I ask myself whether I had ever really seen him—whether it was possible to meet such a phenomenon!" (103).

David Adams sees Conrad as an author who collapses boundaries between Europe and Africa: "Beginning his tale with an analogy between Roman Britain and Africa, and then describing Brussels as a 'whited sepulchre' (13), 'city of the dead' (14), and 'cemetery' (72), Marlow consistently incorporates Europe into the Inferno" (147). It seems to me, however, that consistently it is Africa that is infernal, a point which the numerous examples in this chapter illustrate. Europe is merely lifeless. Though anemic, it is not devoid of markers of identity and historical relevance, as Conrad's Congo is.

The Diabolical Other and the Danger of Emasculation

Eliade includes in his description of chaos a crucial element; he maintains that to the inhabitants of cosmos, only the space they occupy is organized and populated. But the word *unoccupied* in relation to chaos may simply mean "unoccupied by our people" or "peopled by ghosts, demons, 'foreigners'" (*Sacred* 31). Marlow's natives resemble ghosts and demons, with "their eyeballs glistening," "faces like grotesque masks" (30), and "deathlike indifference of unhappy savages" (33). He sees "nothing earthly" in these "black shadows" and "moribund shapes" (35). Later, during his trip up the river, he recalls the men who "were—No, they were not inhuman. Well, you know, that was the worst of it—this suspicion of their not being inhuman" (62–63).[4] Clearly, when the fabricated distinction between the devilish natives and the urbane Europeans becomes blurred, the negative mirror image through which Marlow and other Europeans identify themselves no longer allows for a clear-cut compartmentalizing and ordering process. This axiomatic framework distorts reality, but existence without the comfort of constant encoding of difference looms as too frightening, too complex. Marlow prefers to cling to the comforting myth.

This delusion, invading even the British abolitionist propaganda long before Conrad's times, sustained—conveniently enough—the claim of both moral and scientific foundation for the European imperial drive, what Patrick Brantlinger calls "the myth of the Dark Continent" ("Victorians and Africans" 45). In the same vein, the narrator in "Outpost" describes the Sierra Leone native, Makola, as "taciturn and impenetrable," a man who "cherished in his innermost heart the worship of evil spirits" (3). The Africans make "an uncouth babbling noise," send "quick, wild glances out of their startled, never-resting eyes" (7), and perform barbarian rites with "songs from a madhouse" that "darted shrill and high in discordant jets of sound" (11). In both texts, the narrators fear any possibility of collapsed racial boundaries and choose the ethnocentric normativizing discourse instead.

De Certeau says that the "a priori of difference" typical of travel accounts "is illustrated by a series of surprises and intervals (monsters, storms, lapses of time, etc.) which at the same time substantiate the alterity of the savage, and empower the text to speak from elsewhere and command belief" (*Heterologies* 69). This exercise in ethnography, the account of a "true" witness, comes of course from the location of power. De Certeau makes a similar claim in his commentary on Léry:

The native reenacts the Western phantasm of witches dancing and crying in the night, wild with pleasure and glutting themselves on children. The "sabbath" that Léry evokes is in continuity with what the Carnival of antiquity has since become, now progressively excluded from cities with the development of bourgeois towns, exiled into the countryside, the forests, and the night. This festive, prohibited, threatening world appears again exiled to the other side of the universe, at the outer limit of the conquerors' enterprise. And like the exorcist, his colleague from over here, the explorer-missionary assigns himself the task of expelling witches from the foreign land. But he does not succeed so well in localizing them on the stage of ethnological exorcism. The other returns: with the image of nudity, "an exorbitant presence"; with the phantasm of the *vagina dentata*, which looms in the representation of feminine voracity; or with the dancing eruption of forbidden pleasures. More basically, the native world, like the diabolical cosmos, becomes Woman. It is declined in the feminine gender. (233)

The uncanny, the ghoulish, and the wild appear in Conrad's evocation of the cannibals, naked figures or limbs hiding in bushes, witchcraft, the carnivalesque, darkness, sensuality, desire, and the diabolical female. Kurtz's mistress, "a wild and gorgeous apparition of a woman" (99), with her "bizarre things, charms, gifts of witch-men" (99), her "savage and superb" demeanor, "wild-eyed and magnificent" face and "ominous and stately" posture, is the epitome of a primitive goddess blessing the wilderness that surrounds her, terrible, dangerous, unmediated—and yet defeated by the "imbecile crowd" (109) shooting toward the riverbank. She is, in fact, "like the wilderness itself" (99), looking at the steamer crew "with an air of brooding over an inscrutable purpose" (99).[5] Marlow recalls her face, which has "a tragic and fierce aspect of wild sorrow and of dumb pain mingled with the fear of some struggling, half-shaped resolve" (99). The mistress's resolve could not be fully shaped, nor could her sorrow be anything but "wild" in Marlow's recollection. She is a part of the savage crowd, a part of the jungle, of chaos, and—as a woman—even more treacherous than the other natives so incompetently described in Marlow's account. Conrad's often discussed misogyny finds its vent in the figure of Kurtz's mistress. The diabolical female "with helmeted head" (108), armed with magic and "an uncontrollable desire" (100), displays the last act of valor as she "put out her hands, shouted something, and all that wild mob took up the shout in a roaring chorus" (108–9). Significantly, Kurtz's mistress remains nameless, perhaps as Marlow's attempt to facilitate the listeners' association of this woman with voracious Africa itself.

The urge to "civilize," to introduce traditions and moral codes of "our world" (that is, the center) into the "other world" (the periphery) is also representative of a male desire to overpower and subdue the female element. The colonizers will match Africa's fecundity with their own potency. They will penetrate the wilderness without asking for permission. By analogy, "going native" is tantamount to emasculation, loss of virility, and lack of agency. Kurtz, an elusive and fierce figure in Marlow's narrative, chooses chaos over cosmos and becomes an "enchanted princess sleeping in a fabulous castle" (72), no more real than "inhabitants in the planet Mars" (49).

Reverse Cosmogony

An attempt to render what the hegemonic establishment deems as chaos and to transform it into cosmos is perilous, and it demands outstanding, omnipotent qualities if confusion, emasculation, or even death are to be avoided. Once the "missionaries" (the self-appointed divine agents) approach the task without due care and reverence, the process seems to be reversed—we observe chaos invading cosmos, anarchy and bewilderment taking the place of civility, and devotion to a "cosmicized" moral code. Such is the fate of Kurtz, Kayerts, Carlier, and many other Conrad characters who finally prove to be too unbalanced and absolutely dependent on the immediate presence of arbitrary rules and the means to enforce them. In his isolation from "civilized" society, Kurtz's "nerves went wrong, and caused him to preside at certain midnight dances ending with unspeakable rites" (83), the "wastes of his weary brain were haunted by shadowy images" (110), and "his soul was mad. Being alone in the wilderness, it had looked within itself, and, by heavens! I tell you, it had gone mad" (107).[6] After his exhausting trip to the Central Station, Marlow himself admits that "[being] hungry, you know, and kept on my feet, too, I was getting savage" (43). The heat, hunger, and, most of all, lack of supervision of the representatives of the law create a temptation to abandon one's beliefs in moral order established by the inhabitants of cosmos, those of the European community. As the doctor says to Marlow, "the changes take place inside" (*HD* 58).

Conrad himself seems to question the Manichean construct and expose the essentialist binarisms as fake. The inhabitants of the very disorderly "outpost of progress," Kayerts and Carlier,

were two perfectly insignificant and incapable individuals, whose existence is only rendered possible through the high organization of civilized crowds. Few men realise that their life, the very essence of their character, their capabilities and their audacities, are only the expression of their belief in the safety of their surroundings. The courage, the composure, the confidence; the emotions and principles; every great and every insignificant thought belongs not to the individual but to the crowd: to the crowd that believes blindly in the irresistible force of its institutions and of its morals, in the power of its police and of its opinion. But the contact with pure unmitigated savagery, with primitive nature and primitive man, brings sudden and profound trouble into the heart. To the sentiment of being alone of one's kind . . . to the negation of the habitual, which is safe, there is added the affirmation of the unusual, which is dangerous; a suggestion of things vague, uncontrollable, and repulsive, whose discomposing intrusion excites the imagination and tries the civilised nerves of the foolish and the wise alike. ("Outpost" 5)

The uncharted, wild environment, combined with a lack of authority and supervision, triggers an unusual process: the chaos that the white man himself created and then ventured to restrain and discipline creeps closer and closer to the "cosmicized" world of schools, priests, and prisons and, unnoticed but very effective, gradually takes possession of the hitherto ordered and meaningful realm, revealing flaws and undercutting confidence in the cosmos. Similarly, Kurtz goes "mad" (107) and takes "a high seat amongst the devils of the land" (81) without "solid pavement under [his] feet" (81–82) and without "kind neighbours ready to cheer [him] or to fall on [him], stepping delicately between the butcher and the policeman, in the holy terror of scandal and gallows and lunatic asylums" (82). But it is also important to notice that although Conrad points at the fragile nature of the order imposed by "civilization" (that is, the West) and therefore effectively diminishes the merit of the imperial enterprise, he also indirectly expresses the belief, embedded in the "myth of the Dark Continent," that the foreign land (in this case, Africa) has demoralizing and degenerative effects on the "civilised nerves" of the Europeans. In other words, the African chaos retains its demonic qualities, even though the European invaders soon prove to be no better than the devilish and menacing natives, so resistant to the charm of "civilization."

This revenge of the other upon the invaders is a common trope in Conrad's texts. As William R. Mueller notes, in Conrad's fiction, "storms and seas and jungles seem at times not merely blind, errant forces, but purposeful, consciously motivated antagonists, committed to the destruction of a mankind which goes beyond appropriate limits, which overruns and violates the nonhuman orders of the created universe" (78–79). *Nostromo*, for example, through its depictions of covert invasion, exploration, industrialization, and exploitation, indicates how perilous it is to violate the natural order of the land and the will of its native people. The characters who believe in the "civilizing" mission they initiate are finally swept away

by the wild forces of revolution fueled by insatiable greed, by forces uncontrollable, voracious, as chaotic as the African interior in *Heart of Darkness*. Imposition of one's own "superior" will means either death or a necessity to assimilate, that is, to become a part of the uncontrollable force.
The "cosmicizing" mission in this "Tale of the Seaboard" fails. Mueller
says that in *Nostromo*, the characters "are cursed with a lack of restraint—
for silver, not for ivory and savage rites—and with a rapacity luring them
to cross that cosmic line separating their proper territory from nature's
domain, in this case her mineral kingdom. They lack the wisdom which
intuits boundaries and foresees the consequences of trespass" (82).

Nostromo's Color-Coded Wilderness

Nostromo is a story about a struggle between the chaos of the virgin land
(including natural but violent forces intrinsic to Costaguana) and its native people and, on the other hand, the cosmicizing design of "material
interests" (*Nostromo* 170) represented first by the Spanish conquistadores
(whose descendants are now, in a way, colonized themselves), the Inquisition, and Higuerota's treasure disturbed—or penetrated—by an English entrepreneur aided with American dollars. Charles Gould, however,
wants more than silver. What might seem to be a redeeming motive for
his drive to make profit from the San Tomé mine—that is, the desire to
implement an ethical order, integrity, and justice in Costaguana—turns
out to be equally risky and arrogant. The moral high ground from which
Gould dispenses orders and tries to control what he considers an unruly
and confused population does not provide, in the end, any backbone resistant to error.

The land invaded by the Spanish conquistadores and later by other Europeans hoping to profit from the natural riches of Costaguana resembles,
at times, Conrad's Africa; it is wild, treacherous, and inaccessible, and
it often reveals feminine attributes. The indigenous Costaguaneros are
often like the natives of the Congo in *Heart of Darkness*—uncouth yet
obedient to the foreign powers, an "uncivilized," simple, and mostly mute
workforce. The peninsula of Azuera is "a wild chaos of sharp rocks and
stony levels cut about by vertical ravines" (5); the "vastness" (7) of the
gulf is punctuated with "uninhabited islets" (7) and resembles the "mouth
of a black cavern" (7). It would be difficult to say with certainty whether
Conrad's description of the land as a black, cavernous mouth with sharp,

teeth-like rocks and vertical ravines deliberately suggests a *vagina dentata* figure, but it does invoke an image of a voracious monster ready to swallow innocents, an image—I should add—that is a projection of an irrational fear of the other.[7] Conrad presents Sulaco itself as "the opal mystery of great distances overhung by dry haze" (8). Gould's father thus sums up his antipathy to Costaguana in one of his letters: "God looked wrathfully at these countries, or else He would let some ray of hope fall through a rift in the appalling darkness of intrigue, bloodshed, and crime that hung over the Queen of Continents" (57). We learn that "the fantastic intrusions of the Old Man of the Sea, *vampires*, and *ghouls* . . . had lent to his [Gould's] father's correspondence the flavour of a gruesome Arabian Nights tale" (40). Eliade's description of the collective imagination of chaos as the nebulous or disordered space full of nightmarish ghosts and devils matches, at times, Conrad's rendering of the Europeans' perception of Costaguana. In fact, the very words *devil* and *devils* appear, according to *A Concordance to Conrad's* Nostromo, twenty-three times in the book; *ghost, ghosts, ghouls,* and *ghostly* surface twelve times.

There is a legend in Sulaco, a "strange theory of tenacious gringo ghosts suffering in their starved and parched flesh of defiant heretics, where a Christian would have renounced and been released" (6). The ghosts occupy the mountains, but there is an ominous presence in the water as well, in "the impenetrable darkness of the gulf, in the darkness defying—as men said—the knowledge of God and the wit of the devil" (360–61). The people in Costaguana fear Hernandez "as if he were the devil" (256). During one of the revolutions, Gamacho's speech resembles "the uncouth howlings of an inferior sort of devil cast into a white-hot furnace" (263). Even Nostromo assumes "the appearance of a phantom-like horseman" (65) when his "steed paced the lanes of the slums and the weed-grown enclosures within the old ramparts, between the black, lightless cluster of huts, like cow-byres, like dog-kennels" (65). He appears, at one point, to Captain Mitchell "like a haunting ghost" (326), and to Old Giorgio, sitting in "impenetrable darkness" and "ghostly silence" as a "vision" (312). The Violas sit in "the darkness of the room, striped by threads of quiet sunlight, alight with evil, stealthy sounds," the noise they had "in their ears as though invisible ghosts hovering about their chairs had consulted in mutters as to the advisability of setting fire to this foreigner's casa" (15). Don Pépé's face, in turn, resembles "a leathern mask with a benignantly diabolic expression" (73). It seems to Mrs Gould "as though the government of the country had been a struggle of lust between bands of absurd devils let loose upon the land with sabres and uniforms and grandiloquent phrases" (60). Although the word *absurd* might be quite apt in describing the violent revolutionaries who operate within long-winded, populist, sanctimonious discourse, it also refers to the "nightmarish parody of administration without law, without security, and without justice" (60).

In this Central American "heart of darkness," the "very paradise of snakes" (72), "the lawlessness of a populace of all colours and races, barbarism, irremediable tyranny" (126), few people care about order and moral integrity. Significantly, almost all of those who do are of European descent. They look upon the natives of Costaguana with either condescending superiority or hostile misapprehension. Even the magnanimous Mrs Gould "heroically concealed her dismay at the appearance of men and events so remote from her racial conventions . . . , since so much that seemed shocking, weird, and grotesque in the working out of their purposes had to be accepted as normal in this country" (112). Don Pépé, supervising the Indians working in the mine,

> could distinguish them not only by their flat, joyless faces, which to Mrs Gould looked all alike, as if run into the same ancestral mould of suffering and patience, but apparently also by the infinitely graduated shades of reddish-brown, of blackish-brown, of coppery-brown backs, as the two shifts, stripped to linen drawers and leather skullcaps, mingled together with a confusion of naked limbs, of shouldered picks, swinging lamps, in a great shuffle of sandalled feet on the open plateau before the entrance of the main tunnel. (68)

The classification according to skin color (that is, the various shades of brown) and flatness of the faces, the appalling objectification of the natives—with the emphasis on the "confusion of naked limbs," very suggestive of the portrayal of Africans in *Heart of Darkness*—comes in handy in exercising control over the mute workforce in Sulaco. Conrad endows the white European characters with idiosyncrasies, positive and negative traits of their personalities, but he leaves the members of the native population undefined, nebulous, ghost-like. True, some of the Hispanic native citizens of Costaguana, like Don Pépé himself, possess interesting characteristics that define their behavior and identities, but they are, without exception, persons with some kind of power—over the workers, the bandits, or the mob in numerous revolutions. Those belonging to the realm of cosmos emerge as human beings; those who dwell in the chaotic space of the other—whether slaving in the mine or murdering and plundering in another barbarous uprising—are formless masses of limbs, picks, lamps, axes, rifles, and blood-stained, ragged clothing. The "tame Indians," the "common folk of the neighbourhood" (5), "would lift sad, mute eyes to the cavalcade raising the dust of the crumbling *camino real* made by the hands of their enslaved forefathers" (60) in this "great land of plain and mountain and people, suffering and mute, waiting for the future in a pathetic immobility of patience" (60). When Don Pépé supervises the dangerous paths of Higuerota, the miners, most of whom are Indians "with big wild eyes" (68), address him as "Taita (father), as these barefooted people of Costaguana will address anybody who wears shoes" (68). Those who do not work in the mine "ploughed with wooden ploughs and yoked oxen, small on a boundless expanse, as if attacking immensity itself" (60).[8] These half-enslaved and speechless people are caught in the turmoil of relentless revolutions initiated mostly by the descendants of the Spanish invaders, now considered as "native" to the land as the Indian inhabitants. They are sucked into the whirlwind of upheavals or, as Old Viola calls the revolutions, "outbreaks of scoundrels and léperos, who did not know the meaning of the word 'liberty'" (16), from which they never benefit, directly or indirectly.

The narrator describes the incitement to revolution against the Blancos, reported to have "plotted with foreigners for the surrender of the lands and the slavery of the people," as the "clamour" of "Negro Liberalism" filled with "atrocious calumnies" (108). But slavery to European oligarchs seems to be quite real in *Nostromo*. When Holroyd visits Sulaco in 1885, slavery in some parts of the continent is still legal. Only in 1888 is slavery abolished in Brazil, for example. Conrad doesn't provide any account of abolitionism in his imaginary country, but we know that before 1800 San Tomé mine was worked by Indian slaves. Conrad never tells us how much, if anything, the miners are rewarded by the Gould Concession. He tells us, however, that the newspaper established to counter incitements to popular upheaval against unjust exploitation of the land and its people is funded, at least in part, by American dollars (108).

The Hispanic population of Costaguana can most certainly trace their roots (if we take into account geographical and historical clues that Conrad disperses throughout the novel) to Columbus's "discovery" of Central and South America (1492) and the conquest similar to that of Cortés in

Mexico in 1521. Conrad mentions the Inquisition in Costaguana, which reinforces the theory that the land and its people were subject to Spanish colonization as early as, for instance, Mexico. Old Viola's opinion on the revolutions and violence reflects the fact that he is "full of scorn for the populace" (13). The villagers about to attack his house are for him "not a people striving for justice, but thieves. Even to defend his life against them was a sort of degradation for a man who had been one of Garibaldi's immortal thousand in the conquest of Sicily" (16).

No newcomer seems to be prepared for this turmoil of the land. The European visitors find the deceitfully quiet water of Costaguana engulfed in "an impenetrable darkness" (7). At night, "[sky], land, and sea disappear together out of the world" (7). Like in Conrad's Africa, vision here is often limited; shapes are warped or hazy; good often merges with evil: "The eye of God Himself . . . could not find out what work a man's hand is doing in there; and you would be free to call the devil to your aid with impunity if even his malice were not defeated by such a blind darkness" (7). Higuerota and its surroundings appear to the head of the railway like "an imponderable liquid" (28). In this chaotic space of "trails of dust" (20), the sun "clear and blinding" (20), the riders "disappearing as if they had galloped into a chasm" (20), nothing can be taken for granted.

The Evangelists of Progress

Yet the head of the railway board from London, after an arduous trip over the mountains to Sulaco—this "out-of-the-way place" (25)—through "impassable roads skirting awful precipices" (25), thinks of "all the indifference of a man of affairs to nature, whose hostility can always be overcome by the resources of finance" (28).[9] The new European invaders reenact cosmogony not with the use of deadly weapons, like the Spanish conquistadores before them, but with the American dollars provided by Holroyd, which Charles Gould, this "Idealist-creator of Material Interests"—as Conrad calls him in the "Author's Note" (xxvi)—invests in the restoration of the mine and, he hopes, of "order." Indeed, the Europeans involved in the construction of the mine and of the requisite railway system consider this industrialization of the wilderness as a process equal to creating a universe or at least as a life-giving activity. For them, "the surveying of the railway track had the glamour of the first steps on the path of life" (29); some of them would die in the process, but "the work would be done:

the force would be almost as strong as a faith" (29). The qualifying word *almost* is significant, though, as Conrad immediately adds, "Not quite, however" (29). When the undertaking proves to be impossible—after an engineer pronounces, "We can't move the mountains!"—the engineer-in-chief decides to violate the rights of the villagers and build the railway on their land. Conrad's choice of words is typically very apt in his description of the European engineers' "civilizing" (that is, industrializing) mission in Costaguana. The passage seems to be a clear reference to Matthew 17:14–22, "The Healing of a Boy with a Demon," in which Jesus helps a member of the "unbelieving and perverse generation" when he banishes the demon out of a boy's body and thus explains the people's inability to conquer the profane: "Because you have so little faith. . . . If you have faith as small as a mustard seed, you can say to this mountain, 'Move from here to there' and it will move. Nothing will be impossible for you." The parallels between the gospel and the story of the railway construction in Costaguana hint at Conrad's disbelief in the honesty of the Europeans' declarations of their noble and disinterested desire to bring order and morality, or a spark of "civilization," to the invaded land. The symbolic statement "We can't move the mountains!" and the subsequent decision to interfere with the lives of the Indians and uproot them from their birthplaces in order to continue the construction are the early signs in the novel of the author's awareness of this civilizing mission's duplicitous motives and his disapproval of foreign invasion upon the imaginary Sulaco, but also upon the historical Central American soil. In fact, Eloise Knapp Hay remarks that it was "the Spanish-American War of 1898 which turned his [Conrad's] glaring monocle on the hypocritical aggressiveness of the apostles of New World freedom" (*Political* 166).

Let's take a closer look, then, at the man financing this aggression against Costaguana and its people. Holroyd, a commercial titan who embarks on a civilizing mission from behind his office desk in San Francisco, figures in *Nostromo*, very much like Sir Ethelred in *The Secret Agent*, as an enigmatic, powerful man determined to carry out his design. Sir Ethelred's plan is to nationalize fisheries in England. Holroyd, as long as he receives profit from the mine in Sulaco, "would not drop his idea of introducing, not only justice, industry, peace, to the benighted continents, but also that pet dream of his of a purer form of Christianity" (161), which we can understand as eradicating folksy and backward Catholicism. The engineer-in-chief explains Holroyd's zeal as a desire to retain long-lost youth:

> To be a millionaire, and such a millionaire as Holroyd, is like being eternally young. The audacity of youth reckons upon what it fancies an unlimited time at its disposal; but a millionaire has unlimited means in his hand—which is better. One's time on earth is an uncertain quantity, but about the long reach of millions there is no doubt. The introduction of a pure form of Christianity into this continent is a dream for a youthful enthusiast, and I have been trying to explain to you why Holroyd at fifty-eight is like a man on the threshold of life, and better, too. He's not a missionary, but the San Tomé mine holds just that for him. (214)

Getting rich then, through industrialization and exploitation of another country's natural resources, is literally a sacred mission. Changing chaos into cosmos is no more an attribute of primitive, archaic religions than an element of Christian apostolic zeal. Mrs Gould recognizes the Protestant work ethic and beliefs behind Holroyd's disgust with the "worship . . . of wood and tinsel" (49), as he calls the Catholic religion, and his conviction that God is "a sort of influential partner, who gets his share of profits in the endowment of churches" (49), which she sums up with one word: "idolatry" (49). Writing "from his inviolable sanctuary within the eleven-storey high factory of great affairs" (98) in San Francisco, he triggers—through the American dollars he gives to Gould—a colonizing mission that both Holroyd and Gould confuse with a civilizing project. Again, Mrs Gould aptly names their ideology as the "religion of silver and iron" (49). Thus Conrad—despite his aversion to organized religion, including Catholicism—implicitly gets back at what he would see as the self-righteous and arrogant Protestant mission to prosper and to write off predominantly Catholic nations (such as his imaginary Costaguana and his native Poland) as narrow-minded, infantile, and wild.

Why did Conrad destabilize the dichotomy of the demon and the saint? Why does he subvert the popular associations of "the monster," this allegedly stable signifier of alterity? In a circumventing way—through Holroyd—Conrad not only voices his dislike of American imperial venture but he also strikes back at the culture that often points to the distinction between the blood-drinking, vampiric, and cannibalistic Catholic and the virtuous Protestant, whose good works draw near to the sacred. I'm not claiming that Conrad was a good little Catholic, but I suggest that as a socially conservative Anglophile, he attempts to maintain through this subversion stable delineations of power allocation (that is, to the British—not Belgian, Spanish, or American—empire of "good intentions"), validating, at the same time, his own (Catholic) origin, a ghostly heritage which he abandoned, but by which he was, nevertheless, haunted.

In an astonishingly prophetic speech, Holroyd explains the "cosmicizing" plans of the Holroyd Missionary Fund carrying out "the Protestant invasion of Sulaco" (339) and those of America in general:

> Now, what is Costaguana? It is the bottomless pit of 10 per cent loans and other fool investments. European capital has been flung into it with both hands for years. Not ours, though. We in this country know just about enough to keep indoors when it rains. We can sit and watch. Of course, some day we shall step in. *We are bound to.* But there's no hurry. Time itself has got to wait on *the greatest country in the whole of God's Universe.* We shall be giving the word for everything: industry, trade, law, journalism, art, politics, and religion, from Cape Horn clear over to Smith's Sound, and beyond, too, if anything worth taking hold of turns up at the North Pole. And then we shall have the leisure to take in hand the outlying islands and continents of the earth. We shall run the world's business whether the world likes it or not. *The world can't help it—and neither can we,* I guess. (53)[10]

While Holroyd's speech and his convictions are grounded in a powerful sense of predestination, they also point to the dangerous voraciousness of a sinister capitalist monster lurking, lying in wait to eventually devour the world if an occasion arises. The blind force of Providence leads this "greatest country in . . . God's Universe" to impose its rules on others, to cosmicize not only Costaguana, but the entire world—as Americans are "bound to" follow this divine urge. In fact, Conrad predicts through Gould's words that people like Holroyd "some day shall get hold of Costaguana along with the rest of the world" (56).[11]

In comparison, Gould's own indomitable faith in the sacred power of material interests, although affecting an entire nation, seems rather innocuous. Gould proclaims: "I pin my faith to material interests. Only let the material interests once get a firm footing, and they are bound to impose the conditions on which alone they can continue to exist. That's how your money-making is justified here in the face of lawlessness and disorder" (57–58). Charles Gould is, as Mueller argues, "like the early Kurtz, a man with an ideal before whose altar he is ready to bow down and offer the sacrifice of mind, heart, and hands." Mueller adds: "As Kurtz would redeem savages from savagery, Gould, who also sees himself as something of a missionary, would redeem Costaguanans from the instability, poverty, and ill governance which rides herd over them" (Mueller 89).

My contention is that Gould is not the only Kurtz-like character in *Nostromo.* Guzman Bento, for instance, requests to be addressed as "the Citizen Saviour of the Country" (*Nostromo* 95) and sees himself "elevated on a pinnacle of power and safety beyond the reach of mere mortal plotters" (95). During masses, he sits "in a gilt armchair placed before the high altar" (95), commanding "manifestations of presidential piety" (95). Conrad adds that all women were supposed to "present thanks afterwards in a special audience. The incarnation of that strange god, El Gobierno Supremo, received them standing, cocked hat on head, and exhorted them in a menacing mutter to show their gratitude by bringing up their children in fidelity to the democratic form of government" (96). This grotesque imitation of the godhead of civil order resembles Kurtz's, and even Lord Jim's, elevated place in their respective environments and the incongruity between their own self-image and the real reception of their positions by observers such as Marlow. And there are more Kurtz-like characters in the novel: the president-dictator, Ribiera, who looks like an "exaggeration of a cruel caricature, the fatuity of solemn masquerading, the atrocious grotesqueness of some military idol of Aztec conception and European bedecking, awaiting the homage of worshippers" (83), or Pedrito Montero, who enters Sulaco to "the furious beating of drums" (258), inducing fear of his newly acquired power among the population of Costaguana.

The Aristocratic Club of Sulaco, thriving under the unofficial reign of the Gould Concession, has its quarters, significantly, in a house that was once "the residence of a high official of the Holy Office" (67), that is, of the Inquisition. Conrad also mentions "the heavy stonework of bridges and churches left by the conquerors" that "proclaimed the disregard of human labour, the tribute-labour of vanished nations" (61). The emblematic figure of the attempts made by the church to reclaim its influence is Padre Corbelàn, another Kurtz-like figure. This "fierce converter of savage Indians" (128), as Decoud calls him, "had come out of the wilds to advocate the sacred rights of the Church with the same fanatical fearlessness with which he had gone preaching to bloodthirsty savages, devoid of human compassion or worship of any kind." Apparently, he was successful, as he "baptized whole nations of Indians, living with them like a savage himself" (131–32). He has a "white spot of a scar on the bluish shaven cheeks (a testimonial to his apostolic zeal from a party of unconverted Indians)" that "suggested something unlawful behind his priesthood, the idea of a chaplain of bandits" (131).

Marlow says in *Heart of Darkness* that "all Europe contributed to the making of Kurtz" (117)—a statement that places the blame for the colonial atrocities in Africa not only on the Belgians but on the entire Old Continent and its "cosmicizing" urges. Perhaps of significant importance is the fact that Holroyd, a man with a profile of "a Caesar's head on an old Roman coin" (52–53)—a detail already hinting at his imperial drives—has, like Kurtz, roots all over Europe. Conrad explains Holroyd's parentage as a mixture of German, Scotch, English, Danish, and French blood, "giving him the temperament of a Puritan and an insatiable imagination of conquest" (53). Europe, it seems, excels at producing men thirsting for power who try to achieve salvation through imposition of their own culture and religion upon the other. Thus in *Nostromo*, the most frightening bloodsucking others are not Catholics, as England and Prussia at the turn of the century would have it, but the omnivorous Protestant evangelicals armed with Bibles and cash. Most important, however, Conrad blurs and often subverts the boundary between the saintly and the demonic to underscore the insidious danger of empty rhetoric and self-righteous religiosity in general at work in various colonizing missions.

The Dangers of Scripting Cosmos

One attempt to impose order of a textual, scriptural kind upon the chaos of history in *Nostromo* is "Fifty Years of Misrule," written by Don José Avellanos and, notably, never published.[12] The book apparently does not cover the origins and the entire process of colonization of Costaguana, from the early Spanish explorers, through the Inquisition, through Charles IV, whose "equestrian statue gleamed pale against the black trees of the Alameda, like a ghost of royalty haunting the scenes of revolution" (240), up to the attempts made by the Catholic Church to reclaim its gradually diminishing influence and goods, as well as the invasion of foreigners drawing profit from Costaguana's natural resources. What seems to be covered in the book is an array of contemporary revolutions, and although Conrad calls it "impartial" (Author's Note xxv), the perspective it entails is, inevitably, that of an influential and (in comparison with the Indians) affluent member of the society.

Decoud, though belonging to the same privileged group as Don José, tries to imagine the old days "when the persistent barbarism of our native continent did not wear the black coats of politicians, but went about yelling, half-naked, with bows and arrows in its hands" (155). Like Mrs Gould and Dr Monygham, Decoud realizes that those who attempt to introduce new, "civilized," and "just" laws in Costaguana, to make a "little rift in the darkness" (58, Gould's words)—through investments, jurisdiction, religion—are, in fact, gradually swallowed by the chaotic forces of the land, the "blood-dimmed tide," perhaps because, as Yeats would say, "The best lack all conviction, while the worst / Are full of passionate intensity" (Yeats, "The Second Coming" 7–8). Their position on "the Olympus of plutocrats" (*Nostromo* 47), as Conrad calls the mine, does not shield them from corruption. Mrs Gould "saw clearly the San Tomé mine possessing, consuming, burning up the life of the last of the Costaguana Goulds; mastering the energetic spirit of the son as it had mastered the lamentable weakness of the father" (348).[13] Like the first gringos wandering in search of the treasure in Azuera, who perished in their search, the contemporary forces of "cosmos" are slowly consumed by the lawlessness and mayhem of Sulaco. Throughout the novel, Gould, Decoud, and Nostromo refer to the silver of Higuerota as poison and curse. Gould, from the very beginning of his "mission" in Costaguana, has to "accommodate himself to existing circumstances of corruption so naively brazen as to disarm the hate of a man courageous enough not to be afraid of its irresponsible potency to ruin everything it touched" (98). Therefore, he uses illicit practices and refuses to discuss the ethics of his behavior with his wife, trusting that "though a little disenchanted, she would be intelligent enough to understand that his character safeguarded the enterprise of their lives as much or more than his policy" (98). Gould miscalculates his resistance to fraudulence and duplicity, and falsely assumes that his actions (bribery, plotting, and scheming in order to establish governments that approve of his business practices) do not represent his moral standing. The silver and the power it begets corrupt his reasoning. The history of Costaguana, consisting of cycles of revolutions and relative peace sustained by corrupted practices, is eventually unaffected by the Goulds. Although they influence political decisions, the concession is unable to change what it considers the "profane" nature of that land and its people.

Conrad's Priapic Dance and the "Irruption of Speech"

Gould is unaware of the activities in which villagers engage during festivals and public meetings. For him, they are a uniform, mute, and passive mass. And yet the ferocity and wild passion of the native Costaguaneros underlie the carnivalesque scenes in *Nostromo*. In one of them, we observe the Capataz de Cargadores approaching a "huge circus-like erection" (86), where the crowd of the mine workers "*thickened*; the guitars tinkled *louder*"; the people "*eddied* and *pushed* before the doors of the high-roofed building, whence issued a shuffle and *thumping* of feet in time to the dance music *vibrating* and *shrieking* with a *racking rhythm*, overhung by the tremendous, sustained, hollow roar of the gombo. The *barbarous* and imposing noise of the big *drum*, that can madden a crowd, and that even Europeans cannot hear without a *strange emotion*, seemed to draw Nostromo on to its source" (86).[14] A few moments later, "from the doors of the dance hall men and women emerged tottering, *streaming with sweat, trembling in every limb*, to lean, *panting*, with *staring eyes* and *parted lips*, against the wall of the structure, where the harps and guitars played on with *mad speed* in an incessant roll of *thunder*. Hundreds of hands clapped in there; *voices shrieked*, and then all at once would *sink low*, chanting in unison the refrain of a *love song*, with *a dying fall*" (86).[15]

The highly sexualized picture of the native of non-occidental territories—which de Certeau, Said, and others mention in their analyses of the European colonizers' fascination with and fear of the other—seems to be one of the major techniques of rendering indigenous peoples in Conrad's fiction. But does *Nostromo* offer a slightly modified version of that portrayal? Here Conrad replaces the shameless nudity and unencumbered libido of the African female (the *vagina dentata* trope in his description of Kurtz's mistress in *Heart of Darkness*) with a highly masculinized and homoerotic form of sexual behavior. He thus places his own apparently unambiguous value upon the natives of Costaguana. The carnivalesque becomes an orgy; the potentially procreative act turns into prophylactic or nongenerative gratification through the phallus.

The festivity is centered at a "circus-like erection," a phrase already implying masculine sexuality and some kind of performance; in the case of a circus, it is usually an unusual or even freakish show. This erection attracts a thickening throng, eddying and pushing, thumping, vibrating, and shrieking to a rhythm, to the primitive drumbeat—again, a reminiscence of the wild drumming in *Heart of Darkness*—that fills the Europeans (in Costaguana, as much as in the Congo) with anxiety, excitement, or fear. Both men and women are drawn to the erection; they sweat and pant, their limbs tremble, their lips are parted, until the shrieking voices "sink low" and the love song ends with "a dying fall," a phrase suggestive of a climax and subsequent sexual detumescence.

The intensity of the priapic images could stem from Conrad's undoubtedly stereotyping attitude toward ethnicities and races and, therefore, from his perception of Central or South American culture as highly sexualized and macho-dominant. However, the homoerotic connotations of this description invite an important question about Conrad's attitude toward his indigenous characters: Is it a sign of his disapproval of the lack of traditional social conventions among the natives, a homophobic assault on unrepressed libido? Or is it a gesture of endorsement of the characters' natural, spontaneous, unlimited sexuality expressed in dance?

Conrad's repeated expressions of disgust toward the mob in *Nostromo* probably suggest the first answer. After all, he states, reinforcing his essentialist perception of difference, that "there is always something childish in the rapacity of the passionate, clear-minded, Southern races, wanting in the misty idealism of the Northerners, who at the smallest encouragement dream of nothing less than the conquest of the earth" (224). However, the contrast between his feminized Africa and masculinized Central America, considered through the prism of power allocation in gender relations at the turn of the century, might imply a favoring gesture toward the Latin culture. On the surface, then, the dance scene defies the hegemonic order in Costaguana, and not just social order, but also political control. The sexualized, homoerotic dance may be a voice of dissent. It is no accident that Foucault links stifling of open expression and control over open spaces to the rise of capitalism or, to use Mr Gould's famous phrase, "material interests." Repression, says Foucault, is "an integral part of the bourgeois order" (5). One of the reasons for this repression is that sex "is incompatible with the general and intensive work imperative" (6). In *Nostromo*, desire is supposed to function as a sign of resistance against everything the mine and the reign of the Goulds represent: usurpation of the land, the Protestant work ethic and restraint, panoptic control, materialism, greed, inhumane working conditions, European social conventions and business institutions, and American money. The homoerotic undertones of the scene only strengthen this subversion. Foucault asks: "At a time when labor capacity was being systematically exploited, how could this capacity be allowed to dissipate itself in pleasurable pursuits, except in those—reduced to a minimum—that enabled it to reproduce itself?" (6) Sex and the right to speak about it are generally considered to be forms of political subversion: "If sex is repressed, that is, condemned to prohibition, nonexistence, and silence, then the mere fact that one is speaking about it has the appearance of a deliberate transgression. A person who holds forth in such language places himself to a certain extent outside the reach of power; he upsets established law; he somehow anticipates the coming freedom" (6). What is at stake in Conrad's narrative, then? On the surface, this insubordination, the throbbing, swaying, panting, sweating, and shrieking of the dancers, the letting go of conventions owned and imposed by the European exploiters—all undermine the illusion of full hegemonic control in Costaguana. Surreptitiously, or perhaps not quite consciously, through an extended metaphor of a communal dance, Conrad seems to undermine Victorian social conventions and accepted image of alterity.

But what does Conrad's choice to articulate the desire and to offer a vivid description of the highly sexualized dancing scene tell us about traditional binarisms endorsed by the colonizers? Could this articulation really be a tool for clandestine subversion of these arbitrary dichotomies? Foucault uses the word *appearance* in the passage quoted above. One of the main arguments he suggests in the first volume of *History of Sexuality* is that sex isn't really that which remains unspoken, although we tell ourselves that it is. We fail to account for the explosion of discourse that actually produced and categorized sexuality, and then constructed and portrayed it as something innate and natural yet dangerous and in need of control. I would like to suggest that Conrad is part of that myth— the telling ourselves that sex is unspoken in polite (or civilized) society. Such speech contributes to and perpetuates the power/knowledge regime that constructs sexuality in the first place. Conrad, then, transfers that which he believes to be unspoken in the turn-of-the-century Europe onto a removed and imagined territory, where pleasure can be contained and described. His scene represents what Foucault calls "irruption of speech"

(Foucault 5), an act that only on the surface seems indispensable in transgressing prohibitions and freeing oneself from repression because it is believed to articulate the taboo and reinstate one's voice. In the end, Conrad's dance scene is part of the discourse that creates the normalizing narrative in which sexuality is essential to (racial) identity. Although the dance itself seems to be an act of liberatory transgression, Conrad engages in a codifying and essentializing description through which power is maintained by confession of a secret and classification of it through the gaze (Nostromo's, the narrator's, Conrad's, ours).

In other words, within the narrative, the dance itself could be seen as liberatory in that it takes place beyond the reach of the gaze, beyond the hegemonic control. Conrad's narrative act, however, is not liberatory but restrictive in that it assigns essentialized sexuality to "the native." Although the Costaguaneros' shrieks and drumming disrupt silence and seem to create unencumbered space of self-expression, Conrad's discourse on sex and race participates in oppressive mechanisms of power/ knowledge and essentializes difference. Despite the evidence pointing to Conrad's understanding of the drive to classify and compartmentalize as reductive and stultifying, Conrad circumscribes the space in which the officially constructed dichotomy of master-slave in Costaguana could be disrupted and makes this disruption possible through a description of a highly sexualized body of the native.

Although he goes against codification of alterity when he portrays the perceived chaos of the other invading the cosmos of power, Conrad still maintains the colonizing narrative tendency to gaze, survey, and classify in his description of nonwhite characters. A schizophrenic cartographer of empire and its dominion, he is aware of multidimensionality and complexity of the colonial enterprise, but he nevertheless renders most of his non-European characters on a two-dimensional plain, orchestrating them according to the reductive myth of the other popular in colonial England. Discussing our tendencies to impose order on that which is unknown, Robin W. Lovin and Frank E. Reynolds claim that "cosmogonic myths . . . are attempts to find a pattern for human choice and action that stands outside the flux of change and yet within the bonds of human knowing" (5). They emphasize the "underlying function of bestowing on certain actions a significance that is not proportioned to their empirical effects or to the individual goals of their agents, but derives from their relation to an order of the world that begins with the beginning of the world as we know it" (6). It is important to remember, though, that the prevalent occurrence of false gods in Conrad's writing indicates his awareness that colonizers have proven to be their own worst enemy—especially where cultural pride and blindness have been fortified by "religious" certainty or, in theological terms, by idolatrous attachment to one's own constructed cosmogonic myth permitting disrespect of *other* cosmogonies.

3

"A free lay church in a free lay state"

From the Cosmogonic Discourse to Sacred Secularism in Joyce's Imagined Community

In "Ireland: Island of Saints and Sages," Joyce tells us that "what England did in Ireland over the centuries is no different from what the Belgians are doing today in the Congo Free State" (119). Although there are marked parallels between the colonial status of the Irish and the native tribes in parts of Africa, as I pinpoint in my earlier discussion, the colonized Irish and the colonized African tribes sustained disproportionate forms of oppression due largely to their racial difference. Vincent Cheng and Enda Duffy draw our attention to this distinction. Cheng notes that the discourse about race in Ireland "was inseparable from the 'Irish Question' and issues of Empire and Home Rule" (15), partly because the denominators of "race" ranged between "issues of sociology, biology, ethnicity, genetics, lineage, physical typology, animal species," "social class, status," and other factors (16). Therefore, the word itself "serves as a blank screen or cipher upon which to encode a culture's or an individual's own unacknowledged preoccupations" (17). He returns to Benjamin Disraeli's 1836 speech in which he describes the Irish as a "wild, reckless, indolent, uncertain, and superstitious race" and as barbarians who "hate our order, our civilisation, our enterprising industry, our sustained courage, our decorous liberty, our pure religion" (qtd in Cheng 20). Duffy states that the Irish occupied "an ambivalent middle ground between the 'master' and 'dark' races" (43) against whom the colonizers measured their own supremacy. The indistinguishable racial signifiers—even though, as mentioned in the first chapter, there were multiple attempts on the part of the British to produce an image of the Irish as simianized, intellectually and emotionally inferior—led to "outright hatred rather than condescension" (Duffy 44), manifested in English jingoism and often undisguised ridicule of the fabricated "other."

Echoing to a certain degree the motifs in Conrad's fiction, Joyce's texts—through their reflection of the modernist obsession with fragmentation of space—portray not only artificial binarisms inherent in colonial and religious hegemony but also an endeavor to reclaim national identity in late colonial Ireland as contemporary forms of a cosmogonic drive. Like Conrad, Joyce exposes the atavistic desire to reach the sacred through appropriation of cosmos in imperial enterprises; Joyce, however, also deals with the subaltern subjects internalizing the ideology of the oppressor in their struggle for independence. Significantly, *Ulysses* looks at this process from a late colonial and imminent postcolonial perspective (since Joyce wrote it between 1914 and 1921, on the eve of the proclamation of the Irish Free State), even if the book describes a still subjugated nation in 1904. It therefore offers a portrait of the nation anticipating its postcolonial struggle for autonomy, self-sufficiency, and identity independent of the former colonial power and its dialectical rhetoric.

In mythical geography, the only real space is that within the myth, which in turn relies on essential division of space into sacred and profane, proper and improper. As Foucault ascertains in his essay "Of Other Spaces,"[1] this split was present in Medieval culture and in its insistence on boundary production and what he calls "emplacement" (1), but it is also ingrained in the modern perception of reality. Modernity is "the epoch of juxtaposition, the epoch of near and far, of the side-by-side, of the dispersed" (1), where "life is still governed by a certain number of oppositions that remain inviolable" (2). Modernist poetry and fiction, with their tensions between the ahistorical and archetypal models of humanity, on the one hand, and, on the other, the modern, post-Hegelian, historical conceptions, are nevertheless often saturated with unspecified and unrealized nostalgia for the sacred, as Eliot's *Four Quartets* exemplifies. Foucault points out that "despite all the techniques for appropriating space, despite the whole network of knowledge that enables us to delimit or to formalize it, contemporary space is perhaps still not entirely desanctified" (2). Moreover, the set of relations which we inhabit "delineates sites which are irreducible to one another and absolutely not superimposable on one another" (2). As I will claim in the second section of this book, it is difficult, and sometimes even impossible, to transgress the boundaries between these sites when one embarks on a quest toward the sacred, toward the cosmic center, the fixed identity.

Sacral Nationalism

Discussing the colonization of Ireland, Joyce says that "no one, unless he were blinded by self-interest or ingenuity, can still believe that a colonizing country is prompted by purely Christian motives when it takes over foreign shores, for all that the missionary and the pocket-bible come some months ahead of the arrival of the army and machine-guns" (*Occasional* 116). Joyce is not sure whether nationality is "not really a useful fiction like many others which the scalpels of the present-day scientists have put paid to" (118), but at the same time, he claims that it "must find its basic reason for being in something that surpasses, that transcends and that informs changeable entities such as blood or human speech" (118). This reason—Joyce seems to imply through his discussion of the mystic theologian Dionysius the Areopagite's claim that the limits of nations appeared through a divine force, through the workings of God—goes beyond race and even history, and reaches back to the earliest times when a variety of tribes formed one body under the influence of a local god. In other words, it stems from the cosmogonic myth; hence the drive of the powerful nations (like England or Belgium at the turn of the century) to continue the cosmogonic enterprise and to subordinate such notions as "race" or "civilization" to the reenactment of the myth. The "local god" Joyce mentions in the essay turns out to be of a less mystical nature than Dionysius the Areopagite imagined, as Joyce proceeds to talk about the "second-rate and backward" (119) Irish race that, nevertheless, is "the only one in the entire Celtic family that refused to sell its birthright for a plate of lentils" (119). The local god is, then, simply mammon.

But Joyce's position on nationality and nationalism is more ambiguous. He does admit that nations "like individuals, have their egos" (108) and recognizes that they often attribute to themselves "qualities or glories unknown in other races—from the time when our forefathers called themselves Aryans and nobles to the Greeks who were wont to call anyone barbarian that did not live within the sacrosanct land of Hellas. The Irish, with a pride that is perhaps less explicable, love to refer to their land as the land of saints and sages" (108). He adds, however, in a rather Conradesque fashion, that "it would be easy to make a list of Irishmen who, both as pilgrims or hermits and scholars or sorcerers, have carried the torch of knowledge from country to country" (108) and emphasizes Ireland's "reputation as teacher of spiritual matters" (108), a "school for apostles" (111).[2]

In Conrad, this kind of discourse serves to expose the ethnocentric assumption of the colonizers that the invasion of other territories is a manifestation of their apostolic right to impose more "advanced" forms of civilization upon chaos. Joyce also mocks the colonizers' assumption of divine intervention in the lives of "barbaric" peoples when he ridicules Queen Victoria's excessive emotional stringency and devout behavior in "Cyclops" and when he presents King Edward VII as a laughable woman- izer. The king first appears in "Nestor," when Mr Deasy stares "sternly" at the picture of "Albert Edward, prince of Wales" after preaching to Stephen about the generosity and impartiality of the English (2.266–67). We might assume, having seen Stephen sit "noiselessly before the princely presence" (2.299), that Dedalus is intimidated by the company of the "generous" and "just" Deasy and his virtuous king (2.263). His circuitous reply, how- ever, suggests quiet disapproval of "those big words . . . which make us so unhappy" (2.264) and a refusal of an intellectually curious Irishman and an aspiring artist to engage in an active political debate which he finds extraneous to his creative effort. But Joyce does not drop the subject of Edward VII here. Let us consider the ubiquitous presence of "the royal initials, E.R."—for Edward Rex—on "His Majesty's vermillion mailcars" (7.16–17) all over Dublin, reminding its citizens of their subaltern status, or the king's apparition in "Circe." Here, Edward VII wears "a white jer- sey," on which—rather incongruously—"an image of the Sacred Heart is stitched," a markedly Irish-Catholic symbol, "with the insignia of Garter and Thistle" (15.4449–51), one of which is, according to Gifford, the im- age of St. Andrew bearing a cross (521). The king is also "robed as a grand elect perfect and sublime mason with trowel and apron" (15.4454–55). Gifford tells us that the Masonic apron is a symbol of "innocence and irreproachable conduct" (522). While historically accurate—since Prince Edward was grand master of the Grand Lodge of England—Joyce's use of an emblem of virtue and incorruptibility and his description of Edward appearing "with the halo of Joking Jesus" (15.4476) in this scene smacks of mockery of the king who has earned his reputation as a womanizer, gam- bler, and a rather dubious "peacemaker." In "Cyclops," the citizen, alluding to the reputation of Edward VII as a philanderer and disputing his title of a peacemaker, refers to the king as "more pox than pax" (12.1400–1401), a phrase which Gifford translates as "more venereal disease than peace" (Gifford 360). While Joyce's implicit references to Queen Victoria's assertions of her and her nation's moral superiority hint at his critique of England's imperial mission as inextricable from the search for the sacred, the presence of Edward VII in *Ulysses* suggests how fragile, subjective, and often downright deceitful such convictions of moral incorruptibility are.

Joyce, in addition, seems to recognize these convictions in both colonial oppression and resistance to the colonial power. It is no longer only the colonizer who appears to have a sacred motive; the colonized nation has one as well. Joyce would not remain true to his propensity for irreverent humor if he did not mock Ireland's tendency to perceive itself as the "martyr" or "saint." Like Conrad, he disrupts commonly accepted definitions of the sacred and the nation.

Even young Joyce seemed to understand the arbitrary divisions between the powerful and the subaltern as a result of the innate drive to triumph over others rather than inherent disparities in characteristics of races; he wrote in his 1898 essay "Subjugation," possibly a part of his university matriculation course, that "it may be that the desire to overcome and get the mastery of things, which is expressed in man's history of progress, is in a great measure responsible for his supremacy" (6). He added that "among human families the white man is the predestined conqueror" (*Occasional* 7). It is difficult to determine whether, according to young Joyce, this "predestination" is a disgraceful sign of the white man's sense of entitlement and superiority or an indication of the inevitable fulfillment of proper social roles by different races. Hence this remark of an aspiring writer and still-to-be educated student could be either a critique of the white supremacy or an acquiescence to the "natural" dominance of the "superior" race. Joyce's stance in his more mature writing, however, lends itself to a more substantiated interpretation—though not much clearer, on account of the problematic definition of "race" itself, especially in colonized Ireland.

The Racial Other and the Visual Dilemma

The first chapter of this book addresses the complex character of racial categories and potential difficulties in the comparison between the subjugated African peoples and the Irish, the "blacks of Europe"—a relationship nevertheless explored or, rather, constructed by the British to validate their imperial enterprise in the nineteenth and early twentieth centuries. Elizabeth Butler Cullingford notes that, although the socially and politically constructed affinity between the Irish and the Africans proved rather useful for the anti-Celtic agenda of the colonizers, nineteenth-century colonial observers "found it inconvenient that, despite their African pedigree and prognathous facial angles, the Irish remained stubbornly white" (145), preventing British politicians from openly justifying their occupation with the sacred call to carry the "white man's burden" also on their racially akin neighbors' territories. When Charles Kingsley described the people of Sligo as "white chimpanzees," and complained that "if they were black, one would not feel it [dreadfulness] so much" (Kingsley 107), Carlyle's answer, says Cullingford, to Kingsley's "visual dilemma" was to "black-lead them and put them over with the niggers" (Cullingford 145).

The imperial establishment presented both Africa and Ireland as either uncultivated and unsophisticated territories (hence the recurring pictures of Africa's impenetrable jungles and Ireland's barren swamps) ready to be introduced to order and "civilization" or as treacherous, overpopulated, untamed lands. Sometimes, defying the obviously illogical juxtaposition, both types of description were present at once, to magnify the necessity of the "civilized" British to bring the light of knowledge to these dark, horrifying places. The nothingness, whether physical or moral, had to be filled; the periphery had to become subject to the sacred center; the void had to be transformed into cosmos. In the maps of early modern Ireland, the Gaelic Irish are portrayed as hiding behind their defenses, but we also see "abandoned forts or ruined buildings. In other words, they [the Irish] are gone, the land is now empty and thus open for exploitation" (O'Sullivan 95).

In his essays and fiction, Joyce himself points to the stereotypical picture of the Irish as "strange souls," "artistically and sexually uninstructed," "childish spirits, unfaithful" ("Ireland: Island of Saints and Sages" 125), disoriented and mute, dazed by alcohol, and oppressed further by a second form of hegemonic power: the strict rules of the Roman Catholic Church. In "Ireland at the Bar," he recalls the murder trial of Myles Joyce, a peasant who could not speak English. Public opinion considered Myles Joyce a martyr: "The figure of this bewildered old man, left over from a culture which is not ours, a deaf-mute before his judge, is a symbol of the Irish nation at the bar of public opinion" (*Occasional* 146). Because of the impossibility of meaningful communication between the colonizer and the colonized, so emblematically represented by the passive figure of Myles Joyce,[3] the English press "act as interpreters between Ireland and the English electorate" (146), solidifying, conveniently for the English, the imperial point of view of the Irish "as criminals, with deformed faces, who roam around at night with the aim of doing away with every Unionist" (146). Joyce is also aware of the images of "the baboon-faced Irishman that we see in *Punch*" (*Stephen Hero* 69), reinforcing prejudice and hatred toward the subaltern.

Ireland, as the land of the other and on the periphery, "at the farthest remove from the centre of European culture" (*Stephen Hero* 199), will some day have to choose between England and Europe, says Robert Hand, "the descendant of the dark foreigners" in *Exiles*: "If Ireland is to become a new Ireland she must first become European" (51). Joyce's characters seem to have internalized the inferiority ascribed to them by the British, an attitude that is sometimes hard to distinguish from a motivating dose of self-criticism, but rather palpable in repetitive negative portrayals of the Irish as, for example, passive and helpless animals (like Eveline in *Dubliners*), anti-Semitic belligerent nationalists (in "Cyclops"), and spiritually paralyzed cowards, drunks, and hypocrites. The setting of their oppression is, at times, as nebulous and full of phantoms as Conrad's Congo. In *Joyce, Chaos, and Complexity*, Thomas Rice draws our attention to "Stephen's increasingly futile efforts to encounter his subjectively shaped reality in the real" and Joyce's descriptions of "the 'slight shocks to his boyish conception of the world . . . [that] obscured his mind' (*P* 64)" (72). He also notes that "Stephen's visions of 'goatish creatures with human faces' (*P* 137), a procession of 'masked memories' that pass 'quickly before him' (*P* 157), [. . .] or of 'cloudy shapes and beings' as his 'soul' swoons 'into some new world, fantastic, dim, uncertain as under sea' (*P* 172) at the conclusion of chapter 4 all emphasize the difference between Stephen's conception of the encounter with reality and what he is actually doing: constructing fantasies" (Rice 72). Ireland becomes in this narrative the land of ghosts and foreigners, a phantom land, clouded, misty, unreal, and profane. Even in *Ulysses*, highly naturalistic descriptions of the city and the slice-of-life expositions of the basest and the most human activities are interrupted by the "Circe" episode, a chapter full of phantasmagoric images, role changing, and magic.

In the midst of this parade of ghosts, absurd apparitions, and mortals step in Stephen's "guests. Uninvited. By virtue of the fifth of George and seventh of Edward" (*U* 15.4370–71): Privates Carr and Compton. "Circe" is actually framed by the menacing presence of these two redcoats, just as the "Wandering Rocks" chapter opens and closes with the viceregal cavalcade—one a dramatized reminder of a real threat of violence, the other an exercise in imperial theatricality designed to emphasize and, if necessary, reestablish the subaltern status of its viewers. In his exchange with the soldiers, Stephen remembers, tapping his brow, that "in here it is I must kill the priest and the king" (15.4436–37), exacerbating the squabble with the privates whose insularity and eagerness to fight do not allow them to comprehend his metaphor. Vincent Cheng tells us that "Carr is exhibiting the masculinist, xenophobic, racist tendency to essentialize everything foreign in terms of a single binarized pole, the hated enemy Other (in which place Irish, German, Boer, black, Jew, and so on, are interchangeable)" (232) and that the entire scene in "Circe" in which Stephen encounters the soldiers "proves to be a symptomatic, dialogic panoply of the colonial dynamics, struggles, and currents under the British Empire at the turn of the century" (232).

When Stephen, turning to Private Compton at the beginning of their altercation in "Circe," misquotes Jonathan Swift's words from "A Letter to the Whole People of Ireland" ("Doctor Swift says one man in armour will beat ten men in their shirts" *U* 15.4402), he alludes to the slavery of the Irish under British power. Swift maintains in the fourth of his *Drapier's Letters* that "all government without the consent of the governed, is the very definition of slavery: but, in fact, eleven men well armed will certainly subdue one single man in his shirt" (Swift 182). Following John Locke's contention about the sovereignty of nations in *Two Treatises on the Government*, Swift supports the constitutional independence of Ireland, asserting that if the rights of an Irishman are violated, he should have "the liberty of roaring as loud as he thought fit" (182) and that he has "looked over all the English and Irish statutes without finding any law that makes Ireland depend upon England, any more than England does upon Ireland" (181). Swift writes the letter under a pseudonym and addresses the Irish people "in order to refresh and continue that spirit so seasonably raised amongst you, and to let you see that by the laws of GOD, of NATURE, of NATIONS, and of your own COUNTRY, you ARE and OUGHT to be as FREE a people as your brethren in England" (183).

It is doubtful that the soldiers are familiar with the letter, as Stephen's words elicit no intelligent reply, only a threat of violence. However, after evoking Swift's letter, Stephen says: "I have no king myself at the moment" (15.4470) and calls himself a "judge of impostors" (15.4490–91)—like the soldiers and King Edward—and "Green rag to a bull" (15.4497), clearly resisting any classification and enslavement imposed by the colonizer.

Joyce is aware of the comparison between the Irish and the African slaves, so carefully constructed by the British to maintain the colonial status quo in both territories, but he also hints at important distinctions between the subaltern European and the subaltern African. True, the awareness that other territories under British control, especially Africa, suffered from the same or even greater imperial hypocrisy and brutality led some Irishmen to a sense of brotherhood with and empathy toward the black slaves. In his comparison of African, African American, Irish, and Jewish nationalisms, George Bornstein claims that these groups and their supporters felt affinity with each other, especially in the nineteenth and early twentieth centuries. He recalls Frederick Douglass's tour of famine in Ireland, after which Douglass spoke out against the misery and deprivation of Irish peasants who lived in "much the same degradation" as the slaves in America (371).[4] However, Joyce's compatriots also harbored racial prejudice and irrational fear of the other, best exemplified in their ostracism of Bloom, but also present in race-based projections aimed at presenting a negative, rather than empathetic, image of black slaves or black people in general.

When Molly, for example, ponders one of Mina Purefoy's numerous children, she compares him to "a nigger with a shock of hair on it" and exclaims: "Jesusjack the child is a black" (18.162–63), with as much implied astonishment as disgust. Intriguingly, Leopold Bloom, himself a victim of racist attacks and ridicule based on lack of validation of his ethnic difference, seems at first to espouse the same reductive patterns of identification, at least in the dream world of "Circe." "I treated you white," he says to Mary Driscoll and explains what "white treatment" actually means: "I gave you mementos, smart emerald garters far above your station. Incautiously I took your part when you were accused of pilfering" (15.876–78). One might assume, then, that these acts of kindness are reserved for the white race and somehow inappropriate in one's contact with a non-white person. But what does the narrative context tell us about this striking statement? The chapter combines the absurd with the real and, as many critics have noted, serves as a hyperbolic surfacing of Bloom's and Stephen's fears and desires buried in other chapters of the novel.

If it is common knowledge in turn-of-the-century Ireland that certain races or ethnicities deserve better treatment than others, as constant attacks on Jewish Bloom might indicate, then it should not be surprising that this pattern reappears in Bloom's fantastically altered reenactments of oppression and performance of race. After all, soon after Mary Driscoll is reminded about this "white treatment," she accuses Bloom of attacking her "in the rere of the premises. . . . I was discoloured in four places as a result" (15.885–87). Her "white" turns to bruises as a result of an alleged sexual assault. Moreover, when Bloom "begins a long unintelligible speech" (15.899) and "mumbles incoherently" (15.923)—resembling the Congo natives and their "uncouth babbling noise" in Conrad's narratives ("Outpost" 7)—the stage directions present him as dressed "in a torn frockcoat stained with whitewash" (15.935–36), the last word implying an attempt to make oneself white despite one's essential difference. Here, despite his inability to speak intelligently, Bloom makes an awkward attempt at passing as a white person. J. J. O'Molloy comes to Bloom's defense, saying that his client "is an infant, a poor foreign immigrant" (15.942–43), whose "misdemeanor was due to a momentary aberration of heredity" (15.944–45). Infantilized, othered Bloom might stand a better chance at the trial as someone uncontrollable, irrational, lacking intelligence. O'Molloy further explains that "such familiarities as the alleged guilty occurrence" are "quite permitted in [his] client's native place, the land of Pharaoh" (15.945–47), and he blames Bloom's behavior on "atavism" (15.950), adding that "he is of Mongolian extraction and irresponsible for his actions. Not all there, in fact" (15.954–55), after which Bloom with "a shrug of oriental obeisance salutes the court" (15.960). Therefore, in a relatively short scene, we find atavistic behavior, imagined oriental heritage, otherness, and deviance treated as synonymous with each other. O'Molloy adds soon after that Bloom "wants to go straight. I regard him as the whitest man I know" (15.980). While the previous line of defense implied racial otherness and therefore insanity, this one is intended to hint at Bloom's innocence, or whiteness. Similarly, Moses Dlugacz, another Jew, appears as "ferreteyed albino . . . , holding in each hand an orange citron and a pork kidney" (15.987–88), having undergone an erasure of markers of race and ethnicity. A few pages later, however, Alexander J. Dowie calls Bloom "Caliban!" (15.1760), and the mob shouts: "Lynch him!

Roast him!" (15.1761). And later, in his demeaning submission to Bella/ Bello, Bloom's face acquires new features, new markers of race: "His eyes grow dull, darker and pouched, his nose thickens" (15.2830–31). Within the "real" plot of the novel, before the nightmarish world of "Circe," we witness the fabricated and damaging understanding of ethnic difference (e.g., in "Cyclops"). Although "Circe" erases some racial markers, adds others, and plays with conventions of ethnic otherness, the associations attached to skin color remain the same: "White" implies "proper"; "black" implies "dangerous" or "submissive." Joyce recognizes these arbitrary associations and draws our attention to them.

In "Wandering Rocks," as Father Conmee passes the poster of Mr Eugene Stratton, his thoughts become inspired by the man's "thick nigger-lips" (10.141–42), and he thinks of "the African mission and of the propagation of the faith and of the millions of black and brown and yellow souls that had not received the baptism of water," to whom "the faith had not . . . been brought" (10.144–50). The passive voice in Conmee's musings on the necessity of "enlightenment" of "black and brown and yellow souls" is not accidental here; he transfers what Joyce calls the spiritual paralysis of the Irish onto the "other" races, acknowledging simultaneously the benevolence and sacredness of the Catholic agenda of conversion, as he remembers a book by "the Belgian Jesuit" (that is, Father A. Castelein), *Le rigorisme, le nombre des élus et la doctrine du salut*,[5] whose argument was that the majority of people would eventually be saved. The book itself was attacked, as Gifford notes, by both orthodox Catholics and liberal Protestants, though for different reasons. The dogmatists accused Castelein of being too inclusive in his claim that even those who were not baptized Catholic could be saved. The Protestants opposed his insistence upon the inflexible principle of eternal damnation (Gifford 263). In effect, these optimistic predictions reflect the same kind of complacency and duplicity that the people popularizing the myth of the "white man's burden" obviously displayed. The heathens will be converted; once they assume "our way" and reject the yoke of "otherness," redemption will come to them. Father Conmee, however, himself subject to an agenda of a similar nature (though wielding more power than an average lay Irishman), does not seem to notice any connection between the rhetoric of salvation vs. redemption and the damaging discourse based on the dichotomy between the civilized English and the barbaric Irish.

The "niggerlip[ped]" (10.142) Eugene Stratton, significantly, was a minstrel show star and "a Negro impersonator," who toured Great Britain with a repertoire of "'coon songs' . . . with soft-shoe dancing 'on a darkened, spotlighted stage, a noiseless, moving shadow'" (Gifford 108). His name reappears in "Circe" right before the stage directions in which "*Tom and Sam Bohee, colored coons in white duck suits, scarlet socks, upstarched Sambo chokers . . . leap out. Each has his banjo slung. Their paler smaller negroid hands jingle the twingtwang wires.*" Combining this grotesque picture with an image of their "*Flashing white kaffir eyes and tusks*" and "*smackfatclacking nigger lips*" (15.412–18), we may discern a resemblance to Conrad's infamous metonymical portrayals of the African natives as "eyeballs glistening," "faces like grotesque masks" (*Heart of Darkness* 61), and images of the Indian natives of Costaguana as "naked limbs" and "big wild eyes" (*Nostromo* 68). The men in "Circe," however, are actors, or phantoms, and they finally "*whisk black masks from raw babby faces*" (15.424), a gesture that is a startling affirmation of both difference and sameness, a statement reminding Bloom, Joyce's Irish audience, and the global readers of *Ulysses* that the constructed similarity between the subaltern Irish and the subaltern blacks, whether divined for the purpose of ridicule or as a sign of empathy, ultimately fails because of skin color. It is interesting that Joyce describes the Bohee Brothers as essentially white even though, as Zack Bowen reminds us, James and George (not Tom and Sam, as Gifford would have it) Bohee were in fact black (Bowen 817). While it may be important, and perhaps sometimes even useful, to consider both ethnic groups on the same discursive plane, the most obvious difference that, crucially, carries with it historical, political, cultural, and linguistic baggage cannot be ignored. The baby-faced Irishman, once under the Home Rule, will take off the mask, a colonial artifice, and gradually begin to enjoy the privileges of the Western, white, male, dominant part of society. The native of the Congo, on the other hand, will have to change the entire conception of centuries-long oppressive dialectics attributed to "blackness."

Joyce's *Vagina Dentata*: Manhood, Nationhood, and Female Vampirism

The word *race*—denoting skin color, ethnicity, religion, sometimes even gender—appears in Joyce's description of the Irish themselves, not, as we might expect, just in his recounting of the English stereotypes of the underprivileged neighbors. Simon Dedalus calls his nation "an unfortunate priestridden race" and, to emphasize the Church's audacious betrayal of Parnell (but incidentally echoing the colonizers' epithets for Ireland), a "priestridden Godforsaken race" (*Portrait* 42). It is a nation set apart from "Europe of stranged tongues and . . . of entrenched and marshaled races" (191); a nation in which the very word *race* is synonymous with either the subaltern status or a narrow-minded fanaticism of nationalists such as the citizen in "Cyclops." It is synonymous with half-naked, pregnant, young peasant women standing in doorways, calling strangers to their beds, including the girl in Davin's story, a "type of her race and of his own, a batlike soul waking to the consciousness of itself in darkness and secrecy and loneliness" (208). This "batlike soul" waking in darkness, a vampiric, diabolic (and profane) image of a voracious woman, is reminiscent of the figure of *vagina dentata* typically employed by imperial commentators as an emblem of the wild (usually black) other resisting the colonizers through trickery and dangerous sexual practices.

Admittedly, the theme of *vagina dentata* represents a rather idiosyncratic representation of consumption. Critics have already devoted some time to food, feasting, and even anthropophagy in Joyce's texts. Thomas Rice's most recent book, *Cannibal Joyce*, analyzes a specific form of consumption: "Cannibalism for Joyce," says Rice, "comes to represent both the artist's act of creation (incorporation) and the readers' act of reception (consumption)." Rice discusses "three ways [Joyce's] aesthetic of creative cannibalism manifests itself in forms of cultural transfer: in his manipulations of language, in his uses of literary tradition, and in his exploration of new technical possibilities for the art of fiction" (xiv). I want to add, however, that Joyce explores another form of cannibalism—a very gendered one: the myth of *vagina dentata*, or the fear of the literal and figurative castration by a voracious female. Not only does the toothed yonic image represent Bloom's and Stephen's fear of seduction, castration, and spiritual death, but it also undermines the hypermasculine nature of Irish nationalism. The feminine is not simply a weak link within the struggle for independence that hinges on the male valor and uncompromising warfare; neither is it solely an element to be conquered and penetrated. It is also a threat of corruption of Irish manhood and therefore nationhood, as well as a representation of a castrating lover or a devouring mother. Through this symbol, Joyce indirectly comments on the vulnerability of chauvinistic normative practices of some Fenian leaders, but he also mocks the colonial demonization of Irish Catholics as bloodsucking, disruptive others.

It is King Edward, after all, who appears in "Circe" sucking "a red ju- jube" (15.4454) and levitating "over heaps of slain" (15.4476). But Stephen admits in *Portrait* that "this race and this country and this life produced [him]" (230), that his ancestors "allowed a handful of foreigners to subject them" (231) and took the language of the oppressors. He then defines his race as "the old sow that eats her farrow" (231), ascribing to it not only a specific gender and a species believed to be unclean in the Judeo-Chris- tian culture but also cannibalistic and profane practices, infanticide, and disregard for one of the most protected taboos. Such an equation points toward a reversed cosmogonical process in which the profane chaos de- vours the sacred.

An equivalent of this image of female aggression could be the Hindu folk goddess Kali, "the 'terrible mother' who devours her offspring. She is often depicted with a *vagina dentata* devouring the phallus of the god Shiva while wearing around her neck a chain of skulls and on her hip a belt of severed heads" (Otero 273). Freud would say that the devouring, angry mother castrates in order to compensate for being "castrated," but this kind of misogynistic explanation of "lack" or "envy" reveals yet an- other fear of female domination. Psychoanalysis has long been aware of the projective nature of this kind of fear.

Linking castration with a loss of self and placing that fear in the context of hypermasculine Irish nationalism adds some insight to Joyce's motif of devouring mother. Stephen projects his own feeling of guilt and anger upon the feminized and animalistic Ireland, whose sadistic and cannibal- istic orality mirrors his own insecurities and the already existent instabil- ity of self and nation. Stephen's mother "penetrates" his orifices in chapter 5 of *Portrait* when she carefully washes his ears and nostrils, a kind of touch she finds pleasurable, as he points out to her ("But it gives you plea- sure" 198). In "Circe," a chapter set in a brothel or "mantrap" (15.93), as Edy Boardman calls the place, the mother's apparition, with her "face worn and noseless," mirrors Stephen's fixation on a devouring mouth that produces no speech: "She fixes her bluecircled hollow eyesockets on Stephen and opens her toothless mouth uttering a silent word. A choir of virgins and confessors sing voicelessly" (15.4159–62). True, her mouth is "toothless," but soon Stephen calls his mother a "corpsechewer" (15.4214), and the stage directions tell us that her face draws "near and nearer, sending out an ashen breath" and that she "raises her blackened, withered right arm slowly towards Stephen's breast with outstretched fingers" and "a green crab with malignant red eyes sticks deep its grinning claws in Stephen's heart" (15.4216–21).

Crabs and spiders have been popular representations of female genitalia, especially in European folklore. Legman, for example, discusses a crab in female genitals as northern European motif of *vagina dentata* (Otero 269). Abraham notes that a spider is a devouring yonic symbol in myths and dreams (Otero 269). Similar motifs include snakes, eels, and even piranhas—most figures phallic and potentially deadly. Stephen's mother's weapon is as polyphallic as the teeth it substitutes: outstretched fingers and crab's claws. This demonic other in the end attacks with that which the phallogocentric world of the colonizer *and* the colonized considers as a symbol of dominance.

Is it accidental that Stephen's devoutly Catholic mother reappears in his dreams and hallucinations with a gaping mouth and crab's claws grabbing at his heart? This particular scene in "Circe" points not only to his guilt of disobedience but also to a larger anxiety related to the voracious demon of the Catholic Church and traditional form of Irish nationalism. Let's recall "unmanned" Stephen mortifying his senses and rejecting pleasure after Father Arnall's sermon in *Portrait* or Mulligan's reference to God as a "collector of prepuces" (foreskin, 1: 394) in "Telemachus." Stephen's biological mother, Mother Church, and Mother Ireland are equally dangerous because they demand that he speak for them, repent, and sacrifice his self.

The myth of *vagina dentata* might also reflect a fear of coitus interruptus, an intercourse from which there is no way out. No matter how we understand the word in this context—as a speech act or sex act—what's implied in the image of the yonic teeth is that the intercourse is interrupted before one can withdraw or climax. Joyce also ponders in multiple places a related question of aborting a product of an intercourse, the image of a womb associated with death, not life, as in the passage about the midwives or the long elaboration of abortion in "Oxen," or mothers demonized in the medical students' drunken rant about infanticides and inverted wombs.

And again, we can understand this motif on many levels in Joyce's texts: as a representation of male fear of castration, as a projection of a sense of inadequacy and powerlessness in confrontation with women, with the

Church, with the demands of the nation or with the colonial power, or as the danger of both initiating and aborting a speech act. All of these explanations are inflected, however, with the awareness of hypermasculine nationalist discourse. Irish manhood has long been synonymous with Irish nationhood. As Nancy Curtin points out, national liberation in Ireland "was the test of her sons' manhood," especially around and after the 1790s, when the United Irishmen began engaging in a nationalist campaign whose main component was physical force (37). Curtin adds that "armed filial devotion to the mother-nation" was "a rite of passage to full manhood" (39). If colonialism endangers Irish masculinity, then it is not surprising that this fear of emasculation or castration generates multiple projections, including those of yonic teeth. Sarah McKibben, in her article on Irish nationhood in *Poor Mouth*, cites the romantic nationalism of Thomas Davis and the Young Irelanders who claimed that an imposition of a foreign language amounts to cutting off one's selfhood and corrupting the forefathers' "very organs" and "abridging their power of expression" (McKibben 97), which results in "profound disempowerment and degeneration—amounting to linguistic castration" (98).

If Irish nationalists emphasized their own hypermasculinity, their discourse also implied that those who didn't belong in their ranks were emasculated. Joyce seemed to be familiar with such inflected discourse. The Irish in *Ulysses* see Bloom as a vaguely threatening and emasculated other, "the new womanly man" (15.1798). He is an othered performer, a spectacle, and a projective image of the observers' own fears. Bloom as an emasculated Jew in masculinist Catholic Ireland is himself a *vagina dentata* figure threatening the male- and Catholic-dominated nationalist scene. The stage directions at the beginning of "Circe" refer to him as "doldy" (15.149)—a slang term for an impotent person. (Is this why Molly calls him "Poldy"?) When the cyclists graze him, he is "stung by a spasm" (15.183). Although weakened by other voracious (biological) females, Gerty and Molly—one "drain[ing] all the manhood" out of him (13.1101–2), the other "unmanning" Bloom through her infidelity—he himself poses a threat to traditionally perceived Irish manhood.[6] Dr Mulligan conducts a "pervaginal examination" on Bloom and pronounces him "bisexually abnormal," "virgo intacta," and, paradoxically, "a reformed rake" (15.1781), a phrase suggesting not only a toothed implement but also an aggressive action, an onslaught, as the *Oxford English Reference Dictionary* tells us. *Rake* also denotes a fashionable and promiscuous man or woman, so the fact that Bloom as a rake is "reformed" implies that his sexual licentious-ness and self-indulgence have been mitigated, his aggressive essence un-der control. But in the next line Mulligan adds—rather oddly and with a vague undercurrent of menace—that Bloom "has metal teeth" (15.1782) (perhaps to "eat with relish the inner organs of beasts" but maybe to entice and attack Irish men or Irish manhood in general).

It would be a misunderstanding to assume that employing the mo-tif of the voracious female alone points at an emancipatory tendency in any text. The voracious vagina attacks with polyphallic teeth—a weapon which underscores the castration power as uniquely male. It is "an 'abject' symbol in that it represents the repulsive as distinctly feminine and the horror of 'nonbeing' as decidedly so" (Otero 275). But Joyce seems to be aware of the projective nature of the fear of woman and—through his many-layered employment of the myth of *vagina dentata*—he eventually mocks those practices and perceptions that are othering and unproduc-tive. The devouring mother is simply a condensed fear of linguistic, cul-tural, or literal castration or an aborted, uncommunicative intercourse/discourse, especially the nationalist rhetoric linking armed resistance, liberation, and Irishness in general to manhood and virility.

Hibernian Hybridity?

Following his unflattering comparison of Ireland to a cannibalizing sow, Stephen, right before deciding to "forge in the smithy of [his] soul the un-created conscience of [his] race" (288), calls the Irish "a race of clodhop-pers" (284), indicating their backwardness and intellectual and cultural inferiority and implying their comical nature.[7] While the ploughman's heavy boots could represent hard, menial labor, the *Oxford English Refer-ence Dictionary* also defines a clodhopper metonymically as the plough-man himself: a country lout, a clumsy awkward boor, a clown. This de-scription appears again, indirectly, when Stephen wonders whether the soul of his race "was bartered and its elect betrayed" by "the questioner or by the mocker" (220)—that is, by the oppressor or the oppressed himself, through ignorance, light-heartedness, and mockery; perhaps also through the insistence upon worshipping "the sorrowful legend of Ireland" (205), like Davin's "rude imagination" shaped by "the broken lights of Irish myth" that "moved down the cycles in the same attitude as towards the Roman catholic religion, the attitude of a dull-witted loyal serf" (205). Stephen's portrait of his nation mirrors, in fact, the image constructed by the English, whose king, as Mr Henchy reports in "Ivy Day," "says to himself: 'The old one never went to see these wild Irish. By Christ, I'll go myself and see what they're like.' And are we going to insult the man when he comes over here on a friendly visit?" (*Dubliners* 148). Joyce, says Enda Duffy in his analysis of *Ulysses* as a subaltern text, "mocks imperial stereotypes of the native" while he "delineates their insidious interpellative power" (3).

The subjects of the internalized oppressive attitudes and the acceptance of a collective identity imposed by the colonizer were not alien to Joyce. Whether it was Johnny walking in circles around King Billy's statue or the two vestals eating plums on top of the Nelson column, Joyce's tragic-comic snapshots of perpetuated cycles of repression and domination permeate his fiction. After centuries of being told about their chaotic, uncivilized nature, the Irish begin unconsciously to acknowledge the lie constructed to justify and maintain the colonial power. *Ulysses*, says Duffy, is an example of "the inability of a text written at the moment of decolonization to imagine an epistemologically different subject altogether beyond the pale of the colonialist and masculinist discourses the subaltern author has inherited" (21). Therefore, Duffy claims, the book "is not a manifesto for postcolonial freedom, but rather a representation of the discourses and regimes of colonial power being attacked by counterhegemonic strategies that were either modeled on the oppressor's discourses or were only beginning to be elucidated in other forms" (21). The "resistance" is just a way of "imagining community that has been borrowed by the colonized people from their colonial masters" (31). For example, "most of the anti-British sentiment in the 'Telemachiad' is couched in the middle-class clichés of Irish popular literary culture" (45). *Ulysses*, especially "Cyclops," is a representation of "an Althusserian interpellated subject characterized by a simple dualism," that is, by "the difference between the vulgarian native and the civilized native (Caliban versus Ariel, Black Skin, White Masks), which has been discerned again and again in representations of the colonial subject" (98). The citizen is "the culmination of every degraded stereotype of Irish savagery" (112): he is a good talker in his display of chauvinist nationalism; he is a lazy drunk, perhaps a peasant. The dialectics of chaos/cosmos and profane/sacred finally reproduce themselves, without the previously employed strategies of the colonized party.

Gibson maintains that "Circe" presents "much more of the sense (and, especially, the sound) of actual Englishness" than any other part of the book. "Circe is full of decent, respectable, prim and outraged English and Anglo-Irish voices" (187). He examines multiple examples of these voices, including the presence of the British soldiers and the revealed signifi-cance of Bloom's decision to wipe himself with Beaufoy's Titbits article in "Calypso": Beaufoy appears in "Circe" "palefaced" (15.814)—an epithet emphasizing his Englishness, just as his address does, "'Playgoers' Club, London" (4.503). But "Circe" blurs the boundaries between Irishness and Englishness, too. Consider, for instance, Gibson's claim that Joyce inten-tionally "exposes the anglicized or imported nature of Irish popular cul-ture" (188) through his analysis of echoes of Victorian melodrama and lit-erary iconography. The episode itself, says Gibson, implies that "the more English you look and sound, the more you appear to deserve your place in the sun" (194). Gibson says that Joyce "understands the way in which Anglicization is or has involved a kind of colonization of the soul, a moral and a linguistic colonization" (194).

Joyce's response to the colonial discourse of the English, especially in *Ulysses*, is permeated by a cleverly disguised critique of the marriage be-tween the national and religious fervor. His highly ironic treatment of his characters' outbursts of national pride expressed through constant religious references and allusions is a biting commentary not only on the contemporary national scene but also on Irish history and the mentality of the Irish people, the nationalists' unsubstantiated arrogance and dan-gerous fanaticism justified by religious calls and sacred language. It also anticipates the struggle, already developing when *Ulysses* was in progress, to define a collective identity of a soon-to-be independent nation whose language is that of the former colonizer, and whose culture and institu-tions are still inextricably linked with the aggressive neighbor.

Messianic Zeal and the Fear of Contamination

The emphasis on the messianic character in the process of defining na-tional culture is not a new phenomenon, and it has not been confined to a handful of Catholic countries such as Ireland (or Conrad's native Poland). Sacred and profane languages intertwine in national discourse, but this interdependency did not originate with Christianity. Even pre-Christian myths connect the sacred with the notion of limited, familiar space. Bene-dict Anderson ignored this important fact in his otherwise very insight-ful *Imagined Communities*, pronouncing political ethics detached from religion.[8] But Joyce himself noticed the troubling confusion of religious and secular languages in Ireland, the division between the sacred cosmos and the profane chaos that insinuates itself into the nationalist rhetoric, leaving no discursive space for nonsectarian voices, for comprehensive political agency rather than positivist essentialism, ultimately as reductive as the imperialist propaganda. True, this dichotomy is not always easy to detect, as its expression is often subdued, convoluted, cunningly vocalized. This covert way of blending the two forms of discourse resonates with Michel de Certeau's model of the subtle, persistent activity of the subaltern who, "since they lack their own space, have to get along in a network of already established forces and representations" (*Practice* 18). Anderson's *Imagined Communities* does not focus on these heterogeneous voices present in local (and, according to Anderson, secular) languages, voices analyzed by de Certeau in *Practice of Everyday Life* and *The Mystic Fable*.

De Certeau points out that scriptural practice itself "has acquired a mythical value over the past four centuries by gradually recognizing all the domains into which the Occidental ambition to compose its history, and thus to compose history itself, has been extended" (*Practice* 133). The sacred power of the Voice is now conferred upon the text through the strategies and tactics of its users. Mythmaking relies on transforming a fragmented discourse into symbolic articulations; this practice is not only characteristic of history production but also present in modernist aesthetic, which often proclaims its opposition to grand narratives and artificial systematization.

The tendency to incorporate the sacred language into secular discourse seems even stronger among the nations whose existence has been subdued or officially erased almost immediately after the collapse of the religious and royal (but not yet national) power structures. Even before the power of Irish Celtic clans (under the nominal overlordship of a high king at Tara) and monasteries (which were the centers of missionary and educational work) began to fade, English invasions, which started in the twelfth century, prevented an even superficially partial division between the religious and independent national communities and therefore language to form in Ireland. The multiplicity of the new local, secular languages (often assuming the form of tactics) and the hidden presence of sacred language in national discourse are especially important in "imagined communities" whose existence is repressed, in which official, open expression of national identity is denied, and whose developing secular languages are pushed aside through the process of imposition of the language spoken by the impostors (e.g., through anglicization or russification). Therefore, mythmaking based on rigid classifications such as "cosmos" and "chaos" or "proper" and "improper" is no longer a hegemonic practice, but it assumes the shape of numerous tactics among Irish nationalists aimed at expression of national identity and pride through biblical references and promotion of the Irish language in an almost entirely anglicized Ireland. Joyce reveals the nostalgic and desperate character of these tactics in his ironic descriptions of heated debates in private and public places and in parodies of narrative forms hitherto considered sacred.

"Cyclops" offers one of many accounts of such debates. Joyce portrays the interlocutors in Kiernan's bar as narrow-minded, petty, and avaricious, with the aggressive and fanatical citizen at the forefront. By contrasting the citizen's xenophobia and his inflated devotion to the national cause with Bloom's somewhat naïve message about the universal need for love, Joyce exposes the real dangers of Irish nationalism—parochialism, interpellated fear of the other, violence, and attention to unimportant details coupled with, paradoxically, gigantism, or a tendency to exaggerate, to exceed. Although Bloom's call for peace and love mirrors religious messages about brotherhood and kindness, it is the citizen who consciously uses sacred images, figures, and language in his aggressive speech centered on nationalistic issues and employing highly divisive rhetoric reminiscent of the theme of colonial cosmogony. While talking about the past centuries in Irish trade, "with Spain and the French and with the Flemings before those mongrels were pupped," and glorifying Ireland's history, he promptly asserts that Ireland will be prosperous again, "with the help of the holy mother of God" (U 12.1296–1300). Not only does he aggressively oppose "mongrelization" or pollution of pure Irish blood, but he also supports his right to preserve pure heritage of his nation with a myth distorted to suit his political goals; preservation of racial purity will be rewarded with financial and political fortune. His subsequent prophesy—"Our harbours that are empty will be full again" (12.1301)—has, indeed, biblical or mythical proportions, as it suggests a reenactment of God's wonders depicted in the Old and New Testaments (e.g., that of the pouring of oil into the widow's empty jars in 2 Kings 4:1 or Jesus' multiplying of five bread loaves and two fishes to feed five thousand men with families in Matthew 14:17). The citizen's words themselves sound like a prophecy because they are not supported by any logical arguments, calculations, or propositions. That they are followed by "the last swig out of the pint" and the almost inarticulate cheering of John Wyse Nolan and Lenehan suggests Joyce's critique of mixing the divine and national elements in contemporary Ireland into a half-blind, inebriated, utopian expression of the nation's divine mission.

The citizen also refers to the myth of Kathleen ni Houlihan (*U* 12.1375) and proceeds to talk about Ireland as "the land of bondage" (12.1373), a phrase that comes from Deuteronomy 5:6 ("I am the Lord thy God, which brought thee out of the land of Egypt, from the house of bondage"). It suggests an ironic discrepancy between, on the one hand, the citizen's probably unconscious comparison of Irish people with the Israelites and their desire for homeland and, on the other, his extreme outbursts of anti-Semitism later in the chapter. After Bloom's reply—"And I belong to a race, too . . . that is hated and persecuted. Also now. This very moment" (12.1467–68)—the citizen reacts with an anti-Semitic slur, asking Bloom whether he is talking about "the new Jerusalem" (12.1473). At the same time, he jeers at the English who presented "His Majesty the Alaki of Abeakuta" with "an illuminated bible, the volume of the word of God and the secret of England's greatness" (12.1515–24), an attitude that hints at his conviction that the divine benediction is reserved only for one nation, his own. While he is able to discern comedy in "the white chief woman, the great squaw [Victoria's]" (12.1525) perception of England as the state whose power comes from divine intervention, he is blind to the same comparisons he and his fellow nationalists make. The narrator, for instance, states almost immediately after the scene in which the citizen jeers at Queen Victoria's gift: "God save Ireland from the likes of that bloody mouseabout [Bloom]" (12.1579). The first part of his remark echoes "God Save the Queen," the British national anthem, which also blurs sacred and secular languages.

During Bloom's absence, the citizen speaks again about the dangers of "contamination" of Ireland,[9] generating a dialogue imbued with sacred language that seems highly inadequate to the hateful drunken diatribe:

—Saint Patrick would want to land again at Ballykinlar and convert us, says the citizen, after allowing things like that to contaminate our shores.

—Well, says Martin, rapping for his glass. God bless all here is my prayer.

—Amen, says the citizen. (12.1671–74)

Bloom's presence among the Irish poses a biopolitical problem here: a contamination of the ostensibly unified mythical narrative and the essentialist notions of Irishness. It disrupts the chauvinist normative practices that explore the emotive power carried by the interpellated ideology of racial purity as a tool in the fight for independence. For the citizen, Bloom's pathological Jewishness disrupts the divinely sanctioned and romanticized image of the Catholic nation.

Joyce modeled the character of the citizen on Michael Cusack, the founder of the Gaelic Athletic Association and an ardent nationalist. He figures in *A Portrait of the Artist as a Young Man* as Davin's mentor, one of many who instilled the mixture of national and religious pride in Stephen's friend, "the peasant student" (*Portrait* 204). Davin represents a whole legion of nationalists whose blind devotion to the Irish cause and the Catholic faith and, most of all, whose conviction that these two realms are indistinguishable drove Joyce out of Ireland into a "voluntary exile." Joyce recognizes the danger in the (re-)creation of a national culture striving for independence from the colonizer by adopting the discourse of other hegemonic powers such as the Church and by speaking the language of exclusion.

Another limiting method of analyzing intertwined histories such as those of Ireland and England is a "destructive politics of confrontation and hostility" (Said, *Culture* 18), an attitude Salman Rushdie defines in *Imaginary Homelands* as a "technique of alienation" (2). Resistance becomes yet another form of hegemony—this time imposed from within, as a countermeasure to geographical and cultural imperialism—if the formerly colonized subjects employ the familiar (because experienced firsthand) strategies of appropriation and categorization, of transforming the "profane" into the "sacred." Thus one form of imposed hierarchy is simply substituted for another, allowing for an unceasing perpetuation of the myth of cosmos and chaos, the sacred and the profane, and the pathologies of frenzied religious fundamentalism.

Said's *Culture and Imperialism* and Rushdie's *Imaginary Homelands* try to comprehend and explain the emergence of postcolonial consciousness, the collective awareness Joyce observed before and while writing *Ulysses* and included in the narrative as a late colonial form of resistance in a nation anticipating the Home Rule. Both Said and Rushdie attempt to elucidate the causes and consequences of growing national movements and construe the awakening of narrow-minded nationalisms as groundless arguments whose premises are based on an assumption that there, indeed, existed and exists a privileged (as opposed to morally handicapped, contaminated, or profane) group or race. Joyce's "Cyclops" derides the arbitrariness and assuredness of placing oneself and one's ethnic group within the boundaries of cosmos, of the ordered, the chosen, the sacred, even if this positioning is a form of resistance.

Within the national culture, as in de Certeau's everyday life, strategies (or official discourses and imposed rules) mix with tactics (the unofficial discourses and methods employed by common people). The sacred and the profane are in constant conversation (or, to use Bakhtin's term, in a dialogic relationship with one another), and the boundaries between them often blur. Seemingly secular political ethics form religion on their own. Anderson's own expressions such as "the magic of nationalism" and his assertion of the need to "turn chance into destiny" testify to the peculiar discourse within and outside national culture inevitably tinted with elements of sacred language. The need to replace one system of meaning with another signals an inseparable relationship between the sacred and profane structures: "The century of the Enlightenment, of rationalist secularism, brought with it its own modern darkness. With the ebbing of religious belief, the suffering which belief in part composed did not disappear. Disintegration of paradise: nothing makes fatality more arbitrary. Absurdity of salvation: nothing makes another style of continuity more necessary" (Anderson 11). Anderson adds that, to solve the problem of the disintegrating religious authority, the Enlightenment sought "a secular transformation of fatality into continuity, contingency into meaning" (11). Joyce captures in *Ulysses* the messianic character of Irish nationalism, but for him, it exemplifies the dangerous insularity and stupor of the national movement in Ireland.

Virginia Moseley quotes in her *Joyce and the Bible* the following passage from *Finnegans Wake* (and a cross-reference to the Christmas dinner scene from *Portrait*) as an example of Joyce's acceptance of Ireland's need for a divine savior: "As hollyday in his house so was he priest and king to that: ulvy came, envy saw, ivy conquered. Lou! Lou! They have waved his green boughs o'er him as they have torn him limb from lamb. For his muertification and uxpiration and dumnation and annuhulation. . . . Ah-dostay, feedailyones. . . . Chin, chin! And of course all chimed din width the eatmost boviality. . . . human, erring and condonable, what the statues of our kuo, who is the messchef be our kuang" (quoted in Moseley 39). Moseley's interpretation of the passage (and, consequently, her explanation of Joyce's attitude toward the Irish national cause) rests on her conviction that by "associating Stephen's slaughter of innocence with that of Parnell and of Jesus, Joyce showed Stephen's first realization, perhaps, of Ireland's need for a saviour and of his own mission as its Messiah" (39). She calls this realization a "step towards maturity" (39) and emphasizes its importance "to Joyce himself" (39–40), supporting it with the fact that Joyce was preoccupied "with similar situations in still other of his works" (40). But Moseley ignores Joyce the ironist, Joyce who secretly pokes fun at the messianic character of Irish nationalists by inflating and distorting the connection between nationalism and religion and the implementation of the sacred language in national discourse. Even though the young Stephen in *Portrait* assumes, in a way, the sacrificial role of an exile in order to forge "the uncreated conscience of [his] race" (288), he pities Davin for his inability to distinguish between the religious and national spheres, and ultimately he returns from exile in *Ulysses*. Similarly, there is no messiah in *Finnegans Wake*, only an imperfect delivery man, Shaun, and a circular narrative closing in on itself. *Ulysses* and *Finnegans Wake* unapologetically merge the sacred and the profane and transcend narrow definitions that maintain such artificial dichotomies. Joyce himself, although in self-exile from Ireland until his death,[10] claimed, as Richard Ellmann notes, that if "Ireland was not to be 'an afterthought of Europe' . . . it would have to allow the artist his freedom and would have to muffle the priest" (Ellmann, *James Joyce* 69).[11]

The messianic character of Irish nationalism, so close to the character of the cosmogonic myth, appears as the foundation of John F. Taylor's speech, which Professor MacHugh recalls in "Aeolus" as the "finest display of oratory" (*U* 7.792). Again, it turns out to be just that, an example of a skilled use of fervent and eloquent language, in fact providing no feasible solution to the problem discussed, no detailed guidance, no agency. Responding to Mr Justice Fitzgibbon's speech in a debate about an essay advocating the revival of the Irish language, Taylor remarks that his "learned friend . . . transported" him "into a country away from this country, into an age remote from this age" (7.830–31)—or, to use Benjamin's expression employed also by Anderson in *Imagined Communities*, into "a homogeneous, empty time," which allows for close bonds between invisible compatriots, of whose presence we are, nevertheless, assured. Taylor attacks Fitzgibbon's ideas and indicates parallels between his opponent and an ancient Egyptian "highpriest," exposing, at the same time, similarities between the Irish people and the Israelites. The meaning of the highpriest's words "was revealed to [him]" (7.832–40): "Why will you jews not accept our culture, our religion and our language? . . . You have but emerged from primitive conditions: we have a literature, a priesthood, an agelong history and a polity" (7.845–50). In his oratory focused on the issues of Irish nationalism and preservation of the Celtic culture and language, Taylor employs sacred terminology, references to religious figures and biblical stories, but also the premise of the cosmogony myth (chaos forced to assume the qualities of cosmos), drawing overt comparison between the powerful and disdainful Egyptians and the British or conservative Anglo-Irish oppressors like Fitzgibbon himself, and pointing to analogies between the situation of the Jews, "vagrants and daylaborers" accused of praying "to a local and obscure idol," and the oppression of the Irish Catholics. Thus he bestows on the Irish the title of the chosen people and, indirectly, prophesies the appearance of another "youthful Moses" who will bring them "out of their house of bondage" (mirroring Exodus 13:17) and who will speak "with the Eternal" and "come down with the light of inspiration . . . bearing in his arms the tables of the law, graven in the language of the outlaw" (7.858–69). Underneath this vision, this convergence of religious references and national discourse, there is a startling conviction that Taylor might not even fully realize: the Irish will cast off the oppressors' chains because they are chosen by God. Moreover, they will bring forth "the light of inspiration" along with "the tablets of law"—an image that suggests another vision of another nation, "the light of civilization" promised to the world by the imperial Britain. Here the interpellated salvationist rhetoric again takes for granted the cultural/religious homogeneity of the Irish and creates its own alterities and exclusionary practices.

But there is much more at stake in this account of Taylor's speech than the exposure of the messianic zeal in Irish nationalism. MacHugh recalls a speech whose foundation or inspiration is the ancient oratory, delivered by men for a male audience. Ancient oratory, as Thomas Habinek maintains in *Ancient Rhetoric and Oratory*, is a form of nonviolent reenactment of masculinity and a performative attempt to solidify or legitimate social conventions. Habinek stresses the importance of the body on display as an integral and essential part of this performance. Significantly, in "Aeolus," the body of Taylor is missing from the account. We encounter in MacHugh's account fleshless words, a disembodied voice. Even the physical proof of Taylor's speech—a transcript or a recording—is missing. In an oppressed but still thoroughly logocentric and patriarchal society, this account of ghostwriting and ghost speaking may carry with it a tacit fear of emasculation. There are no men in action here, no fists thumping, no threatening shouts, no promise of action. Turn-of-the-century Ireland, emasculated by its powerful colonizer, produces windy rhetoric and unsuccessful insurrections.

When Professor MacHugh's account of Taylor's speech ends, Stephen remembers "Hosts at Mullaghmast and Tara of the kings" (7.880) and likens Daniel O'Connell with Moses. His words, however, directed to "miles of ears of porches" are "scattered to four winds" and become "dead noise" (7.881–82). In the first phrase, Joyce evokes the poisoning of Hamlet's father and thus reverses the traditional associations of such dichotomies as contamination/purity or chaos/cosmos to expose the potential dangers of nationalist rhetoric. Although the message is valid and important, it is dispersed, rejected, ineffective. Gifford notes that "O'Connell's words have been 'scattered' in the sense that his reliance on and hope for an orderly constitutional achievement of repeal (and a measure of independence for Ireland) were, to say the least, blasted, and his words, for all their oratorical success, wasted." He was subsequently imprisoned for "seditious conspiracy" (Gifford 150). Therefore, his messianic function was not achieved. Joyce, by juxtaposing Professor MacHugh's proud reminiscence (that itself is a piece of fine oratory) of Taylor's prophecy with Stephen's recollection of Ireland's fallen messiah, exposes the futility of elevated rhetoric, empty oratorical displays, pointless effusions, and outbursts of nationalistic slogans mixed with religious language, or the "aquacities of thought and language" (U 17.240) that fill Stephen with disgust.

The persistent, stubborn presence of sacred language—both archaic and biblical myths of the chosen people—in political discourse helps maintain the pivotal role of myth in nationalistic movements such as the Celtic Revival in Ireland or in literature propagating national uprising and the struggle for independence (e.g., Adam Mickiewicz and other Polish Romantics). James Joyce shows his irreverence toward both Irish folklore (the Celtic revival's return to Irish legends), regarded by many involved in the nationalist movement as sacred, and traditional English literary form, sanctified and fossilized by centuries of British culture. His use of myth, the loose connection between the characters and plots of *The Odyssey* and *Ulysses*, is not aimed at creating an ostensibly unified and "uncontaminated" picture of an independent nation; rather, it reveals the rifts, breaches, and ruptures in the ideology that presupposes national independence through homogeneity and obedience of its followers.

But Joyce is also "concerned with the 'strangers' and their legacy" (Gibson 182) and expresses his resistance toward the revered English literary tradition as an imposed form by ridiculing narrative styles and literary figures venerated in Britain. He would ultimately give voice to his resistance to rigid literary forms and English literary tradition through the formal and linguistic experimentations in *Finnegans Wake*. But we also find an extended parody of the English prose in "The Oxen of the Sun" and the formal experimentation within "Circe," a chapter concerned with "the colonized unconscious" (182). The chapter ridicules and transcends both religious and national discourse, relying to a great extent on production and sustenance of a unifying, collective identity, and valorizing traditionally understood masculinity. "Circe" is insubordinate, profanatory, and exhibitionistic. Its coronation scene merges and then distorts sacred and profane languages that have previously appeared in *Ulysses*: "The Bloom who is welcomed as 'successor' to Parnell (*U* 15.1513–14) and echoes John F. Taylor's terms (*U* 7.845–73) in proclaiming 'green Erin' to be 'the promised land' promptly lapses into the tones of English military triumphalism (*U* 15.1525–30)" (Gibson 200). His newly gained power as "emperor-president and king-chairman, the most serene and potent and very puissant ruler of this realm" (*U* 15.1471–72) and the strong approval of John Howard Parnell as "Successor to [his] famous brother" (15.1513) put him in charge of both British and Irish chauvinist rhetoric. The omnipotent monarch becomes the founder of the holy city, the cosmocrator transcending all limits of "the house of bondage" and merging national and religious functions that are bestowed upon him. "Bloom's bodyguard distribute Maundy money, commemoration medals, loaves and fishes, temperance badges, expensive Henry Clay cigars, free cowbones for soup, rubber preservatives in sealed envelopes tied with gold thread, . . . 40 days' indulgences, . . . coupons for the royal and privileged Hungarian lottery" (15.1568–77). The absurd fusion of references to the sacred and the profane in Bloom's benefaction culminates when "Women press forward to touch the hem of Bloom's robe" (15.1585) in order to express their reverent submissiveness, and Bloom the emperor proceeds to perform good deeds (Christian, if not Christ-like) when he "consoles a widow," "kisses the bedsores of a palsied veteran," and "gives his coat to a beggar" (15.1605–13). After Bloom, "His Most Catholic Majesty" (15.1629), suddenly becomes an esteemed Jewish law-giver, dispensing advice on bladder problems and astral physics, mortgages and taxes, he proclaims a new state emerging from the chaos of injustice, persecution, and violence; in this newly created cosmos he stands for "the reform of municipal morals and the plain ten commandments. . . . Union of all, jew, Moslem and gentile. . . . Compulsory manual labor for all. . . . Tuberculosis, lunacy, war and mendicancy must now cease. General amnesty, weekly carnival with masked licence, bonuses for all, Esperanto the universal language with universal brotherhood. No more patriotism of barspongers and dropsical impostors. Free money, free rent, free love and a free lay church in a free lay state" (15.1685–93). Significantly, his hallucinatory transformation of chaos into cosmos is based not on elimination or conversion but on inclusion of the other. His call for a cosmopolitan and anti-nationalist utopian state transcends religious, linguistic, statutory, and economic limitations. Not surprisingly, after this decree, Bloom is pronounced "an Episcopalian, an agnostic, an anythingarian seeking to overthrow our holy faith" (15.1712–13), and his royal and godlike persona disintegrates, perhaps because it does not conform to the traditional cosmocratic prescriptions based on exclusion or alteration of difference.

Joyce's parody functions in *Ulysses*, and with a doubled force in "Circe," as both a critique of the British imperial drive and, according to Gibson, a biting remark on "Irish collusion in and subservience to colonial power" and "a Catholic culture of sacrifice, of dereliction, weariness and bitterness" (207). Gibson mentions "Old Gummy Granny, parody of the figure of the poor old woman, which Joyce clearly saw as an abortion begotten in its present form by Revivalism out of Catholic Mariolatry" (210–11). The chapter's absurd mixture of state and religious functions, random blending of denominations and rituals in the midst of chaos and ever-changing scenes and actors is Joyce's peculiar summation of the book's main accusations veiled by comedy and satire—that of his compatriots' fanatical adherence to the Catholic dogmas and national fervor, of defining one in terms of the other, of the nationalists' xenophobia. The carnivalesque allows him to attack both English imperialism and Irish parochialism.

Ulysses, with its versatile themes and narrative strategies, successfully transcends these reductive ideologies. Paradoxically, though it employs a popular mythical narrative as the basis of its plot, it also exposes the hegemonic and self-destructive practices of mythmaking, polarizing, and othering that are at the core of (re-)creation of collective consciousness. Tom Nairn defines nationalism as "the pathology of modern developmental history, as inescapable as 'neurosis' in the individual . . . and largely incurable" (359). Joyce seems to attempt a healing process through exposing and laughing at the "disease" of English and Irish nationalism. In "Ireland: Island of Saints and Sages," he asks whether "nation" is not "really a useful fiction like many others which the scalpels of the present-day scientists have put paid to" (118), thus foreshadowing medical terminology used by Nairn in his definition. After exposing the limitations and dangers of the binary division between chaos and cosmos, Joyce urges us to abandon the rhetoric of the sacred and the profane, to transform humanity's drive to overcome the profane into a drive beyond any prescriptive and harmful categories. His implied call to avoid the fiction of communitarian unity and to read culture and nation as a multivalent discourse echoes in Said's *Culture and Imperialism*:

> If at the outset we acknowledge the massively knotted and complex histories of special but nevertheless overlapping and interconnected experiences—of women, of Westerners, of Blacks, of national states and cultures—there is no particular intellectual reason for granting each and all of them an ideal and essentially separate status. Yet we would wish to preserve what is unique about each so long as we also preserve some sense of the human community and the actual contests that contribute to its formation, and of which they are all a part. (32)

The contrapuntal analysis—the awareness and consideration of "overlapping experiences and interdependent histories of conflict" (67) and the ability to encompass a multidimensional recognition of the premises and messages included in a text—acknowledges the hybrid and multifarious nature of cultural and historical discourse and constitutes a countermeasure against "rhetoric of blame," a defense mechanism deriving from "the limitations of the attempts to deal with relationships that are polarized, radically uneven, remembered differently" (18). It might also explain to some extent the tendency among some modernist authors and their characters to seek new ways of identity formation in a forbidding milieu of imperial propaganda and intensified nationalist and religious indoctrination, as they transform the traditionally understood pilgrimage into other forms of questing toward self-recognition.

II

PILGRIMAGE

4

Tenuous Itineraries

Modernism and exile. To pronounce these two words in one breath is to acknowledge the importance of displacement and fragmentation in literary and cultural production of the first half of the twentieth century. Is movement possible within and across the rigid boundaries constructed by hegemonic establishments? Are modernist characters and narrators capable of transgressing the preexisting limitations and definitions? Are only the subaltern characters entrapped, or does the fabricated binarism of colonial culture prevent also the privileged from independent decision making? Is traditional pilgrimage a sure method of progress, or does modernity necessitate a polysemous character of the quest? This chapter provides a theoretical overview of several assumptions about pilgrimage toward the center and a preliminary discussion of the (im)possibility of arriving at a set destination.

In chapter 1, I analyze the dangerously tenacious relationship between imperialism and the drive toward the sacred, and I argue that the colonial endeavor to chart sociopolitical spaces of power and oppression is often inscribed within mythical boundaries of chaos and cosmos. This mythical construct assumes that cosmos is the center, the realm of being and meaning, whereas chaos is a non-place ready to be conquered and formed, a nebula with no epistemological and ontological significance. The desire of those inhabiting the center to conquer and convert that space of nonbeing in mythological accounts sometimes stands in reverse relationship to another kind of desire, one to move from chaos toward the sacred center, to embark on a pilgrimage toward it, and therefore to acquire meaning and to reach self-identification.

Two terms, the *center* and *telos*, appear in many texts on pilgrimage in relation to the search for the sacred and the need to escape the profane. Although the first term is often associated with stasis, a focal point in space, and the second with movement, both center and telos are often described as fixed points toward which pilgrims, adventurers, or thinkers progress. The polarization of the world into self and other fabricates the center as the permanent place of being, while the margin remains a place of nonbeing. In traditional pilgrimage, the progress, or the quest to reach self-recognition, occurs from the margin toward the center. The telos of this progress is, then, the center, unless the social and colonial hierarchies are abolished.

Traditional Pilgrimage

A traditional pilgrim, in Mircea Eliade's words, is a suffering ascetic who always seeks a path toward himself or toward "the 'centre' of his being" (*Patterns* 382). To reach the center, he says, "is to achieve a consecration, an initiation" (382). The desire to escape the profane space is underlined, to a certain extent, by the fact that the center is synonymous with power and knowledge, including self-knowledge. Connected with fall into experience, the quest in the archaic world was an endeavor to find the self by either uniting the conscious with the unconscious or by entering the sacred realm that bestows meaning and revelation upon the seeker. This journey often involved a search for the father or the father figure that also commonly preconditioned identity building. Obstacles and unintentional, perilous detours in the passage toward the center were and still are requisite elements in the process of self-definition—a passage that originates, in part, from "the nostalgia for Paradise" or from desire to be "at the heart of the world, of reality, of the sacred, and, briefly, to transcend . . . the human condition and regain a divine state of affairs: what a Christian would call the state of man before the Fall" (383).

Victor Turner's theory of pilgrimage also accentuates the pilgrim's attempt at liberation from mundane, earthly social structures.[1] It is a process of self-identification, as well as assertion of one's "solidified" self, inasmuch as it could be compared to rites of passage, especially the archaic rite of initiation (*Image* 8). Turner's explanation of two crucial terms, the *liminal* and *communitas*, elucidates the parallels between the rite of passage and pilgrimage and sheds light onto the atavistic search for the sacred in general, in all its forms, including the attempts to turn chaos into cosmos, whether through appropriation of the other, through naming, or entering cyclical (nonchronological) time. Turner employs Arnold van Gennep's distinction of three phases in a rite of passage: separation, transition, and incorporation. The stage of separation delineates a boundary between the sacred and the profane. In this stage, "the detachment of the ritual subjects (novices, candidates, neophytes or 'initiands') from their previous social statuses" (Turner, *Process* 16) is as indispensable as the inversion of secular relationships, or the reversal of situations (e.g., a movement from war to peace, from plague to health and prosperity). Van Gennep calls the second stage transition, "margin," or "limen" (Latin for "threshold"). It is a period of ambiguity and "social limbo" (16). The stage of incorporation is signified by a return to a "new, relatively stable, well-defined position in the total society" (16). Turner claims that these stages, especially the liminal transition stage, are also parts of pilgrimage. Although he emphasizes the "symbolic inversion of social attributes" that "characterize separation," he says that "blurring and merging of distinctions may characterize liminality" (18). In this in-between stage, initiands and pilgrims assume a "non-status": they lose their names, disregard their appearance, and display other signs that underline their "uniformity, structural invisibility and anonymity" (19). Beyond the normative power structure, they learn to recognize powers that the profane social ties have weakened or silenced. Pilgrims of the modern era, like initiands in tribal societies, experience a disengagement from a comparatively stable position in life and their social status, and pass into a liminal or threshold condition: "they are 'dying' from what was and passing into an equivocal domain occupied by those who are (in various ways) 'dead' to quotidian existence in social systems" (122).

Turner's theory has as its basis the pilgrim's access to a space without profane social structures, a space of *communitas*, "the underpinning experience that allows pilgrims a sense of socially unencumbered selves that then contributes to a universal sense of human self" (Juschka 2). Turner suggests that stifled and hidden by the social self there is a "human self that is unfettered by history, gender, race, or class and that this is the self that becomes evident in the communitas experience of pilgrimage" (Juschka 2). Communitas, Turner says, is a liminal phenomenon occurring during the exile part of the ritual and among the pilgrims in progress, in which people are united by their abandonment of profane status and normative structures of their societies. They are released from mundane limitations;

they enter space where they distinguish "individuality posed against the institutionalized milieu" (*Image* 153–54). Liminality may also involve ludic or subversive actions. Here, "elements of culture may be recombined in numerous, often grotesque ways, grotesque because they are arrayed in terms of possible or fantasied rather than experienced combinations" (20). Turner adds that "in liminality people 'play' with the elements of the familiar and defamiliarize them. Novelty emerges from unprecedented combinations of familiar elements" (20). The initiands/pilgrims free their own perceptive and creative abilities from normative constraints and obligations. For many, liminality represents "the breakthrough of chaos into cosmos, of disorder into order," while for some it is "the scene of disease, despair, death, suicide, the breakdown without compensatory replacement of normative, well defined social ties and bonds" (*Process* 44);[2] thus liminality can be both liberating and destructive. No wonder, then, that those modernist authors whose characters explore the possibility of transcending hegemonic control and arbitrary colonial and class-related limitations are drawn to the theme of pilgrimage and create new forms of questing as a means to escape entrapment within racial, class, and gender conventions.

Bauman's Strollers, Vagabonds, Tourists, and Players

The character and purpose as well as the personal and political implications of pilgrimage have been undergoing constant changes since the very inception of this quest among the premodern societies. With the onset of Christianity and other teleological systems, archaic cyclic myths of traveling toward the center in search of meaning gave way to chronological progress (e.g., from birth to death, from sin to redemption). Power distribution connected with the process shifted, depending on political systems, church and state relations, individual destinations, and other factors. Furthermore, the very quality and, inevitably, the goal of this progress changed, as did the way in which thinkers and writers addressed the lack of relative stability of meaning. Pilgrimage has become attuned to the erratic reality and arbitrary binaries producing alterity, disorder, incompletion, and inarticulation. Zygmunt Bauman's theory of new forms of pilgrimage in modernity and postmodernity helps elucidate the erratic and often aborted progress of Conrad's and Joyce's characters; it also explains the appeal of the quest theme to modernist authors in general, aware, as Yeats was in 1919, that "the centre cannot hold."[3]

Modernists, Conrad and Joyce in particular, expand the traditional understanding of pilgrimage and provide, through their characters' movement along busy streets or treacherous rivers, a *collective* metaphor for identity building: progress that anticipates the movements of the figures named by Bauman's "From Pilgrim to Tourist—or a Short History of Identity" as the stroller, the vagabond, the tourist, and the player. To define oneself in the hegemonic matrix, one has to employ provisional maneuvers to either challenge or evade inflexible boundaries. Pilgrimage is an attempt at self-discovery irrespective of imposed and presumably fixed identity, an image of self dictated by the parochial and othering society.

"Ambivalence," says Bauman, "the possibility of assigning an object or an event to more than one category, is a language-specific disorder: a failure of naming (segregating) function that language is meant to perform" (*Modernity and Ambivalence* 1). Conrad and Joyce escape the lure of clear-cut classification, and they do not confine their characters to the role of a pilgrim on an uninterrupted path toward the center. While Jim, Verloc, Stephen, or Bloom display characteristics of Bauman's four traveler figures, they do not neatly fit into these exclusive molds. Instead, the fluidity of these characters and their purposes allow them to assume the molds that seem to be convenient or beneficial at certain times. Therefore, an attempt to define Verloc or Bloom in terms of these four figures is not synonymous with imposing an artificial structure upon *The Secret Agent* or *Ulysses*. Quite to the contrary, such parallels with multiple forms of contemporary pilgrimage indicate the random and unpredictable nature of these characters' milieux and explain their—and their creators'—decision to displace the center in their novels.

The premodern pilgrim's driving force was delayed gratification, fueled by belief in the possibility of reaching the truth about himself and the universe. This quest for meaning was facilitated, ironically, by the pilgrim's access to an inhospitable environment; the territory he had to, or rather he chose to, traverse was a desert or a land with desertlike qualities—lacking interruption and diversion, cohesive, though not compact, formidable, but also formative. Anxiety and frustration aside, the delay of gratification was energizing and motivating. People who embarked on a quest "had a stake in solidity of the world they walked; in a kind of world in which one can tell life as a continuous story, a 'sense-making' story" ("From Pilgrim" 23). Therefore, the "world of pilgrims—of identity-builders—must be orderly, determined, predictable, ensured" (23).

In the modern era, the figure of the *flâneur* replaces the traditional pilgrim. Bauman describes the *flâneur* (the stroller) as representing a surface-level interaction with the urban scene: "he is *in* the crowd but not *of* the crowd" ("From Pilgrim" 26). He is the epitome of superficiality, pretence, and inability to form genuine bonds with other people, mostly because he perceives them as actors, and life itself as a form of drama staged right before his eyes. His behavior seems to be an ironic reversal of that of the pilgrim, who gropes in an incomprehensible universe for meaning and objective.

Bauman's second figure, the vagabond, is masterless, rootless, always a stranger. "What made vagabonds so terrifying," Bauman further explains, "was their apparent freedom to move and so to escape the net of heretofore locally based control" ("From Pilgrim" 28). The movements of the vagabond "are unpredictable; unlike the pilgrim, the vagabond has no set destination. You do not know where he will move to next, because he himself does not know nor care much" (28). Vagabonds belong to "the post-traditional chaos" and the realm of "the Other" (28), subversive and superfluous in a meticulously controlled space.

The vagabond's alienation and compulsive walking resemble those of the tourist, the figure in constant motion. Bauman notes significant differences between these two figures, though. The tourist's movement is purposeful (or, at least, he believes so). Moreover, "unlike the vagabond who has little choice but to reconcile himself to the state of homelessness, the tourist has a home." He must have an "indubitably 'owned' place to go to when the present adventure is over." This familiar and safe place assures him that whatever happens to him elsewhere, "in the tourist land," whatever mask he assumes, his "'real face' is in safe keeping, immune, stain-resistant, unsullied" ("From Pilgrim" 30). The tourist, while on his journey, experiences both homesickness and the fear of homeboundedness, that is, of "being tied to a place and barred from exit" (31). Home, adds Bauman, "lingers at the horizon of the tourist life as an uncanny mix of shelter and prison" (31). His primary aims are new sensations and incidents;[4] when the bizarre becomes familiar, he seeks new experience offering excitement and pleasure. The aesthetic criteria in the tourist's world win over moral dimensions.[5] At the same time, the tourist's new experiences have to be not only strange but also innocuous, with clearly marked escape routes (29). Ashcroft, Griffiths, and Tiffin also claim that "the tourist, ostensibly in search of the new, is actually seeking the already known" (98). He moves forward to discover and to domesticate that discovery, to make it comply with his expectations or preconceptions.

If the purposes of the tourist's movement are, as Bauman says, a search for new experience and a "taming" of new perceptions and sensations, the underlying premise of this endeavor to change the new and the unknown into something recognizable (into a world ordered according to the standards of the "seeker") presents a paradigm of desire to free oneself from the realm of the profane ("disordered," unfamiliar space) and enter the realm of the sacred ("ordered," familiar) in the process and reenactment of cosmogony. But while cosmogony is based on change, tourism relies on an acquisition of necessary information and a certain form of adjustment of vision, not a simple appropriation of the new environment.

Finally, Bauman's fourth figure, the player, treats each new experience on the itinerary as a game. In the player's world, "nothing is fully predictable and controllable, but nothing is totally immutable and irrevocable either." In the relationship between the player and the world, "there are neither laws nor lawlessness, neither order nor chaos. There are just moves—more or less clever, shrewd or tricky, insightful or misguided." The player's methods are more heuristic than algorithmic: "The player's world is the world of risks, of intuition, of precaution-taking" ("From Pilgrim" 31). Time in this world is no longer linear or continuous, but consists of fragments, separate games. The game goes on even if he stops playing, but if he plays to the end, he needs to make sure that the game will not affect anything beyond its realm. The player must also remember that "the purpose of the game is to win and so the game allows no room for pity, compassion, commiseration or cooperation" (32).

The De-Centered Quest

All these modes of modern and postmodern quest escape the traditional eschatological nature of pilgrimage and schematize new methods of identity formation. Disillusionment and fragmentation lead to desperate attempts to make our progress faster and easier; the search for the sacred is rarely the ultimate aim of this quest—there seems to be no axis in the disjointed and incoherent world.[6] Bauman's concept of the pilgrim compelled to continue his journey by delayed gratification derives, it seems, from the Lacanian concept of identity formation. A desire gratified is a desire annihilated; this moment of satisfaction is accompanied by denial and resistance. Therefore, pilgrimage (especially as a process of identity formation), in its unattainability of telos, is paradoxically a kind of preservation movement for humanity. Jean-François Lyotard goes even further in his contemplation of teleology, claiming that "any narrative whatsoever begins in the middle of things" and that "its so-called 'end' is an arbitrary cut in the infinite sequence of data" (*Peregrinations* 2). Lyotard adds that the "delusion that we are able to program our life is a part of an ancient fidelity to something like a destiny or destination" (3).

While the premodern pilgrim found the passage toward the center extremely challenging and requiring absolute determination—yet promising reward at the end of the journey—the modern pilgrim faces an obstacle of a different nature: he no longer *believes* in the center. Or, as Bauman would characterize the predicament of contemporary society, *there is no center*. It is illusory, lost in the barrage of fragments and superficial, provisional projects. If there is a center, it is impermanent or simply empty.[7] Modernist pilgrimages acknowledge this impermanence and void. Caught between discipline and contingency, totalitarian dehumanization and egalitarian disavowal of violence, the regulatory lure of metaphor and instantaneity of desire, not all modernists sought to tame entropy with Eliot's "mythic method," and not all modernists sailed to Byzantium. Some—like Conrad and Joyce—accepted and utilized in their texts the feared instability of signifiers, fragmentation, and chaos. In their texts, mythical allusions and patterns often emphasize and even celebrate disorderliness and complexity of human experience.

Michel de Certeau says in *The Mystic Fable* (vol. 1) that pilgrimage is generated by *absence* from desire to attain that which is missing: "One sole being is lacking, and all is lacking. This new beginning orders a sequel of wanderings and pursuits" (2). Robert M. Torrance also describes the primary nature of pilgrimage as "the deliberate effort to transcend, through self-transformation, the limits of the given and to realize some portion of this unbounded potentiality through pursuit of a future goal that can neither be fully foreknown nor finally attained" (xii) and "this business of seeking, of setting off in determined pursuit of what we are lacking and may never attain" (3). Lyotard's peregrinations through the subjects of law, form, and event in his lectures entitled "Clouds," "Touches," and

"Gaps" are themselves underlined by the lack of an authentic center. We delude ourselves, Lyotard claims, that we can predetermine our lives. This self-deception stems from our attachment to the elements of destiny and destination present in the age of the epic and tragedy whose periodic rhythms decayed and disappeared a long time ago.

Paradoxically, the existence of the "religious void" or "vessel" (Eade and Sallnow 15) in the process of pilgrimage, regardless of the variety of ways in which the process itself is understood, is—I argue—formative and meaningful and may assume at least two functions. The empty center has the potential of being filled; that is, its meaning can be created and shifted by those in power in order to contain the subaltern and to perpetuate hegemonic mechanisms within certain cultures, but also by those who apparently cannot speak. Through their attempts to create meaning and to "name" the center, they turn into agents. Moreover, the very absence of the authentic, forever "fixed" telos, even if humanity seems to be engaged in teleology of one kind or another, draws our attention to that which is absent, empty, or chronically unstable. Thus absence creates presence; that which does not come to the surface and is not realized becomes the subject of a variety of discourses (among them, the questions of agency and communication).

Pilgrimage, therefore, encompasses the intertwined questions of power, liminality, fragmentation, and the center (or a lack thereof). As a result, whether considered literally, as journeying toward the shrine or other holy places, or symbolically, as self-development and progression toward a deeper knowledge of the self and others, or realization of one's goals, this process of questing is inextricably connected not just to anthropological science and, marginally, esoteric theories but also to other areas of research, such as postcolonial, New Historical, gender, and cultural studies, queer theory, and multidimensional debates on the nature of nationality/nationalism. Pilgrimage and the process of defining its telos are prompted by, but paradoxically also produce, the clash between the margin and the center, the "improper" and the "proper," the exiled and those who belong.

The Subaltern Pilgrim

Traditionally, the pilgrim has been associated with the subaltern, the ostracized, the exiled. Colin Morris remarks that *pilgrim* derives from the

Latin word *peregrinus*, which "was an unspecific term, meaning a traveler, stranger, alien, or immigrant" (Morris 1). He adds that "such people were not necessarily involved in a religious journey, and did not even have to be traveling at all. When Cicero contrasted the *civis* (citizen) with the *peregrinus*, he was apparently thinking of the 'pilgrim' as a resident alien" (1). This lack of belonging—later ascribed mainly, but not exclusively, to the process of traveling from home to the shrine—and "passing through," connects, as Erin Moure observed, to the etymology of the "pilgrim" as a stranger (McCance 2). People who embark on a quest are not implicated, socially or politically, in the land they traverse, and therefore, although strangers in that environment, they enter some kind of Turnerian liminal or liminoid sphere, one that is indispensable for them to negotiate or contemplate the subject of power.

Such a sphere appears in Homi Bhabha's discussion of postcolonial migration, exile, and social displacements in *Location of Culture*. Bhabha discusses, among many elements, "a return to the performance of identity as iteration, the re-creation of the self in the world of travel, the resettlement of the borderline community of migration" (9). He maintains that although the "'middle passage' of contemporary culture, as with slavery itself, is a process of displacement and disjunction that does not totalize experience" (5), the "interstitial passage between fixed identifications opens up the possibility of a cultural hybridity that entertains difference without an assumed or imposed hierarchy" (4). If we translate Bhabha's proposition that the "Third Space" opens up a possibility to elaborate strategies of selfhood into the discourse of pilgrimage as a metaphor for identity creation or re-creation (often, as in the case of Conrad and Joyce, hindered by strategies of oppression), this questing enables individual development unmediated by mundane social hierarchies. Because Conrad, Joyce, and many of the characters in their fiction belonged to the subaltern stratum in many respects (ethnicity, race, gender, class, education, mental development), their emergence in the liminal space is potentially formative, even if they do not manage to reach their destination. This space—where profane boundaries can be obliterated—allows for or promises self-discovery, no matter what form of questing these characters choose: a passage through a desertlike environment, the *flâneur*'s walk through the city, the tourist's bus ride, the exile's wandering across numerous borders, and many other.

Pilgrimage in Conrad's and Joyce's texts is inextricable from a broader argument of power relations in societies affected by ethnic, racial, gender, and class inequality. There, the individual and collective "pilgrimaging" is a continually unaccomplished quest for relief from the profane world of uncertainty, alienation, and subordination. Do Conrad and Joyce present pilgrimage as solidifying social hierarchies and fortifying political divisions, or do their characters enter the realm of the liminal and engage in some kind of egalitarian community building? Can they abandon, even temporarily, the damaging binarisms of their plutocratic, chauvinistic, and dogmatic environments? Do they believe in the existence of an approachable center? Marlow, Kurtz, Jim, Dedalus, Bloom, Molly, and a few others will provide some answers about the nature of pilgrimage in Conrad's and Joyce's fiction.

5

"Circles, circles, circles"

Conrad's Pilgrimage

Conrad's long essay "Geography and Some Explorers," which was first published as "The Romance of Travel," describes the author's passage through the Torres Straits in 1888 and provides an account of the changing nature of sailors' pilgrimages through explored and unknown territories.[1] In some ways, Conrad's portrayal of the long-forgotten world of sea voyage reflects the pilgrimages of his characters, often thrown into a new and hostile environment, searching for a landmark in the treacherous and hazy surroundings, toiling to achieve their destinations. Conrad romanticizes the contingencies and perils of questing when he evokes in his essay "the fascination of the first hazardous steps of a venturesome, often lonely, explorer" (*Last Essays* 1). His examples include "the awful geographical incertitudes of the first explorers in that new world of waters" (9), their voyages "prompted by an acquisitive spirit, the idea of lucre in some form, the desire of trade or the desire of loot, disguised in more or less fine words," Captain Cook's single-minded and undisguised "search for truth" (14), and his own "romantic explorations of my inner self" (17) inspired by stories of adventure whose protagonists, "with varied motives, laudable or sinful," bore in their breasts "a spark of the sacred fire" (31). Conrad's personal pilgrimage through the partitioned Poland, the coast of Marseille, the world's seas, harbors, and metropolises, and finally into the quiet English countryside influenced his fictional accounts of travel and deracination. His exile (voluntary, like Joyce's, despite the presence of a foreign power in Conrad's native Poland) is reflected in his themes of alienation, deterritorialization of self, redemption, and quest for self-invention.

That Conrad's characters often feel compelled to move on through seas, jungles, and cities by rational and irrational forces seems to be one of the unchangeable patterns in his fiction. In "Geography," the writer recalls the Gulf of Panama, "one of the calmest spots on the waters of the globe. Too calm. The old navigators dreaded it as a dangerous region where one might be caught and lie becalmed for weeks with one's crew dying slowly of thirst under a cloudless sky" (6). Similarly, for Marlow, Kurtz, and the harlequin in *Heart of Darkness*, Winnie in *The Secret Agent*, or Jim in *Lord Jim*, the Central Station, the Inner Station, the Brett Street home and shop with shady wares, the sinking ship with pilgrims on board, or any place on earth where people might hear the gossip about the *Patna* accident might turn out to be their own treacherous Gulf of Panama. Therefore, immobility means death or near death: from malaria or other mysterious illnesses, from a bullet, a spear, a rope on the gallows, or death by drowning. However, a sense of mortality and an immediate danger are not the only reasons for these characters' progress. Marlow's seafaring and his inexhaustible memory of places, people, events, and impressions, Kurtz's journey through and, finally, appropriation of the unknown forces in the heart of Africa, the harlequin's unchanging restlessness, Jim's search for self-redemption, the revolutionaries' walks through slimy London and Geneva streets, Winnie's mad escape in darkness, Yanko's quest toward Keiser's America, Wait's last sea voyage in the cabin of death, and the journeys of numerous other characters—Almayer, Razumov, Heyst, and Lena, to name just few—are all quests toward the center that in most cases is unattainable, delusory, or empty.

Conrad's Ghostly Nomads: Toward Hollow Revelation

The journey in Conrad's fiction, even if it repeatedly lacks, as we will see later, a crucial spiritual component, often displays typical features of the rite of passage, especially the initiation rite, with its three main components: separation, transformation, and return. The Russian sailor—the harlequin in *Heart of Darkness*—breaks away from the mundane social formation in order to be suspended in the transitional, liminal world of ambiguity and deracination. The harlequin is separated from the relative comfort of Western civilization, from his ancestry, and—in the end—from Kurtz, who "enlarged [his] mind" (140), and he wanders under the cover of abundant nature, destitute and lonely, but "excellently well equipped for a renewed encounter with the wilderness" (140) with his peculiar pilgrim's insignia: cartridges, Towson's *Inquiry*, and Marlow's English tobacco. Similarly, Jim, "a friendless, homeless man" (*Lord Jim* 133), after abandoning eight hundred pilgrims on the *Patna* and after his disgrace at the trial, severs all ties with his familiar environment and embarks on his own lonely pilgrimage "generally farther east" (2); his "keen perception of the Intolerable drove him away for good from seaports and white men" (2), prompting a question about why his disgrace might be more tolerable among nonwhites; he "was protected by his isolation, alone of his own superior kind, in close touch with nature" (128). Both the harlequin and Jim occupy a liminal space, as they temporarily abandon their proprietary needs, break free from social conventions, and choose a nomadic, erratic existence. They embark on a pilgrimage to enlightenment and redemption, but these goals are elusive, and even their voluntary, sacrificial deracination and self-flagellation do not make the telos any closer. The Russian sailor remains a blind follower, a mimic (resembling, to a certain extent, Joyce's clownish Malachi Mulligan), while Jim—until his final sacrifice—is suspended between his shameful past and imagined, glorious future, unable to make a step, frozen in the bizarre state of aloof detachment and unfulfilled desire to prove his courage.

The quests of the Verlocs, the anarchists, and the two members of the London police in *The Secret Agent* are also marked by their isolation and inability to communicate with others, but here exclusion and silence take place at the heart of the empire. Truly isolated characters in the novel (those whom Conrad never gives a chance to crave or ask for anybody's affection and understanding) are either mentally or emotionally handicapped, like the half-witted Stevie, lost in drawing circles or obediently following orders, and the misanthropic Professor, whose mind is preoccupied with the production of a perfect device to annihilate the weak.[2] In the end, Stevie's quest will turn out to have a more deadly, though equally pointless, outcome. What links Stevie's progress with other quests in Conrad's fiction is the liminal experience of uncertainty, anonymity, grotesqueness, ludic or subversive behavior that characterize the journeys of other characters, whose travels are dreamlike, hazy, veiled in mysteries.

Let's look closer, then, at Conrad's grotesque Russian sailor. In "Harlequin in Hell," James Morgan claims that this character appears to be "a prototype representing a stage of psychological development Marlow experiences through his journey into the heart of darkness and passes beyond," a conclusion derived from, or helped by, Jung's analysis of Harlequin as "an archetype of initiation" (2). According to Jung, this figure is a slightly sinister "ancient chthonic god," who "descends 'to the crazy primitive world of the witches' sabbath'" on his "wild journey through man's millennial history," traversing "rubbish and decay" and "half-born or aborted possibilities of form" (3).

Harlequin's pilgrimage, I want to argue, is modernism itself. It is an attempt to traverse the "stony rubbish" (Eliot, *Waste Land* 20) and "heap of broken images" (22) through individuation and metaphor. It is an attempt to encompass incoherent reality and opaque surfaces and to express them through collage, atonality, impasto brushstrokes intended to reflect the play of light rather than dwell on specific details; it is an acquiescence to lack of coherent sense of depth and celebration of intersecting surfaces. It may ultimately lead nowhere in particular, but the pilgrim is aware of his transitionality and the freedom that comes from shedding the mask that society ascribed to him and rejecting the convenience of fabricated binarisms.

The Russian sailor is, after all, nameless, with "no features to speak of" (*Heart of Darkness* 122), a puzzle, "an insoluble problem" whose "very existence was improbable, inexplicable, and altogether bewildering." This pilgrim in motley, in "particoloured rags," feels a constant need "to exist, and to move onwards at the greatest possible risk, and with a maximum of privation"; what drives him forward is "the absolutely pure, uncalculating, unpractical spirit of adventure" (126). After the harlequin disappears into darkness, Marlow comments: "Sometimes I ask myself whether I had ever really seen him—whether it was possible to meet such a phenomenon!" (140). The Russian sailor, Kurtz's follower and servant who has been denied voice, does not reach the point of genuine liberation and assertion of his own power in his African quest, as he always appears an intangible, incongruous, fleeting ghost in his master's shadow, even in Kurtz's absence.

Morgan argues that although Marlow implicitly identifies himself with the harlequin, he finally denies "the homo totus Harlequin represents" (5). What goal, then, does Marlow reach at the end of his quest? Morgan's response is as vague as Kurtz's last words. Is Marlow's ultimate telos the Inner Station itself? The hut guarded by heads rotting on poles? Is it Kurtz, the "hollow sham" (*Heart of Darkness* 147), someone whose existence

Marlow confirms only by his voice, who seems a shadow "draped nobly in the folds of a gorgeous eloquence" (155)? Is it really someone whose final whisper, "The horror! The horror!" (149)—the significance of which is clear only to Kurtz himself—is a pronouncement that renders so many varied interpretations that its meaning remains, like Marlow's story, imprecise, enveloping his experiences with fog? Or is it Marlow's final lie, his refusal to uncover the appalling practices based on racist ideologies, this indirect acquiescence to perpetuating the oppression of the natives? If, as Morgan claims, Marlow's quest, unlike the Russian sailor's, ends with an acquisition of some ultimate knowledge, why doesn't he reveal it to his listeners aboard the *Nellie*? Why does the reader remain, just like the harlequin, in the dark?

After Kurtz's death, Marlow admits that he "remained to dream the nightmare out to the end" (150). He further comments: "Destiny. My destiny! Droll thing life is—that mysterious arrangement of merciless logic for a futile purpose. The most you can hope from it is *some* knowledge of yourself—that comes too late—a crop of unextinguishable regrets" (150). Either the pilgrimage from the profane world of arbitrary social roles toward the ultimate knowledge and self-formation remains incomplete or, if Marlow does reach its telos, it turns out to be empty and "hollow at the core" (131).

Kurtz's last pronouncement may indicate that he alone has reached the genuine endpoint of the quest for comprehension. We encounter him as he is still immersed in the liminal experience, both creative and destructive, alluring for those who long to shed their old artificial selves and, sometimes through subversive and ludic behavior, acquire real knowledge about their identities. When such pilgrimage ends with real or symbolic death, it becomes a genuine rite of passage. Kurtz's abandonment of the "civilized" life of the European metropolis and all the connections he might have had with the servants of the empire, his communion with untamed nature, and his involvement in the "unspeakable rites" could open up his mind to the real nature of humanity, unencumbered by societal limitations.[3] In the absence of traditional Western values, though, he inscribes his own visions of power and spirituality, mainly through fear. Paradoxically, then, he attempts to reach the sacred through what the Christian world would call sin: greed, theft, murder, possibly even cannibalism. Admittedly, Marlow also reaches the point of death, which he manages to evade, but this experience does not provide him with any final self-recognition, as he himself admits:

> I was within a hair's breath of the last opportunity for pronounce-
> ment, and I found with humiliation that probably I would have noth-
> ing to say. This is the reason why I affirm that Kurtz was a remarkable
> man. He had something to say. He said it. Since I had peeped over
> the edge myself, I understand better the meaning of his stare, that
> could not see the flame of the candle, but was wide enough to em-
> brace the whole universe, piercing enough to penetrate all the hearts
> that beat in the darkness. . . . True, he had made that last stride, he
> had stepped over the edge, while I had been permitted to draw back
> my hesitating foot . . . perhaps all the wisdom, and all the truth, and
> all sincerity, are just compressed into that inappreciable moment of
> time in which we step over the threshold of the invisible. (151)

Marlow, then, only manages to glimpse a half-truth, a superficial picture of himself and others, whereas he claims Kurtz's gaze to be "wide," "pierc-ing," penetrating, and all-encompassing. The English sailor perhaps has a chance to reach the final destination of his quest and draw a final conclu-sion from his own experiences (and those of humanity), but he also has the opportunity not to take that risk and to return to the profane world without completing the process of self-formation. His near-death experi-ence remains, therefore, formless and devoid of meaning.

Equally meaningless seems to be Lord Jim's travel toward the rising sun. Jim maintains his anonymity among most people he encounters on his journey—and, in a way, with the reader, too, for we never learn his surname.[4] His motives (among them, the reason for his jump) are un-clear; he lives in the realm of moral ambiguity. This "seaman in exile from the sea" (*Lord Jim* 2) leads "the magic monotony of existence between sky and water" (6), and in the most challenging trial in his life, he is in-capable of resisting "a sinister violence of intention" (6), "a purpose of malice, with a strength beyond control" (6), or, as he calls his act of cow-ardice later in the novel, "that mistake" (58). Things just happen to him. Turner's "structural invisibility," typical of the liminal stage of initiation rites and therefore of pilgrimages, is demonstrated in Jim's absolute lack of agency during the accident and until the final scenes of the story. Jim recollects the critical moment on the *Patna* as if it were a dream or, rather, a nightmare, orchestrated by supernatural powers and resisting erasure, lingering in his mind and affecting his somnambulistic progress farther and farther east.[5] The passage before his jump is a stream of "days, hot, heavy, disappearing one by one into the past, as if falling into an abyss for ever open in the wake of the ship" (10–11); the quest after the accident is a "journey towards the bottomless pit" (131), "some mysterious, inexplicable, impalpable striving of his wounded spirit" (133). He has to free his hands "for a grapple with a ghost" (143). A strange kind of fatality casts "the complexion of a flight upon all his acts, of impulsive unreflecting desertion—of a jump into the unknown" (168). Jim himself seems to "gaze hungrily into the unattainable" (13). His eyes are "unabashed and impenetrable" (55). Marlow is never able to see him clearly.[6] Jim is "nothing but an erring spirit, a suffering and nameless shade" (157). Curiously, despite this inability to define Jim with any precision, Marlow assures us several times that he is "one of us" (56), thus reinstating the uncompromising systematization inscribed in the colonial endeavor and including Jim in the superior class (of white European professionals? adventurers? romantics?) despite all the shortcomings of his character.

Initially, it seems that Jim finishes the stage of transformation and achieves a perfect moment of self-understanding, "as if some conviction of innate blamelessness had checked the truth writhing within him at every turn" (57). Marlow infers that "he was partly stunned by the discovery he has made—the discovery about himself" (59), but he never manages to understand precisely whether Jim really arrives at any conclusion and, if so, what kind of revelation he experiences, probably because of Jim's intermittent displays of guilt and defense, self-pity and self-loathing, and his desperate but unsuccessful attempt to explain his action on board of the *Patna*. The aim of his wanderings is "not relief" but "something not easy to define—something in the nature of an opportunity" (146). At some point during his pilgrimage toward redemption, Jim possibly expects to forget and be forgiven for the terrible "mistake" that banishes him from society, shatters his own conception of his character and abilities, and leaves him defenseless. As he asserts, "this thing must be buried" (138), displaying a desire for "a clean slate" (135) that Marlow calls "a high-minded absurdity of intention which made [his] futility profound and touching" (143).

And yet Jim's attempt "to deliver himself" fails (252). After a long and turbulent quest, he "passes away under a cloud, inscrutable at heart, forgotten, unforgiven, and excessively romantic" (308). His truth has always been intertwined with the world of dreams which "carried his soul away with them and made it drunk with the divine philter of an unbounded confidence in itself" (14). Jim's quest is driven by a *demand* to attain truth; however, Marlow himself dismisses the meaning of the very word *truth*, unable to define the border between veracity and delusion. This appears to be Marlow's acquiescence to a failure of understanding both the self and the world of his pilgrimage. The sacred center, the telos, of the quest of humanity is, in fact, a ghost. It entices us and drives our journey, but turns out to be an illusion, as "all assertion in this world of doubts is a defiance, is an insolence" (173). Those engaged in an escape from the uncertain, intangible, or ungodly appear to be "running. Absolutely running, with nowhere to go" (113). Stein, an entomologist on his own pursuit of a "perfect specimen" (154), tirelessly ordering and classifying his findings, contrasts a butterfly which "finds a little heap of dirt and sits still on it" with a human being, unable to remain "on his heap of mud" (155): "He want [*sic*] to be so, and again he want to be so. . . . He wants to be a saint, and he wants to be a devil—and every time he shuts his eyes he sees himself as a very fine fellow—so fine as he can never be. . . . In a dream." (155). He thus sums up the futility of Jim's quest and, in general, human attempts to reach the ultimate truth: "A man that is born falls into a dream like a man who falls into the sea. If he tries to climb out into the air as inexperienced people endeavour to do, he drowns—*nicht wahr*? . . . No! I tell you! The way is to the destructive element submit yourself, and with the exertions of your hands and feet in the water make the deep, deep sea keep you up" (156). The significance of human quest, then, according to Stein, lies not in single-minded and self-assured arrival at the telos or in an abandonment of desire but in a constant endeavor to reach the inaccessible and an awareness that mortals are destined to remain on their "heap of dirt" or in the "deep sea." Rejection of dreams and illusions guarantees at least peace of mind. And yet Marlow himself admits that "it is respectable to have no illusions—and safe—and profitable—and dull" (165).

Paralyzed Pilgrimage in *The Secret Agent*

Illusions and desire for self-invention fuel other quests in Conrad's fiction. Conrad molded all of his characters in *The Secret Agent* as pilgrims. Some members of the establishment, some renegades against it, they are engaged in a perpetual act of walking, seeking, pursuit. Their goals are sometimes clearly defined—e.g., catching the incompetent terrorists responsible for the Greenwich outrage, or reaching for power through a development of a perfect detonator—but sometimes they resemble an ideological fantasy, e.g., bringing about an ideal society based on social equality, mutual respect, and the healing power of science. These characters are, like Jim, the harlequin, or Marlow, suspended in midair, forever lingering in the liminal stage of their quests. The subaltern remain in their disadvantaged position. Even though *The Secret Agent* is set at the center of the empire, the native inhabitants of its colonized territories are literally nonexistent in the book (and mostly immobile and mute in *Heart of Darkness* and *Lord Jim*). Conrad does not even test their ability to protest and transgress rigid boundaries. Without a counternarrative or a representation of their own native myth, they are the backdrop for other traveling characters. The subaltern in *The Secret Agent* are working-class or lower-middle-class walkers, some of them too idle or dim-witted to set precise goals for themselves. Therefore, they submit to the demands of manipulative individuals; Verloc tries to fulfill Vladimir's request to destroy the observatory, the temple of modern science, and Stevie follows Verloc's orders to carry out the plan, thus triggering the "domestic drama" (*Secret Agent* 222) that Sir Ethelred recognizes in the public affair of the bombing.

In the gloomy and inhumane metropolis—the microcosm of an early twentieth-century profane world inhospitable to pilgrims—Karl Yundt, Alexander Ossipon, Michaelis, Verloc, and the Professor, a group of armchair anarchists, discuss at their regular meetings the injustices of the current sociopolitical system and prognosticate about the future of the proletariat. The backstage of their movements is London, a blurred and formless space offering no relief of concrete answers and definitions. Its "dusty windows" offer "the sightless, moribund look of incurable decay" (82), a truly wasteland-like panorama. It is a world of "dusky alley[s]" (82), "a good deal of raw, unwholesome fog" (86), and "alien wilderness of the streets" (Rignall 145), a place "experienced as a kind of elemental confusion where forms are slipping back into a primeval slime" (144), a town Conrad compares to "a wet, muddy trench" (*Secret Agent* 135), in which people proceed as if in a soporific trance. Mr. Verloc's gaze is "somnambulistic" and "expressionless" (177). He "retraced the path of his morning's pilgrimage as if in a dream—an angry dream." (37). The Assistant

Commissioner is "going to and fro with the air of a thoughtful somnam-
bulist" (222). Notably, Heat calls the Professor a "lunatic" (97). Like the
African jungle in Marlow's story, London itself is a monstrous and wild
environment promising a descent into the unexplored territories of the
mind. Is this pilgrimage toward self-revelation and acquisition of power
realized?

Initially, some characters, especially Verloc, Winnie, and her mother,
do not seem to be capable of embarking on such a quest. Winnie's mother,
after all, due to "the impotent condition of her legs" (153) is "staggering"
(242) and "inactive" (6), and Conrad refers to her as a "motionless being"
(7). Conrad also introduces Mr. Verloc as a man "thoroughly domesticated. Neither his spiritual, nor his mental, nor his physical needs were of
the kind to take him much abroad. He found at home the ease of his body
and the peace of his conscience" (5). We learn about his idleness, to which
he is devoted "with a sort of inert fanaticism, or perhaps rather with a fanatical inertness" (12). Throughout his meeting with Mr. Vladimir, he remains "motionless, as if feeling himself surrounded by pitfalls" (18), fighting "that sensation of faintness running down [his] legs" (28–29). Conrad
tells us that, as a young man, Verloc traveled to Europe frequently, and
he "generally arrived in London (like the influenza) from the Continent,
only he arrived unheralded by the Press" (6). Here, Conrad locates the
motif of contamination not in the mysterious and foggy African interior
but in Europe and the center of the biggest colonial empire. However, it
is not the gluttonous empire itself but an intellectually dull agent of the
working class that is compared to the influenza. Brian W. Shaffer notices
that Verloc's name itself suggests "a syphilitic" in French (446). Underbred
and apathetic, Verloc is an offense to the imagined purity of Englishness,
insinuating himself into its ethnos and ethos. His quest is nothing more
than a potentially deadly viral pollution of the discursive image of an imperial, efficient, just, and virtuous nation.

We would expect Verloc, one of the vice presidents of "The Future of
the Proletariat," to be involved in some kind of quest, even if his physique
indicates a degree of indolence.[7] We expect him to work for the better-
ment of the oppressed classes, for the equality of humankind, especially
because Heat calls him "a rather well-known hanger-on and emissary of
the Revolutionary Red Committee" (130); yet, when Ossipon says that
Verloc "was the centre for general intelligence" but was "more useful than

important" (74) and calls him a "man of no ideas" (74), it becomes apparent that Verloc will not directly affect any social change, just as his mind is "evidently unrefreshed by the wonders of foreign travel and a countenance unlighted by the joys of homecoming" (182).

Nevertheless, Conrad compares Verloc to the prototypical pilgrim, Ulysses, and Winnie to Penelope. Her "wifely talk" is "artfully adapted, no doubt, to the circumstances of this return as the talk of Penelope to the return of the wandering Odysseus." We learn, however, that Mrs. Verloc does no weaving, though she entertains suitors: Michaelis, Yundt, and Ossipon (183). There is a stinging irony in this juxtaposition of the mythical pilgrim to an overweight dealer in pornography, a lazy, smug, and "domesticated" double agent who deludes himself about his significant role in "protection [of] this complacent, opulent society" (12). Verloc lacks Odysseus's adventurousness and wit. The secret agent's only apparent dream is to be unperturbed by embassies, policemen, or pangs of conscience (the last turns out be an astonishingly easy task). In another mocking description of Verloc, Conrad likens him to "a peripatetic philosopher" (230): "Mr. Verloc, strolling along the streets of London, had modified Stevie's view of the police by conversations full of subtle reasonings. Never had a sage a more attentive and admiring disciple" (230). We know, of course, that he never arrives at any revelation or meaningful conclusion because the "mind of Mr. Verloc lacked profundity" (*Secret Agent* 233). Until his death, he remains apathetic and uninquisitive, deluded about his wife's supposed deep affection toward him, about his power over her and others, and about his survival skills. Verloc's encounter with death produces no stunning revelation, no Kurtz-like dramatic whisper; his sole utterance after Winnie plunges her kitchen knife into his breast is "Don't" (263).

Neither is Winnie a prime embodiment of the mythical loving and devoted wife fending off suitors during Odysseus's wanderings. The "suitors" themselves are remarkably innocuous because of their physical handicap, age, or cowardice. Winnie, however, does have a "singleness of purpose" (179) that, until Stevie's violent death, constitutes the sole meaning of her life. Hers is a quest of fierce maternal instincts toward her half-witted brother, an endeavor to protect him at all costs. She abandons possibilities of individual independence and submits herself to Verloc's "benevolence," immersed in the nebulous, nightmarish metropolis, where moral and social principles of justice and equality are distorted. When she suddenly loses the outlet for this powerful emotion, after an initial feeling of freedom, she remains motionless, "leaning negligently against the mantelpiece in the attitude of a resting wayfarer" (261). And in a moment of blinding rage, when she approaches Verloc, a kitchen knife in hand, she descends, like Conrad's travelers in the heart of Africa, into the abyss of the unconscious, into the atavistic ritual of revenge: "Into that plunging blow, delivered over the side of the couch, Mrs. Verloc had put all the inheritance of her immemorial and obscure descent, the simple ferocity of the age of caverns, and the unbalanced nervous fury of the age of barrooms" (263).

Again, Conrad's description of primal and ferocious femininity is not as innocuous as it may initially seem. Winnie, after the impulsive and almost involuntary act of murder, relinquishes her agency and remains mute, except for pathetic pleas for help when she runs into Ossipon. Conrad does not grant her a moment of self-investigation. Instead, when Winnie's quest to secure her brother's happiness ends with an explosion and a murder, she finds her personal mantra in "The drop given was fourteen feet" (294). The fear of the gallows paralyzes her actions and arrests her thoughts; she remains a cipher, her identity obliterated with Stevie's death. Winnie is not victorious and enlightened but possessed with fear. She rejects her freshly won independence in favor of another illusion: her belief in Ossipon's chivalric love for her. Her suicide remains forever labeled by the press as a mysterious "act of madness and despair" (*Secret Agent* 307).

Stevie, though sensitive to other people's (and animals') plights, goes through life unbothered by profound questions of identity, personal objectives, or eschatology. His main concern is to please Winnie and her husband, follow his duties without a mishap, and draw endless circles on a piece of paper.[8] Stevie's lines lead nowhere and defy the concept of progress toward a telos, unlike, say, Yeats's converging and diverging spirals that mark the passage of time and herald systematic cultural shifts. We see "the innocent Stevie . . . drawing circles, circles, circles; innumerable circles, concentric, eccentric; a coruscating *whirl* of circles that by their *tangled* multitude of repeated curves, uniformity of form, and *confusion* of *intersecting* lines suggested a rendering of cosmic *chaos*, the symbolism of a mad art *attempting the inconceivable*" (45, emphases mine). His drawings are chaotic; order, design, and purpose are missing. This absence of an ultimate goal in Stevie's production is very symptomatic of the way Conrad portrays the modern quest. If humanity moves at all, if it searches for meaning, it proceeds in circles, in a repetitive, purposeless motion, devoid of effort, intellectual curiosity, and spiritual need to find the ultimate telos, the sacred. And if, as Yeats prophesied, "the centre cannot hold" or, even worse, the center does not exist or is empty, then the human race is caught in the whirlwind of confusion and anarchy, where interpersonal communication and spiritual foundation lose their significance.

Mr. Vladimir sums up this predicament in his conversation with Verloc, claiming that people "dislike finality in this country" (25); the Professor shares this conviction when he says to Ossipon that mankind "does not know what it wants" (305). Pilgrimage through London does not offer any possibilities for identity formation; on the contrary, it obliterates, gradually or suddenly, any vestiges of self-assertion. As Rosenfield notices, a "sense of annihilation of self is the psychological effect of the journey into the underworld" (100). In Conrad, London's murky alleys, like Africa's fog, obscure perception and render intellectual inquiry and sound moral judgment nearly impossible.

In *The Secret Agent*, the only persons unguided by personal, mercenary, or nihilistic motives prove to be highly ineffective. One of them, Stevie, is blown to pieces after Verloc convinces him that eradication of policemen is a requisite step to save humanity and ensure justice. Stevie's identity is obliterated when he becomes "a heap of nameless fragments" (87) scraped off the sidewalk with a shovel. The other, Michaelis, crippled by his unusual weight, is "the hermit of visions in the desert of a penitentiary" (50)—and later, of his solitary cottage—unquestionably unrealistic visions which, apart from condescending remarks at the lady patroness's parties, evoke pity or disdain among fellow revolutionaries. Michaelis, the "gentle apostle" (51) famous for his grotesque appearance, writes a biography in his hermitage, living "on a little milk and crusts of stale bread" (232). He divides the book into three parts entitled "Faith," "Hope," and "Charity," where he elaborates on "the idea of a world planned out like an immense and nice hospital, with gardens and flowers, in which the strong are to devote themselves to the nursing of the weak" (303). Although Conrad's description of Michaelis as a dreaming hermit places him in the realm of liminal detachment from the worldly concerns of ambiguity and grotesqueness, this "ticket-of-leave apostle" never regains touch with reality. He is "like those saintly men whose personality is lost in the contemplation of their faith. His ideas were not in the nature of convictions" (107). True, he is confident "of the future, whose secret ways had been revealed to him within the four walls of a well-known peniten-tiary" (107), but when asked to elucidate his prophecy, he "could not give the great and curious lady a very definite idea as to what the world was coming to" (107).

The other London revolutionaries have equally vague plans for the progress of society in this center of the empire. Their quest consists in walking along damp, slimy streets and engaging in futile debates with each other, one could say—following Stein's words in *Lord Jim*—simply in order to keep their heads above water, because any decisive move might drown them. John Rignall points out that Conrad's "versions of the realist *flâneur*" indeed "dramatize the difficulty of composing experience into meaning except in terms of absolute negation" (141). They "all tread the dangerous edge between a limited bourgeois normality and a frightening abyss where nothing has value or meaning" (142). The details they per-ceive "resist recuperation into any general pattern of meaning" and offer "glimpses which do not quite add up to a coherent vision" (142). Without a coherent vision of what lies ahead on the pilgrim's path, the very es-sence of quest disappears, together with any potential for renewal and empowerment.

Pilgrimage Redefined: Conrad's Peripatetic Characters

But perhaps Conrad noticed that the hostile, fractured society necessi-tates new forms of questing. Conrad's characters, the good-for-nothing revolutionaries among them, embody Zygmunt Bauman's categories of the modern pilgrim, which I discuss in detail in the previous chap-ter. These walkers' patterns of behavior and the nature of their modern "quests" often mirror the stroller's surface-level attachment to the reality he perceives, the vagabond's masterlessness, the tourist's thirst for new experience, and the player's tactics.

As mentioned before, Bauman's *flâneur* operates on the surface. He does not form any bonds with the environment, simply because such of-ten demanding attachments require excessive effort. The strollers, who seem to be the modern antitheses of the premodern pilgrims, perceive other people as surfaces, superficial marks exhausting the need to under-stand the other. Conrad argues in the "Author's Note" to *The Secret Agent* that man, in reality, not just in the novel, is "not an investigating animal. He loves the obvious. He shrinks from explanations" (viii).

Both Mr. Verloc and his wife "refrained from going to the bottom of facts and motives" (245), refusing to exercise their intellectual faculties and engage in an honest conversation. Their domestic and public lives are veiled in mysteries. They do not question their status quo and, accordingly, they never arrive at any answers about the meaning of their existence and the spiritual value (or lack thereof) of their marriage, partly because of "Mrs. Verloc's philosophical, almost disdainful incuriosity"—ironically labeled "the foundation of their accord in domestic life" (237)—but also due to Verloc's sheer idleness. Indications of his complacency and super-ficiality of perception are present at the beginning of the novel, when we trace his walk westward toward the embassy, as he "surveyed through the park railings the evidence of the town's opulence and luxury with an ap-proving eye" (12), the "polished knockers of the doors" that "gleamed as far as the eye could reach," "the clean windows" that "shone with a dark opaque luster" (14), and "a thick police constable, looking a stranger to every emotion, as if he, too, were part of inorganic nature" (14). Verloc "held on steadily, without a sign of surprise or indignation" (14). The de-scription of his walk ends with the assertion that Mr. Verloc's "mission in life was the protection of the social mechanism, not its perfectionment or even its criticism" (15). His is the world of the modern *flâneur*, whom Bauman calls "the man of leisure" ("From Pilgrim" 27), the realm of "the fleeting fragments of other persons' lives," of "simulation" (26), where appearance equals reality and nothing is questioned. Similarly, Jim's life before the jump and, to a certain extent after the accident, his inability to distinguish facts from fiction, such as the light adventure stories in which he was immersed as a young man, and his apparent inability to form pro-found relationships with others place him in the role of the modern stroll-ing spectator.

Both London and the African interior seem also to contain a plethora of masterless, deracinated, alienated vagabonds—the unpredictable and subversive figures who have no set destinations and who devote their lives to a pursuit of freedom from laws and conventions and an escape from the panoptic supervision of modern society. The Professor in *The Secret Agent* accuses other anarchists of being "unable to think independently" (68), of acting as "slaves of the social convention, which is afraid of you. . . . It governs your thought, of course, and your action, too, and thus nei-ther your thought nor your action can ever be conclusive" (69). Whereas their character is "built upon conventional morality" and "leans on the social order," his character "stands free from everything artificial. . . . I depend on death, which knows no restraint and cannot be attacked" (68). His "astounding ignorance of worldly conditions" (80) and misanthropic nature aid his goal to "break up the superstition and worship of legality" (73)—mostly through his blatant disregard for London law enforcement and the unpredictability of his movements, but also, more shockingly, through his work on the development of a "perfect detonator" (69).

This nihilist's quest is, in essence, anti-teleological. His anti-absolutist conviction of epistemological failure, his destructive repudiation of all ethics, and his angst make him an anti-pilgrim, a vagabond with no purpose. The Professor's house, "the hermitage of the perfect anarchist" (82), is expendable, as the only valuable thing it contains is a padlocked cupboard with a stock of explosives. Free from social bonds, nameless and deadly, he walks with "the nerveless gait of a tramp going on, still going on, indifferent to rain or sun in a sinister detachment from the aspects of sky and earth" (96). He is "lost in the crowd, miserable and undersized," when he contemplates "his power, keeping his hand in the left pocket of his trousers, grasping lightly the India-rubber ball, the supreme guarantee of his sinister freedom" (81). His goal to design a perfect detonator and his dream "of a world like shambles, where the weak would be taken in hand for utter extermination" (303) might be some sort of telos, but a self-destructive one.

This drive to purify the human race of vice does not quite align with Bauman's concept of the indifferent vagabond. The Professor's apparent indifference to the masses and his disdain of the crowds are displays of his temporary inability to carry out his plan to which he devotes his undivided attention and skills. Yet we learn that to "destroy public faith in legality was the imperfect formula of his pedantic fanaticism; but the subconscious conviction that the framework of an established social order cannot be effectually shattered except by some form of collective or individual violence was precise and correct" (81). Aware that stirring a united outrage against order is impossible, he clings, nevertheless, to the reverie of "ruin and destruction" (311) that would shake the moral and legal backbone of society.

The Professor's mad plan to "Exterminate, exterminate!" (303) bears an eerie resemblance to another masterless figure in Conrad's fiction. Kurtz's intentional deracination, his yearning for freedom from conventions, and his moral and spiritual vagabondage make him in the end an apostle of chaos. Like Bauman's vagabond, who "is pushed from behind by hopes frustrated, and pulled forward by hopes untested" ("From Pilgrim" 28), he is unpredictable and subversive.[9] However, Kurtz departs from this modern form of pilgrimage, a form we might call an anti-quest, in that he does set roots in the soil (or tries to do so), even if it is foreign, and his settlement disrupts the already imperfect colonial arrangement in the Congo. When he realizes that he is going to be taken back to "civilization," he escapes toward the drumbeats and the incantations by the fire. Nevertheless, Marlow, after ambushing him in the forest, calls him "this wandering and tormented thing" (143). Kurtz's flight from the last chance to return to the European society may represent his disdain for Western conventions and his free-spiritedness, but it may also underline his attachment to the station, its ivory, and its people, which would defy the very nature of vagabondage.

Superficial connections with the surrounding reality and a constant motion are also features of Bauman's tourist. "Like the vagabond," Bauman says, "the tourist used once to inhabit the margins of 'properly social' action" and "has now moved to its centre." The tourist's movements are more "pulled" than "pushed"; he has a "purpose (or so he thinks)," which is new experience, "the experience of difference and novelty—as the joys of the familiar wear off and cease to allure" (29). Marlow, although he would probably disdain being called a tourist, manifests this drive to face and explore the unknown. As a child, he would lose himself "in all the glories of exploration" and become enticed (or "pulled") by "many blank spaces on the earth" (52). Although at the time of his trip to the Congo this territory is no longer blank, its river still enchants him "as a snake would a bird—a silly little bird" (52). Marlow assures his listeners that he "always went [his] own road and on [his] own legs where [he] had a mind to go" (53), but he also admits that the Congo fascinates him so much that he used all available means to be able to explore it. However, the tourist retreats from the point of his destination as soon as the strange becomes domesticated and no longer frightening or exciting. Marlow never attains such an extensive familiarity with the Congo. Until the end, Africa looms before him as unexplored and unexplorable, mysterious, bizarre. He never tames his surroundings, as the tourist would do.

Conrad also presents the "Apollo-like" (309) Ossipon as a version of the tourist.[10] At one time "a wandering lecturer to working-men's associations upon the socialistic aspects of hygiene . . . , special delegate of the more or less mysterious Red Committee, together with Karl Yundt and Michaelis for the work of literary propaganda" (46), this enthusiast of Lombroso preys on the naiveté of the ladies he ensnares with his robust form and eloquence. His search is for new sexual experiences, preferably with women who can support him financially. Unable to forge truly intimate, long-lasting relationships, he rejects Winnie's offer to run away to the continent and be her protector. His jump from Winnie's carriage, however, like Jim's infamous fall, leaves him scarred, not physically, since we learn that he "marched without a limp out of the station" (299), but emotionally. Just as Marlow questions his own sanity in the Congo, Ossipon "was becoming scientifically afraid of insanity lying in wait for him amongst these lines" of the newspaper report of Winnie's suicide (307). We see him in the last chapter, walking "without looking where he put his feet, feeling no fatigue, feeling nothing, seeing nothing, hearing not a sound" (311). He does not return to the world of new sensations and exciting encounters, the world of the tourist, where "tough and harsh realities resistant to aesthetic sculpting do not interfere" ("From Pilgrim" 30).

The characters in *The Secret Agent* who embody the characteristics of the player, and who perhaps most frequently rely on risk taking, intuition, and a drive to win in their quests—or, should I say, conquests—seem to understand that in life, like in play, they can control and predict very little. They devise their own moves in response to the overwhelming chaos of their surroundings and other players' decisions. Chief Inspector Heat, in his struggle with the so far untouchable Professor and with the Assistant Commissioner, the remaining key players in the game, contemplates his maneuvers and appears to realize that the goal "is to guess the moves of the adversary and anticipate them, prevent or pre-empt" (31).[11] Sometimes fate thrusts clues into Heat's hands (*Secret Agent* 90), and sometimes he changes tactics or plans on giving up the game altogether,[12] as if he knew that his life game was divided into a succession of moves. Heat realizes that his job of catching criminals "had that quality of seriousness belonging to every form of open sport where the best man wins under perfectly comprehensible rules." But there are "no rules for dealing with anarchists" (97). Heat, falling into the pattern of Bauman's players (the last group of the modern pilgrims), is possibly aware that those "who refuse to obey the conventions do not rebel against the game; they only opt out and cease to be players" ("From Pilgrim" 31). His game is to eliminate the danger that London revolutionary circles pose for the city and to outwit the Assistant Commissioner, who has his own private agenda in the investigation of the Greenwich outrage. However, "he meant to get hold of [the Professor] in his own time, properly and effectively, according to the rules of the game" (122).

That Heat is involved in a game with the Assistant Commissioner follows from their verbal duel at the latter's office, when Heat feels the strong "indignation of a betrayed tight-rope performer" and is "affected by the assurance that the rope was not shaken for the purpose of breaking his neck, as by an exhibition of impudence" (124). The Assistant Commissioner engages in this round with undeniable pleasure, missing the excitement of his previous post in the colonies, which had the "saving character of an irregular sort of warfare or at least the risk and excitement of open-air sport" (*Secret Agent* 113).[13] At stake is his wife's friendship with the lady patroness, but he also derives a certain perverse pleasure from the play for its own sake. This "foreign-looking chap" (214) with "a long, meagre face with the accentuated features of an energetic Don Quixote" (115) seems destined to live in the world of superficial moves and useful tactics, unlike Heat, the crusader, who participates in the game not just to satisfy his ambition but also to make London's opulence safer from thieves and anarchists.[14] The Assistant Commissioner might, however, realize the ultimate pointlessness of his movements in a metropolis resembling "a slimy aquarium from which the water had been run off" (147) when he thinks, "Horrible, horrible!"(100) while looking down at London from his office window. But it is doubtful that, like Kurtz's last utterance, this thought carries any profound significance, any inspired (vague as it is) summation of his entire life. The players in Conrad's fiction mirror Bauman's elucidation of the shallow and short-lived pursuits of the last of the modern pilgrims.

In all the movements of the modern versions of the pilgrim, the absence of the goal that traditionally a pilgrim would pursue—that of spiritual renewal and self-assurance or self-formation through contact with the sacred—is so glaring that one may suspect Conrad of omitting these elements intentionally in order to draw the reader's attention to the spiritual sterility of modern society. Either his characters are at ease in the profane world of miscommunication, selfishness, nihilism, racism, and murder, or their attempts at escaping it are weak-willed and ineffective. Implicated in this plight of humanity is the question of power. Incompetence and irresolution in the characters' quest, as well as their frequent inability to actually determine what it is that they want to pursue, render them truly inferior, unable to arouse themselves from torpor. Therefore, they remain in their limbo and fail in their ill-planned pilgrimages toward the illusive or empty telos.

6

Teleology without a Telos?

Constitutive Absence in Joyce's Pilgrimage

Among numerous commentators about the plight of the displaced self and the Sisyphean quest for meaning is James Joyce, a voluntary exile himself, a wanderer, seeker, a pilgrim of sorts, albeit one who has rejected formalized religion. His Leopold Bloom—an Irishman, a Jew, and a cuckold, a "homeless" and alienated character—attempts to escape the double oppression of colonized, predominantly Catholic Ireland through literal and metaphorical forms of pilgrimage. In the act of walking, in movement through his urban world, he strives to arrive at independent self-identification. When his telos, however, proves to be empty or false, he redirects his steps and shifts his gaze onto another one. Hence the disappointment upon reaching an unfulfilling goal turns into a new promise of a formative center. The empty center becomes a constitutive absence, a driving force to redirect and move toward a new telos. But why does he pursue it at all?

Joyce's personal pilgrimage through Dublin, Paris, Trieste, Pola, Rome, and Zurich, his disenchantment with Dublin's factionalism, and the stifling limitations imposed by the Catholic Church, by England, and by his destitute and rowdy father influenced his portrayal of Bloom and Stephen's restlessness. In the country whose citizens are either Catholic or Protestant, pro-Union or anti-Union, pro-Treaty or anti-Treaty, pro-Parnell or anti-Parnell, there seems to be no niche for those who acknowledge plurality and diversity, who choose to explore their selves rather than blindly follow ideologies, who realize that succumbing to limitations imposed by society, religion, and politics equals spiritual and artistic death. Joyce himself escaped Dublin; instead, he placed Stephen Dedalus and Leopold Bloom within this milieu. His surrogate selves explore the city's paths and their own identities.

Almost all of Joyce's characters in *Ulysses* attempt to subvert or evade their fragmented world through literal and metaphorical forms of pilgrimage. They strive to arrive at independent self-identification, but their telos proves to be ultimately unachievable or "empty." The characters' dislocated selves, revealing ontological anxiety and frustrated pursuit of the sacred union between the father and the son, display important qualities of the pilgrim as well as certain modalities characteristic of all four categories analyzed by Bauman: the stroller, the vagabond, the tourist, and the player. Each character's pilgrimage is informed by other methods of seeking an identity or, in some cases, of escaping a fixed identity. This transformation from the identity seekers in archaic culture into the homeless in contemporary society is one of the central themes in *Ulysses*. Here, as in Conrad's *Secret Agent*, wandering through the city is a metaphor for seeking an identity. The characters experience anxiety resulting from the lack of center as well as a ceaseless endeavor to approach it.

In "Semus Sumus: Joyce and Pilgrimage," Julia Bolton Holloway presents a thorough and pertinent survey of the figure of the pilgrim in *Ulysses* and *Finnegans Wake*. She analyzes influential sources employed by Joyce in his direct and indirect references to pilgrims, but disregards the very nature and purpose of Joyce's quest motif. In fact, she focuses on the pilgrim and his predecessors rather than on the progress itself. However, her discussion is valuable as an encyclopedic enumeration of references to pilgrim figures in the novels, as well as a detailed analysis of their sources. She mentions James Joyce's namesake, Saint James of Spain, a pilgrim traditionally depicted with a book, a staff, and a hat. Stephen, Holloway notices, wears a pilgrim's hat and carries a traveler's staff (his ashplant). He also bears the key to the Martello tower, "a pilgrim emblem of the Romeville journeying" (215). Not only is he associated with symbols of the Judeo-Christian pilgrim, but his hat and staff are also reminiscent of the Greek *xenos, ptochos, paroikos* (stranger, beggar, pilgrim) in exile (217). While Stephen "is on the brink of his Daedelian flight, about to set forth on *ailithre* into exile," Holloway adds, "Bloom is the exile from Jerusalem . . . who plans a 'retourney postexilic' (*FW* 472)" (216), as well as Moses, who carries "the lighted candle, the Paschal candle which liturgically reflects Mount Sinai's pillar of fire by night and pillar of cloud by day, beside Stephen's Aaron's rod as they chant '*In exitu Israel de Egypto: domus Jacob de populo barbaro*'" (220). Joyce, through his references to pilgrims, "conflates the Bible and the Odyssey, the Hebraic and the Hellenic, with himself" (216). I would argue that such mock-heroism and the conflation of cultural references indicate the collapse of confidence in a fixed center, as well as the recognized need to approach the center through multiple means and modes of behavior. In the end, this recognition of pluralism leads to Bloom's, as well as Joyce's, decenteredness.

If Joyce indeed portrays both Stephen and Bloom as pilgrims, we need to address the nature of the world in which they travel, the manner of their journey, and the aim of their quest. In the past, Bauman asserts, the environment conducive to pilgrimage and meditation was the desert: the "land not yet sliced into places" and "the land of self-creation" ("From Pilgrim" 20), a "nothingness waiting to become something" (21). The pilgrim had to reject the distractions of the city to choose the place that would offer unlimited potential and unrestricted space for progress. The desert is a world without restrictions and imposed rules. Stephen Dedalus and Leopold Bloom, however, are aware that in their quest, arbitrary boundaries and preconditioned categories prevent them from making progress toward self-revelation and preclude their movement toward the center. In the city, in both literal and metaphorical senses, buildings and even streets are obstacles; they mislead and divert attention. Dublin in *Ulysses*, much as London in *The Secret Agent*, with its kaleidoscope of colors, sounds, shapes, and prejudices, is inhospitable to the pilgrim, although it is an interesting place for the stroller and the vagabond. It is the epitome of erratic and aborted identity: seeking, dwarfed by boundaries and panoptic supervision; hence Joyce's reproach of the moral paralysis of Ireland, of parochialism and narrow-mindedness in its people. In his letter to C. P. Curran, Joyce says that in his writing, he wants to "betray the soul of that hemiplegia or paralysis which many consider a city" (Ellmann 22).

"Know thyself": Stephen's Urban Pilgrimage

This modern city becomes, however, the backdrop for Bloom's search for a son figure and a witness to his quest for self-identification. Both Stephen and Bloom, in a way, strive to achieve a condition close to that of premodern desert-wandering hermit-pilgrims. Stephen's *non serviam*, his indomitable statement of rejection of "a false homage to a symbol behind which are massed twenty centuries of authority and veneration" (*Portrait* 277), expresses his desire to enter the world unhindered by the obstacles raised by religion and tradition. Paradoxically, this would be the world hospitable to the pilgrim, encouraging self-exploration and unencumbered identity building. He asserts at the end of *Portrait* that he will not conform to three forms of oppression that hinder his progress: "I will not serve that in which I no longer believe, whether it call itself my home, my fatherland, or my church: and I will try to express myself in some mode of life or art as freely as I can and as wholly as I can, using for my defence the only arms I allow myself to use—silence, exile, and cunning" (*Portrait* 281). His call "Away! Away!" makes him an anti-pilgrim, one that does not attempt to approach the sacred but tries to escape that which his culture considers sacred: the Church and the homeland. But this self-exile from his environment also foreshadows pilgrimage to "distant nations," a process that could make possible an unencumbered search for identity, fulfilling his pledge "to forge in the smithy of [his] soul the uncreated conscience of [his] race" (288).

In *Ulysses*, Stephen proceeds to dwell on his initial insubordination and intensifies his denunciation of arbitrary signs and prescribed behavior. He prepares himself for the solitary pilgrimage toward self-identification and freedom for his creative spirit, shedding the burden of liturgical symbols and gestures, a rejection we have already observed in *Portrait*. True, his refusal to kneel at his mother's deathbed haunts him throughout his progress, but as both Eliade and Bauman assert, one of the characteristics of pilgrimage is—or rather was, in premodern times—its challenge. The quest toward the center usually involves sacrifice and difficulties. The very delay of gratification provides a source of anxiety but also of energy.

When Buck Mulligan says that he is "hyperborean" as much as Stephen (*U* 1.92), he implies more than just their disregard for rites and symbols. Hyperborean, a member of the legendary race following Apollo, living in a land of plenty beyond the north wind (*Oxford English Reference Dictionary* 696), appears in Nietzsche's *Der Wille zur Macht*, in part 1, entitled "The Antichrist," as a feature of the *Übermensch*: one refusing to be enslaved by traditional Christian morality (Gifford 15). Apollo, with his golden lyre, silver bow, and knowledge of healing art, was also variously seen as the god of truth, the god of art, and the sun god. His oracle in Delphi was a destination of many pilgrims and was regarded as the *center of the world* (Hamilton 30). Again, we can observe a paradox in Stephen's rejection of what is considered sacred in his culture in order to enable his pilgrimage toward the center, or self-recognition (which is, indeed, hyperborean in nature). Stephen's quest, his search for Apollonian truth, is ultimately a pilgrimage to a center and is inevitably connected with art and the attempt at perfect representation.

Joyce's direct and indirect allusions to Apollo thus hint at a possible course of Stephen's pilgrimage. The motif of quest toward identity building surfaces when Joyce gives us Stephen's thoughts after Mulligan's song parodying "Baile and Aillinn" by William Butler Yeats. The words "Know thyself" (*U* 9.1153) acknowledge the necessity of searching for truth and self-recognition, as they reverberate one of the two mottos on the temple of Apollo at Delphi (Gifford 254).[1] In order to attain creative powers and ultimate truth, self-truth in particular, Stephen aspires to Apollo-like qualities. The arrogance and risk of such desires are suggested in the fiery sermon in *Portrait*: "Lucifer . . . was a son of the morning, a radiant and mighty angel; yet he fell: he fell and there fell with him a third part of the host of heaven: he fell and was hurled with his rebellious angels into hell. What his sin was we cannot say. Theologians consider that it was the sin of pride, the sinful thought conceived in an instant: *non serviam: I will not serve*. That instant was his ruin" (*Portrait* 133). Stephen will repeat the words of Lucifer several times in *Portrait* and *Ulysses* and will insist that this denial is the requisite step toward self-knowledge and freedom indispensable in the process of creation. He has to defy God in order to assume godlike qualities himself. In other words, he has to defy the traditional center, or telos, in order to achieve it.

In "Scylla and Charybdis," Mulligan calls Stephen "wandering Aengus of the birds" (*U* 9.1093). Aengus was the Irish god of youth, beauty, and love, and in some ways an Apollo-like deity. In Yeats's "Song of Wandering Aengus," the god is "old with wandering / Through hollow lands and hilly lands" (17–18), following "a glimmering girl / With apple blossom in her hair" (13–14). Aengus's pilgrimage is directed toward the unattainable, ghostlike girl in order to "pluck" (22) the "golden apples of the sun" (24). It comes to a halt when he learns after many tribulations that the maiden, Caer, daughter of Ethal Anubal, lives alternatively in the form of a girl and a swan, changing her form every year. When he finally finds her, he himself is transformed into a swan, and they fly together, "uttering as they go a music so divine that all hearers are lulled to sleep for three days and nights" (Rolleston, *Celtic Myths* 121–22). Mulligan's nickname for Dedalus suggests that—at least in Buck's view—Stephen is still in the process of transformation, waiting for his divine swan song, pursuing the ghost of sacred inspiration.

Fissures and Connections: The Readerly Desire for Cosmos

Stephen's transformation does not depend, however, on some spiritual father-son (re)union. True, although Bloom (the Odysseus-father) and Dedalus (the Telemachus-son) differ in terms of intellectual potential and temperament, Joyce introduces numerous connections between the two lonely characters to suggest their symbolic relationship. Peake notices that "as Stephen had contemplated on Sandymount beach his romantic isola-tion, so Bloom on the same beach contemplates his outcast state, and masturbates, the physical emblem of romantic isolation. The parallels are not exact, but there is enough to suggest how the sense of friendless and fruitless isolation and resignation develops in the two men" (115–16). William Tindall devotes an entire chapter of his *Forces in Modern British Literature* to the modern representations of search for a father. Stephen, "who has lost both earthly and heavenly father" (222), finds Bloom, who "symbolizes the father on at least three levels, Homeric, divine, and per-sonal" (223n.).

But, Joyce's creation of Blephen/Stoom in the night world of "Ithaca" notwithstanding (17.549), there may be too prominent a rift between these two men's intellectual capacities and artistic sensibilities to con-sider their meeting as a full integration of two very different selves into a seamless father-son dyad, one sacred center of the universe. The sec-ond line in "Ithaca" gives us Stephen and Bloom "united both at nor-mal walking pace" (17.2), but the same paragraph describes these men as "approaching" (a key word in Stephen's heretical essay in *Portrait* in which he hints at the impossibility of ever reaching the sacred) and as "disparate" (17.7), essentially different, without relation or basis for com-parison. Latin *disparatus* means, after all, "separated, unequal." A few lines below, the catechetic voice asks whether Bloom—not Stephen and

Bloom together—discovered "common factors of similarity between their respective like and unlike reactions to experience" (17.18–19), the reply to which lists their similar preferences and (dis)beliefs, observed by Bloom himself. The next question, however, does not center on either Bloom's or Stephen's subjective perception of each other; instead, it seems to require a detached, objective answer, "Were their views on some points divergent?" (17.27), and is followed by an enumeration of their disagreements, including "civic selfhelp" and "eternal affirmation of the spirit of man in literature" (17.29–30). While Bloom, the "waterlover, drawer of water, watercarrier" (17.183), ponders water's "properties for cleansing, quenching thirst and fire, nourishing vegetation" (17.215), Stephen, a "hydrophobe, hating partial contact by immersion or total by submersion in cold water," expresses his dislike of "aqueous substances of glass and crystal" and distrust of "aquacities of thought and language" (17.237–40), which we could understand as a circulatory, watered-down use of speech. Apart from hinting at Stephen's rejection of the cleansing ritual of baptism here, Joyce also indicates that Stephen distrusts what Bloom in fact engages in at different times in the novel. Isn't the hackneyed phrase "the university of life" (17.555) an example of (however temporary) aquacity of thought and language? Aren't Bloom's insistence on linking the climate with people's character (e.g., 5.32–34) and his frequent evocations of essentialist Oriental images examples of diluted and oversimplified conceptions of race and ethnicity, the kind of misunderstanding that is at the core of his own ostracism?

Moreover, Stephen's anti-Semitic song in "Ithaca" about "the jew's daughter" who "took a penknife out of her pocket / And cut off [Harry Hughes's] little head" (17.813–26) evokes "mixed feelings" in "Unsmiling" Bloom, "the father of Millicent" (17.829–30). Stephen, disrupting any unity that these two men might have experienced, performs lyrics which combine the stereotype of Jewish cannibalism with the myth of *vagina dentata* rooted in racial otherness. We also learn in the same chapter that "four separating forces between his [Bloom's] temporary guest and him" are "Name, age, race, creed" (17.402–3), and the question "Did either openly allude to their racial difference?" is answered: "Neither" (17.525–26). That question itself does not include any speculation whether there indeed exists a racial distinction. It assumes an essential difference between the two men. The answer tells us that the difference is quietly acknowledged but not openly discussed. Why? If there really is a mystical bond between Stephen and Bloom, why does the text reveal all these fissures in their relationship and gaps in their supposed commonalities? As readers, we tend to overlook these cracks and inconsistencies in order to embrace the mythical union of father and son and validate the underlining fable about Odysseus and Telemachus as uncomplicated and undisturbed by "obstacles" such as race, ethnicity, age, or personal preferences.

Similarly, we might be tempted to read the fragmented city of "Wandering Rocks" as finally synchronized in the last section of the chapter through the viceregal cavalcade, a gravitational force that brings all the loose pieces into one coherent center. The disjointed narrative is, after all, neatly framed with two forces of hegemony in Catholic colonized Ireland: the priest and the powerful colonial agent. Both occupy a privileged position of surveillance. The first section of "Wandering Rocks" is filtered through Father Conmee's vision, revealing either his human interest in other people's lives or an attempt to contain them within his own cosmology. He asks the boys about their names, notices the details of Professor Maginni's flamboyant dress, and ponders on imperfect pilgrimages on his apparently perfect, "idyllic" (10.104) walk. He sees "two unlabouring men" in a pub window (10.94), a "towhorse with pendent head" (10.102)—a very Dickensian and Conradian image—"a bargeman with a hat of dirty straw" (10.102), and these images seem to fit nicely into place, following "the providence of the Creator who had made turf to be in bogs whence men might dig it out and bring it to town and hamlet to make fires in the houses of poor people" (10.104–6). Although the chapter suggests movement and circulation, Father Conmee's eyes see things and people set in their places, where they belong, static and compliant.

Conmee is a *flâneur*, albeit one with authority. When he thinks about the unbaptized lost souls, "a waste" (10.151), his theology reveals a great deal of old Victorian efficiency, the economy of grace.[2] He is a self-possessed, self-centered pilgrim; he wants the world to satisfy his expectations: the field's lych-gate displays vegetables for his own delight; the cabbages curtsey to him; the sky shows him its clouds (10.181–82). At the same time, he divests himself of ethical engagement when he "blesses . . . gravely" a man and a woman climbing out of a bush, flustered and covered with hay straws (10.203). His is a passage of condescending inspection, one mirrored later by the viceregal cavalcade.

On the surface of the narrative, Lord Dudley's passage brings every-thing together: the characters mentioned in the fragmented chapter, oc-cupying different positions within Dublin, are linked by the focal point of the colonial I/eye. Within the narrative, however, the characters remain as disjointed as usual, some missing the cavalcade or being missed by the eye of Dudley (Bloom and Professor Maginni, "outpassed be a viceroy and unobserved," 10.1240), others (Dilly and Gerty) seeing only obscured parts of it. As Budgen notes, the characters in this chapter "seem to be per-forming actions with a minimum of willpower. It is as if they were borne towards their ends floating on an invisible tide, actively swimming neither with nor against it" (130). The last section does not confer any agency on them, and the only way to see them as forming a coherent whole is to examine Joyce's bird's-eye, enumerative and, in a way, manipulative look at the city as united through the cavalcade. It is then up to the author and his readers to combine the fragments into a meaningful whole, a cosmic center. Perhaps on a subconscious level, we become accomplices to the cosmogonic drive; we inhabit the world in which only the known/the coherent is real.

Fritz Senn notes in "Charting Elsewhereness" that Joyce's "interloca-tions" within the chapter have both a coordinating and disorienting effect (155). The allotropic scenes, the ones that belong elsewhere, the intru-sions without narrative markers that defy our expectations of narrative paragraphing and sequencing, are "alternatives within the episode, paths not taken by the main narrative"; they are also "reminders that numerous events are constantly taking place outside of one's perceptual range" (159). Joyce could be telling us, then, that the belief in one common telos of humanity is founded upon a myth, that in reality, our goals are plural and multifaceted. The characters' potentialities are idiosyncratic and can only be united through an arbitrary imposition of an aesthetic or linguistic grid. The multiple centers in "Wandering Rocks" come together in one overarching narrative of Dudley's procession because we will it so.

Bloom's Mobile Center

If the tenth chapter of *Ulysses* reminds us of the multiplicity of the center and our desire to make it whole, the progress of Leopold Bloom suggests another deviation from the traditional cosmological narrative. In most anthropological accounts, the center is a fixed place of convergence. For Bloom, however, it is mobile. This mobility provides constant though un-realized hope for reaching the real, formative center. If the one he attains does not provide what it has promised, he abandons it in favor of an-other. The expectations of its significance are simply (dis)placed onto an-other center, in the hope that the next one will prove to be genuine. Thus Bloom walks through the city in search of a place charged with meaning, but finds his destinations (*Freeman's Journal* offices, the maternity ward, the brothel, and, finally, his own home) not fulfilling the expectation of a transformative or constructive place. The driving force of Bloom's soli-tary progress is delayed gratification, fueled by a belief in the possibility of reaching the truth about himself and the universe. The center in such a universe is illusory, lost in the barrage of fragments and superficial, pro-visional projects. Its impermanence can be alleviated by shifting its as-sumed significance onto another place, still ahead, not yet associated with disappointment. *Ulysses* itself, as Stephen Morrison claims, is concerned with "contesting the notion of transcendent and stable origins and with destabilizing the very idea of fixed centres." It is a book that "hinges on [its] 'null space'" (Morrison 1).

The gypsies who pass Stephen in "Proteus" evoke the image of the lonely, wandering peoples with no nationality and no future, preparing the way for Bloom's entry into the novel in the following chapter. He, in-deed, belongs to a race of pilgrims, without clear-cut borders of a native land; he is a member of a "non-national nation"—as Zygmunt Bauman defines the Jews—that has become a prototype of "otherness." Bloom's otherness relates to the process of pilgrimage; the already mentioned ety-mological study of the word *pilgrim* traces it to the Latin *peregrinus*—that is, a traveler, immigrant, stranger, an alien visitor (Morris and Roberts 1). Like Stephen, Bloom decides not to go home, in fear of seeing his wife in an embrace with Boylan. Thus he is itinerant and alienated in two ways: he does not belong to the Irish Catholic society, nor does he feel that he belongs in his home. John Orr remarks:

> Plunged into the detritus of city life, [Bloom] watches it circle around him, repetitive and without semblance of order, either advancing to the margins of meaning or leading his mind into daydream, into the mythic wanderings of the imagination. He shares Stephen's absence

but his goes deeper. Jew and cuckold, his confrontation with the city resembles an interior estrangement, a failure to belong to what he cannot fail to cling to. . . . At first sight, Bloom's senses seem to blend harmoniously with their surroundings, making him a natural inhabitant. But the harmony proves to be deceptive. The close encounter with city life occurs because he lacks anchorage in the two most significant features of Catholic Dublin—the church and the home. (53)

Bloom is ostracized by the society of Dubliners because of his Jewish origin, gentle nature, and inability to participate in the low-key, irreverent pub banter with its puns, shallow witticisms, and profanities. He is also estranged from his wife and distant from other Jews, since he does not observe their traditions, but he keeps traveling through the city despite impediments, mostly on foot, carrying, instead of the typical insignia of a pilgrim (a staff, a wallet or a bag, sometimes a book), a potato, a bar of soap, and a letter from Martha. These are objects that emphasize the mock-heroic character of Bloom's pilgrimage. However, the undiminished tragedy of his estrangement and his desperate need for affection make his progress far from comic. His goal does not seem to be religious, but it is, undoubtedly, spiritual. He states his mission in a hostile environment of bigoted, binge-drinking Dubliners dominated by the citizen, proposing that the answer to "Force, hatred, history, all that" is "Love" (*U* 12.1481–85). His plea for universal love mirrors his more personal quest for reconciliation with Molly and union with a son. The bar becomes yet another center with no sense of *communitas* or fulfillment.

Stephen and Bloom's missions are aborted, incomplete, or still at the stage of plans and daydreaming. Both are caught in the vortex of a society that does not seem to have a center that can hold. When Bloom visits All Hallows Church, his profane thoughts turn into contemplation of Catholic rites. The syntax of organized religion, though comforting in its inviolability, is signification without meaning, form without essence: "Good idea the Latin. Stupefies them first. Hospice for the dying. They don't seem to chew it: only swallow it down. Rum idea: eating bits of a corpse. Why the cannibals cotton to it" (*U* 5.350–52). He watches people blinded by faith, yet peaceful and united: "Now I bet it makes them feel happy. Lollipop . . . Then feel all like one family party, same in the theatre, all in the same swim. They do. I'm sure of that. Not so lonely. In our confraternity" (5.359–64). The last metaphor brings to mind Stein's philosophical remark in *Lord Jim* in which he places humanity in deep water and describes its futility to "reach the air." Bloom notices that what keeps some people (Catholics, in this case) afloat is the repetition of rites, this time, the sacrament of the Eucharist, one that remains empty for nonbelievers. Bloom is aware of the comfort and peace that religious rites can provide, but like Stephen, he rejects false and artificial forms of self-realization. He rejects the center of conventional religion that silences real emotions and damps down one's true identity. The Church is compared to a theater; hence the comfort it promises is artificial, fake, a result of a performance, perhaps an act of simony. Bloom leaves the church, and though he does not repeat Stephen's phrase "I will not serve," he admittedly cuts himself off from the stupefying ceremonies and immerses himself in the pulsating life of the street, free from the oppressive power of Church hierarchy.

Other locales of Bloom's wandering are also unrewarding. His pilgrimage to the cemetery does not result in any spiritual revelation on the nature of life and death. Instead, Bloom muses on semi-scientific explanations of postmortem physiological changes. The initial destination for his lunch repels him; he does not manage to purchase the lotion for Molly; his journey to the newspaper proves to be fruitless, and so is his stay in the bordello. The list of his unsuccessful quests is much longer, but one of his most important quests—the search for a son—although nearly realized, turns out to be momentary, as Stephen rejects Bloom's invitation to stay in his house overnight. When Stephen and Bloom join each other, the constant flux of Dublin seems to stop for a moment. Yet this union, although based on the profound need for human contact and understanding, is temporary and fragile, partly because of their intellectual incompatibility.

Bloom perceives the pilgrimage of his race as fruitless and terror-ridden in his ghastly vision of a "barren land, bare waste" and "the cities of the plain: Sodom, Gomorrah, Edom. All dead names. A dead sea in a dead land, grey and old. Old now. It bore the oldest, the first race. . . . Wandered far away over all the earth, captivity to captivity, multiplying, dying, being born everywhere" (4.219–26). The cities of the plain (Sodom, Gomorrah, Admah, Zeboiim, and Bela) were destroyed by God, whose design is expressed in Genesis 18 and 19: "And he overthrew those cities, and all the country round about, and all that dwelt in the cities, and the plants springing out of the ground." Instead of edifice, we find ruins; instead of identity building, there is the wrath of God, who denies us any self-construction that does not follow his laws.

However, this enumeration of the cities annihilated by God in Genesis does not necessarily imply lack of the center, the ultimate goal of pilgrimage, but a drive to abolish obstacles on the pilgrim's path and to remind him to look ahead instead of looking back, just as Lot is instructed by angels to "go forth; lest thou also be destroyed with the iniquities of the city" (19:15). Although Bloom's nostalgia and Stephen's lingering trauma suggested by recurrent apparitions of his mother hinder their quest for independent self-definition, they both reject another form of "looking back," the mechanical repetition of religious rites in favor of a search for something more immediate and genuine. At least in the half-dream of "Ithaca," Bloom's thoughts converge around an imagined center, Flowerville (17.1580) or Bloomville (17.1613), where he would be "pruning, staking, sowing hayseed, trundling a weedladen wheelbarrow without excessive fatigue at sunset amid the scent of newmown hay, ameliorating the soil, multiplying wisdom, achieving longevity" (17.1584–87), and where he would achieve the status of a "gardener, groundsman, cultivator, breeder, and at the zenith of his career, resident magistrate or justice of the peace with a family crest and coat of arms and appropriate classical motto (*Semper paratus*), duly recorded in the court directory (Bloom, Leopold P., M.P., P.C., K.P., L.L.D. *honoris causa*, Bloomville, Dundrum) and mentioned in court and fashionable intelligence (Mr and Mrs Leopold Bloom have left Kingstown for England)" (17.1609–15). But Flowerville and the corresponding activities and titles remain a construct in Bloom's imagination, a desired desire, perhaps little more achievable than the discarded notion of Agendath Netaim. And although the narrator in "Ithaca" calls Bloom a "centripetal remainer" and Stephen a "centrifugal departer" (17.1214), let us remember that the word *centripetal* does not imply an achievement of the center but a drive or motion *toward* it. It denotes *direction*, not achievement of a goal. Moreover, Bloom's thoughts about possible departure (17.1955–2027) are examples of a temporary centrifugal tendency, a reactionary force, a desire to escape, as the Latin root of the word *fugere*, to flee, indicates.

Bloom goes back to bed, lured by "the superior quality of human (mature female) . . . calefaction" (17.2037–38), where his wife ponders their homelessness, the constant hassle of their moving from house to house, fleeing from landlords. Her repetition of the word *yes*, including the final "yes I said yes I will Yes" is an affirmative gravitational force, but a vague one. It provides a narrative anchor within the chapter, but this very unambiguous word is often placed in ambiguous contexts, its meaning shifting with new thoughts that come to Molly. It is not exactly an empty center, but Molly constantly destabilizes its meaning. In this "overpotentialized text" of *Ulysses* (Derrida 579), Joyce celebrates the disrupted coherence of the center while making it clear that this lack of stability is a source of anxiety for many.

"Without a possibility of ever reaching": Telos Deferred

According to Bauman, premodern pilgrims started their quest for the sacred *ab nihilo*, so that their progress could be a path of self-construction and the "pilgrim and the desertlike world he walks" could "acquire their meanings *together*, and *through each other*" (22). Moreover, the pilgrimage toward self-discovery, any pilgrimage for that matter, is always in progress, unfinished. The pilgrim's progress is continuous, determined, incessant. The teleological character of pilgrimage does not preclude the pilgrim's inability to reach his ultimate goal. For pilgrims "the truth is elsewhere; the true place is always some distance, some time away" (20). What enables these projects is the distance between the here and now and the future for which we strive: in other words, the discontent with and deprecation of the present state; it is the constant awareness of delayed gratification, "the never-to-be-bridged distance between the ego-ideal and the realities of the present" (22).

Bloom and Stephen are homeless daydreamers, dislocated and pursuing distant, ultimately unsatisfied aims. Perhaps Stephen will escape a Marsyas-like punishment for attempting to rival gods and produce art of divine quality, simply because his telos will be constantly delayed. After all, he admits the hopelessness of our (or our souls') attempts to approximate the sacred in his heretical essay in *Portrait*. Only after Mr Tate's accusation does he correct the phrase "*without a possibility of ever approaching nearer*" into "*without a possibility of ever reaching*" (*Portrait* 90), although the second statement still asserts the futility of human endeavor to approximate divinity. Stephen's evocation of Aristotle's words about "an actuality of the possible as possible" being "a movement" (*Ulysses* 2.67) might be acquiescence to this infinite quest. Thus the telos in Stephen's and Bloom's pilgrimage may be viewed as constitutive absence, a kind of gravitational force that pulls them into its direction, without allowing them to achieve the destination of their quest.

Bloom's incomplete unions with a son figure and Molly may simply be inevitable, as the final goal is continuously postponed. Mulligan refers to him as the "wandering jew" and the "ancient mariner" when he spots Bloom in the library (*U* 9.1209–11). This allusion to Coleridge hints again at the restless progress of Leopold. *The Rime of the Ancient Mariner* does not define the sailor's destination when he begins the journey with his crew; it is a tale of a quest without a telos or, at least, with a telos that remains unknown to the reader. However, when the mariner returns to the shore, wanders "like night, from land to land," and embarks on his quest to tell his story to "the man that must hear me," confessing that "till my ghastly tale is told, / This heart within me burns" (Coleridge 437), the goal of this pilgrimage is known: it is redemption. And, like Bloom's goals (or Jim's desires in Conrad's novel), it is "always some distance, some time away" (Bauman, "From Pilgrim" 22).

Ulysses suggests that the pilgrim's access to the center might be blocked, nonexistent, his path stopped in midair, like the Kingstown pier—a "disappointed bridge" (2.39)—or aborted like the misbirth Stephen imagines in "Proteus." While Bloom thinks of "his navel, bud of flesh" (5.570) in a down-to-earth, rational way, and even reflects that "Dirt gets rolled up in your navel" (5.502–3), Stephen's musing on the same subject (the *omphalos* in "Telemachus") leads him to a far different conclusion: the evidence that "the center cannot hold" and is disintegrating. Bloom's comment on dirt in the navel might, then, indirectly lead the reader to think of the center as contaminated. On a broader scale, it may be contaminated by modernity itself, but Joyce's constant critique of Dublin's parochialism and jingoism, as well as Ignatius Gallaher's phrase "dear dirty Dublin" ("A Little Cloud," *Dubliners* 75), suggest other "pollutants" here. Significantly, Bloom goes to "the mosque of the baths" (5.549) to cleanse himself. In the end, though, he will not be able to wash off the chauvinism, blind devotion to religious doctrine, and violent nationalism inherent in Joyce's Dublin.

In "Telemachus," Joyce alludes to the efforts of the Celtic revival movement through his reference to a navel—"To ourselves. . . . New paganism. . . . *omphalos*" (1.176). While "To ourselves" seems to refer to the Irish

"Sinn Fein" ("We ourselves"), *omphalos*, a Greek word for "navel," appears in *The Odyssey*; Calypso's island is called "navel of the sea." However, it also refers to the oracle at Delphi ("the navel of the earth") and "the center of prophecy in ancient Greece" (Gifford 17). Therefore, a navel equals the center and the origin of the world. Moreover, as some late nineteenth-century Theosophists claimed, the omphalos is also "the place of the 'astral soul of man,' the center of self-consciousness and the source of poetic and prophetic inspiration" (Gifford 17). Thus the navel that Stephen contemplates links the national movement of the literary revival, the search for absolute truth and self-definition, with—as "new paganism" suggests—the rejection of traditional religion and assertion of sexual sensations as the new force of life.[3] But in "Proteus," Stephen notices two midwives carrying a bag, and he imagines that it contains a "misbirth with a trailing navelcord, hushed in ruddy wool," adding that the "cords of all link back, strand-entwining cable of all flesh" (3.36–37). He subsequently "reflects on the network of navel-cords linking all humanity together, back to Eve. . . . The network is like a telephone system linking all men to a central exchange, the navel-less belly of Eve" (Blamires 14). The navel as a central point of humanity or the universe, as a source of truth and aesthetic inspiration, is ultimately fruitless; it leads nowhere: its cord is severed because the fetus is dead (and it is a result of an accident, hence the "*misbirth*"). It offers no link with the center. Let us also remember that Mulligan calls the Martello tower an *omphalos* (*Ulysses* 1.544). It is, however, a false navel that Stephen will not seek further (He says, "I will not sleep here tonight. Home also I cannot go" [1.739–40]).

This disturbing surmise suggests that a straightforward presentation of the characters in *Ulysses* as pilgrimlike needs to be more complex and informed by the changes that the environment of the pilgrim has undergone. How did the world become inhospitable to pilgrims? Bauman says that they "lost their battle by winning it," by striving to "make the world solid by making it pliable." The pilgrims "turned the space in which identity was to be built into a desert" (Bauman, "From Pilgrim" 23). Therefore, pilgrimage is no longer a conscious choice but a necessity, "less still is it a heroic or saintly choice." We embark on a pilgrimage to avoid being confused and lost in the desert, "to invest the walking with a purpose while wandering the land with no destination" (21).

Hence the progress in modernity displayed directional features. The delay of gratification was, anxiety and frustration aside, "an energizing factor and the source of identity-building zeal in so far as it was coupled with the trust in the linearity and cumulativeness of time." People who embarked on a quest "had a stake in solidity of the world they walked; in a kind of world in which one can tell life as a continuous story, a 'sense-making' story." Therefore, the "world of pilgrims—of identity-builders—must be orderly, determined, predictable, ensured" (23). The perceived ordering project of modernity seems to be the result of that yearning. The rigid dichotomies and all-too-easy classifications are desperate attempts to escape the presumably perilous world of ambiguity. But Bloom does not agree to this world, and perhaps because of this dissent, he recognizes the center as false and embarks on new quests, to a more promising center. As Bauman asserts, "The other of the modern state is the no-man's or contested land: . . . the demon of ambiguity. Since the sovereignty of the modern state is the power to define and to make the definitions stick—everything that self-defines or eludes the power-assisted definition is sub-versive" (8). Bloom's relentless search for a true center is therefore a form of subversion, while the citizen's anti-Semitic rant in the bar is simply a sign of conformity to artificially imposed boundaries designed to maintain clarity and order.

Critics often characterize modernity as a never-ending, unaccomplished process to unify, to impose order, to discover meaning. Bauman presents a picture of modernity as a domain of the Protestant (therefore, neither Stephen nor Bloom), "that pattern-setter . . . for the modern man," as a space "of nothingness waiting to become something, if only for a while; of meaninglessness waiting to be given meaning, if only a passing one" (21). Similarly, Marc Augé explains that "what is new is not that the world is lacking meaning, or has little meaning, or less than it used to have; it is that we seem to feel an explicit and intense daily need to give it meaning" (29). Bauman speaks of modern society as a "space without contours, ready to accept any contour offered, if only until other contours are offered; . . . virgin land yet to be ploughed and tilled; . . . the land of the perpetual beginning; . . . the place-no-place whose name and identity is not-yet" (21). The goal of the modern man is to give "form to the form-less," make "a whole out of the fragmentary," lend "continuity to the epi-sodic" (22), a task never accomplished and therefore perpetual. However, by turning the space into the desert, modern pilgrims made the outcome of their task very ephemeral because "the desert, though comfortingly featureless for those who seek to make their mark, does not hold features well. The easier it is to emboss a footprint, the easier it is to efface it. A gust of wind will do. And deserts are windy places" (23).

In the unstable world of desacralization, the industrial and technologi-cal revolutions, national and social upheavals, especially in Ireland torn by multiple factions and battling ideas about its national and religious allegiances, the "gusts" of change are particularly poignant. The pilgrim is probably safer to take surfaces for granted and to avoid deep contempla-tion. This choice involves a terrifying prospect of effacing one's identity in the realm of instability but also the excitement of shunning ossified identities devoid of opportunities of change and reversal. One strategy that Bauman describes is "depicting daily life as a succession of minor emergencies" and the resolve "to refuse to be 'fixed' in one way or the other. Not to get tied to the place. Not to wed one's life to one vocation only. Not to swear consistency and loyalty to anything and anybody. Not to *control* the future, but to *refuse to mortgage* it" (24).

From this point of view, Bloom's numerous jobs (a salesman of trinkets, packaging man at Kellet's, stationer, an actuary for a cattleman, collector of accounts of convents, canvasser for the *Freeman's Journal*), his succes-sion of dwelling places (52 Clanbrassil Street, Pleasants Street, Lombard Street West, Raymond Terrace, City Arms Hotel, Holles Street, Ontario Terrace, Eccles Street), his detachment from his religious and traditional background, and his attempt to escape his identity as a cuckold and a Jew all suggest a pursuit of an ever-shifting center. So are Stephen's reluctance to continue teaching, his aborted career as a medical student, his artistic ambition, and his multiple addresses (at least two present in *Ulysses*). But Bloom's pilgrimage is not simply a form of escape from a "mortgaged" future, for he displays courage and compassion, as well as yearning for a moment of unity with others and understanding of himself. Bauman's real-estate metaphor is not, then, all-encompassing and universal. Bloom wants to be self-identified and defined by others not in terms of what or who he is *not* (e.g., as a non-Catholic, non-Irish, virtually non-husband), but through positive assertion (e.g., as an Irishman, a husband, and a father).

Drifters and Gamers in *Ulysses*

Joyce expands the traditional understanding of pilgrimage and provides, through Bloom's movement along Dublin's streets, a *collective* metaphor for identity building: progress which anticipates the movements of the figures named by Bauman as the stroller, the vagabond, the tourist, and the player. To define oneself in the hegemonic matrix, one has to employ provisional maneuvers to either challenge or evade inflexible boundaries. In Bloom's case, movement toward the center is an attempt at self-discovery irrespective of imposed and presumably fixed identity, an image of self dictated by the parochial and othering society.

Bauman, in his exposition of the figure of *flâneur*, points out that "strolling means rehearsing human reality as a series of episodes" and that the stroller "practiced the 'as if' life and the 'as if' engagement with other people" (56). This "as if" engagement with others and superficiality of cognition are very prominent in the movements of multiple characters in "Wandering Rocks" and throughout *Ulysses*, as we follow, for example, Blazes Boylan through the city. We catch only superficial, synecdochic, decontextualized glances of him, which may suggest that Boylan's progress has none of the metaphysical depth of the premodern pilgrim's quest.

Strolling, says Bauman, "means rehearsing meetings as mis-meetings, as encounters without impact" (26). The episodic, disjointed, seemingly accidental nature of action in "Wandering Rocks" and "Circe" makes the characters in these chapters, as well as their perception of the city or the bizarre happenings in the brothel, seem equally inconsequential and, in some cases, anonymous. The formal arrangement of nineteen short sections of "Wandering Rocks," where an assortment of characters make their way through the streets of Dublin, allows for multiple perspectives but also sets pitfalls for a lackadaisical reader. Richard Brown lists "loose ends, chronotopic ruptures, false identifications" among the "reader-traps" in the chapter (58), also noting that the episode itself may be seen as a process, comparable—I would add—to the act of walking through the city. The apparent randomness and anonymity of most encounters in "Wandering Rocks" turn the characters into typical strollers, gliding over the surface, unconcerned with genuine emotions and motives behind the passers-by, content with the scenery, stage props, and actors, but indifferent to the meaning of the play itself. Significantly, the chapter full of ruptures and false identifications is located as the central point of *Ulysses*, as if Joyce wanted to draw our attention not to abundance but to lack, not to coherence but to estrangement.

Father Conmee, looking at Dublin's surfaces and thinking about the necessity to protect the lost, unbaptized souls from hellfire, is a version of Conrad's Verloc on his way to the embassy, surveying London's opulence that needs to be protected. With the same satisfied, aloof eye, they monitor their surroundings and ascertain their own redemptive powers. When Conmee mechanically raises his hat "to the Blessed Sacrament" (10.81) of Saint Joseph's Church as he thinks about the devout and bad-tempered "virtuous females" (10.80), it is an empty gesture, a force of habit, instead of a fully conscious spiritual rite. He pays attention to the aesthetic pleasures of his passage through the city, as he "disliked to traverse on foot the dingy way past Mud Island" (10.114) and "liked cheerful decorum" (10.121). But Joyce also gives us Conmee's remembrance of his rectorship in Clongowes and other reminiscences, such as young Dignam's thoughts of his father's "tongue and his teeth trying to say it better" right before his death (10.1171–72), and through this, he superimposes the past upon the present. "Wandering Rocks" is no longer just a cartographic enumeration of names and places, a mirror image of a city on one day in 1904. Here, through blending of history and mock prophecy (the throwaway "Elijah is coming" floating down the Liffey "sailing eastward" [10.296] toward the bay) in contemporary Dublin, Joyce defies the common purpose of imperial cartographers, that is, to represent a territory devoid of historical significance and individual or collective narratives; a territory rendered through markers of space, not time; a land open to invasion; a land of no epistemological value.[4] In this spirit, Haines reports to Mulligan that a Viennese professor, Julius Pokorny, "can find no trace of hell in ancient Irish myth. . . . The moral idea seems lacking, the sense of destiny, of retribution" (10.1082–84). Here is an example of a member of a powerful nation romanticizing the past of its subaltern through his particular attention to Celtic folk, but denying it its imagined collective telos without checking the facts. This implied anti-teleology of the ancient Irish myth is only half-true, as Gifford notes (281).

Is there something of a colonizing drive in *flâneur's* self-satisfied walk, focused on surfaces and interpreting them according to his own will? If the stroller turns "the fleeting fragments of other persons' lives" into "stories at will," stories that are, significantly, his own, as "it was his perception that made them into actors, let alone the plot of the drama they play" (Bauman, "Pilgrim" 26), then the readers themselves take part in this process (and so do the critics), trying to assemble disjointed movements and figures they encounter during their stroll through the pages of the book into a meaningful totality of experience. Joyce constantly fuels our possessive drive to inhabit a text and make it our own, thus making us accomplices in a sense-making process of collecting scattered fragments into a coherent whole.

One chapter in *Ulysses* fulfills the role of a component-assembling, story-making "reader" (*flâneur*) of what seems at the beginning an emotionless array of events and encounters in *Ulysses*. The "continual sense of 'elsewhereness'" (Senn 155) comes into play, literally and figuratively, in "Circe," the episode of the wandering mind. What justifies the bizarre tale in "Circe," composed of characters and events collected from (and beyond) the entire novel, including the apparently incongruous chapter 10, is the meticulous engineering (not at all obvious to an unobservant reader) underlying the entire parade of people, objects, places, and situations in the book. Fritz Senn mentions that in "Circe," "the characters, as well as the text itself, perform a mental version of what in 'Wandering Rocks' remains predominantly physical movement in space" (156).[5] Through a recollection of the real *flâneur* figures and projection of their presence in Bloom's mind, "Circe" embarks on its own procession through the unconscious.

The stroller "was the creator without penalties attached to creation" (Bauman, "From Pilgrim" 26), a model offering an opportunity, it seems, for Stephen to fulfill the goal of his Luciferian quest and, as *flâneur*, to achieve the demiurgic power in his art "*without ever approaching nearer.*" Bloom himself often perceives "strangers as 'surfaces'—so that 'what one sees' exhausts 'what they are'" (26), partly as his defense mechanism against further hostilities, partly because of his frustrated sexual life. His perception of women throughout the book reveals that he pays particular attention to *surfaces* in these contacts. However, his compassion and melancholy, as well as his persistent, though often subconscious, quest to reunite with a son, make him depart from this model of the *flâneur*-pilgrim.

The stroller—like Joyce himself—is a playful mocker. *Ulysses* is, after all, a mock-epic, a tragic-comic rendering of perhaps the most popular of mythical pilgrimages, the quest of Odysseus in Homer's *Odyssey*, so the narrative as a whole joins its two central characters in enacting the role of the *flâneur*. But Joyce, despite his mockery, does not dismiss the life he describes in *Ulysses* and other books as superficial and imitative, for his and his characters' pilgrimages equally evoke other features of Bauman's model for the modern pilgrim. Joyce's quest "began in the merest lyric and ended in the vastest encyclopedia. . . . He is by turns gay, morose, trusting, suspicious, uxorious, and misogynous" (Ellmann, *James Joyce* 2). His judgment on the world he describes is often hidden behind the mockery, but, as Ellmann emphasizes, "Joyce's court is, like Dante's or Tolstoy's, always in session" (3).

Joyce himself displays certain qualities of the vagabond, masterless and restless. Vagabonds belong to the realm of "the other," subversive and uncalled for in a meticulously controlled space. Joyce called himself a "vagabond" (*Selected Letters* 26) and referred to his situation as that of "voluntary exile" (56). Like their creator, Stephen and Bloom fit this category inasmuch as they are solitary and determined "walkers" or "seekers." Bauman stresses that the vagabond is "a stranger; he can never be 'the native,' the 'settled one,' one with 'roots in the soil'" ("From Pilgrim" 28), a description that is consistent with both Stephen's voluntary spiritual exile and Bloom's actual painful detachment, ostracism, and deracination. However, Stephen and Bloom are restrained by a variety of imposed bonds and obligations, and they are not entirely liberated from them, even at the end of *Ulysses*.

If Joyce gives us Boylan as a *flâneur* figure in juxtaposition to Stephen and Bloom, so also does he offer us the citizen as a reflection of these characters' vagabond status. In chapter 12 of *Ulysses*, the citizen deliberately sets himself outside the society dominated by the British imperial power, and although his aim to liberate Ireland might seem clear enough a goal, he remains listless yet unpredictable and menacing. And another, less threatening figure that similarly acts as a vagabond-pilgrim in juxtaposition to Stephen and Bloom is Cashel Boyle O'Connor Fitzmaurice Tisdall Farrell, looping his name through the streets, always outside the lampposts, "murmuring, glasseyed" (10.919–20), insane. Surprisingly, in "Sirens," Bloom expresses his desire to "walk, walk, walk. Like Cashel Boylo Connoro Coylo Tisdall Maurice Tisntdall Farrell. Waaaaaaalk" (11.1124–5), perhaps half-consciously admitting that setting oneself intentionally outside the society (and following instinct as one proceeds) does not constitute as painful a failure as being rejected by others. Cashel, whose only aim in the book seems to be walking, is probably unaware of his isolation.

The vagabond's alienation and compulsive walking are somewhat related to those of a tourist, though certainly more subversive, menacing, and erratic. Joyce himself, both in art and in his own life, seems to inhabit the tourist-land as he ventures into the realm of bizarre language formation and techniques in *Ulysses* and, most strikingly, in *Finnegans Wake*. At the same time, however, he retains anchorage, a safe haven, in tradition; his tireless search for new modes of representation goes hand in hand with his employment of mythical figures and stories, traditional tropes, and, quite often, realistic and naturalistic descriptions. Like his characters, Joyce shifted the goals of his own quest whenever he found the old ones unfulfilling.

Although he refuses to return home and chooses to wander through Dublin streets instead, for fear of confrontation with Boylan, Bloom always has the "nest" to come back to, and he does so after the night in the redlight district. However, that he "entered the bed . . . prudently, as entering a lair or ambush of lust or adders" (17.2113–18) as much as "reverently" because the bed is a place of "conception and of birth, of consummation of marriage and of breach of marriage, of sleep and of death" (17.2119–20) indicates his ambivalent relationship with *home*. In a more metaphorical sense, Bloom is the most itinerant and homeless character in Joyce's fiction: deracinated, untied to any religion, fatherless, and sonless. He gropes for any signal that could define his real self, but, as a stranger, he fails to find his place in the community. He has a choice between, on the one hand, clinging to definitions and descriptions produced by others and denying the creation of an autonomous self or, on the other hand, positioning himself against biased Dubliners, as a Christ-like figure, full of compassion and innate righteousness. Neither path seems to lead to any anchorage in his society. In this sense, Bloom has none of the security afforded to the tourist.

Haines—"The seas' ruler" (*Ulysses* 1.574), "a ponderous Saxon" (1.51), an ardent enthusiast of the Irish culture, with a "cold gaze" but "not all unkind" (1.634–35), and Murphy, the sailor of dubious identity conversing with Stephen and Bloom in "Eumaeus," are tourists as well. Both have embarked on long but exciting escapades (if we believe the sailor's colorful accounts), away from Oxford and Queenstown harbour, but the masks they assume are short-term, unbinding identities they can shed at any moment and return home from "the tourist land." Bloom, after all, calls Haines "that English tourist friend of [Mulligan's]" (16.264–65). This English supporter of Celtic revival, expressing his sympathy for the Irish who, as he himself admits, have been treated unfairly—for which "It seems history is to blame" (1.649)—comes from a place of ossified intellectual tradition and strong national pride to which, after his voyages among manuscripts, Irish songbooks, and drunken medical students, he can always return, as he admits to Stephen: "Of course I'm a Britisher . . . and I feel as one" (1.666).[6] He listens to Mulligan's morning song, "The ballad of joking Jesus," with delight, but is careful enough not to participate in Buck's blasphemy directly, even if, as he admits, he is "not a believer" himself (1.605–6). He is but another example of the "palefaces" (as Stephen calls the tourists from England), albeit educated in Irish literature and language, who flock hotels and historical sites, and who provide background to Stephen's encounter with Almidano Artifoni in "Wandering Rocks": "Two carfuls of tourists passed slowly, their women sitting fore, gripping the handrests. Palefaces. Men's arms frankly round their stunted forms. They looked from Trinity to the blind columned porch of the bank of Ireland where pigeons roocoocooed" (10.340–43).[7]

Amidst the panorama of Dublin's nightlife figures assembled in the cabman's shelter near Butt Bridge, a sailor who introduces himself as D. (W.) B. Murphy of Carrigaloe spins a yarn in a fashion remote from that of Conrad's Marlow, about his journeys around the world.[8] This arouses questions and admiration and inspires Bloom's thoughts on Irish tourism and possible ways to improve travel experience on the island.[9] Murphy says that he came to Dublin from Bridgewater and that he "circumnavigated a bit since [he] first joined on" (16.458–59). His tall tales of adventures in the Red Sea, China, Russia, and North and South America, of "maneaters in Peru that eats corpses" (16.470), culminate when he produces a postcard of Bolivian Indians: "a group of savage women in striped loincloths, squatted, blinking, suckling, frowning, sleeping amid a swarm of infants (there must have been quite a score of them) outside some primitive shanties of osier" (16.475–78). The tourist-sailor replicates the old ethnocentric model of a seasoned traveler returning from remote voyages and framing distant lands in tall tales of the grotesque and the bizarre. In this spectacle of the other, the tourist/traveler recognizes his anti-self against which his own identity is formed. Murphy's story, we learn, is probably fictitious: Bloom notices that the postcard is addressed to "*Señor A. Boudin*" (16.489) and thinks that "it was quite within the bounds of possibility that it was not an entire fabrication though at first blush there was not much inherent probability in all the spoof he got off his chest being strictly accurate gospel" (16.826–29). Murphy the "globe-trotter" (16.575), like a proper tourist, admits to having a wife and a home: "Fort Camden and Fort Carlisle. That's where I hails from. I belongs there. That's where I hails from. She's waiting for me, I know. *For England, home and beauty*. She's my own true wife I haven't seen for seven years now, sailing about" (16.418–21).

Although the modern "quest" of the tourist is conditioned by adjustment of vision, not the perceived territory, this process of temporary accommodation is incomplete in *Ulysses*; just as its pilgrims are unable to reach "the center," some tourist figures are unsuccessful in the process of familiarization and are unable to find genuine satisfaction in their voyages. Stephen's parable, which he calls "*A Pisgah Sight of Palestine or The Parable of the Plums*" (7.1058–59), describes two "Dublin vestals . . . elderly and pious" (7.923), who, after saving up some money, leave their home on Fumbally's lane to embark on a trip to the top of Nelson's Pillar in order to enjoy the view of Dublin from there. They take their umbrellas, buy brawn, bread, and plums and, just like well-mannered and law-abiding tourists, pay their admission to a guard at the turnstile. As they ascend the dark, winding staircase, they already feel discomfort, but move on, "praising God and the Blessed Virgin, threatening to come down" (7.945–46). Once on top of the pillar, they fear it might topple, and "it makes them giddy to look" (7.1012). They feel none of the excitement they expected when they look down, nor when they look up at the statue of "the onehandled adulterer" because it "gives them a crick in their necks" (7.1017–23). That the two Irish spinsters' encounter with the phallic monument of a British admiral ends in "a crick in their necks" is not surprising. The tall Doric column, commenced in 1808 at a central location in the city, supported a statue of a naval hero who was unpopular among the Irish, and it was a political embarrassment for Dubliners until it was blown to pieces in 1966 (Egan 2006). The women in Stephen's story finally sit down on their petticoats and eat the plums, spitting the stones between the railings, down on the streets of Dublin. They reach the goal of their trip, the phallic symbol of the empire keeping a watchful eye on the Dubliners below, but it proves to be unfulfilling and disappointing, just as the mini-narrative itself, apparently with no climactic ending, a form resembling the gnomic conclusions of stories in *Dubliners*. If understood as a political allegory, the tale points to the Pisgah sight of Irish independence and unattainable telos of self-governance and satisfaction on the collective quest for sovereignty.

If there's no guarantee of lasting happiness and self-fulfillment in the tourist land, perhaps Joyce's players achieve some sense of accomplishment. All of Joyce's characters are burdened by factors independent of their will (such as inexperience, patriarchy, social position, religion, and desires) and therefore cannot assume a completely detached, unaffected position. Some, however, treat their lives as a series of episodic games. The ability to stay unaffected is one of the features of Lenehan's life, consisting of a series of bar hopping and afternoon chats in public houses. Considered by many "a leech" ("a sponger" by Molly), he "had a brave manner of coming up to a party of them in a bar and of holding himself nimbly at the borders of the company until he was included in a round. He was a sporting vagrant armed with a vast stock of stories, limericks and riddles" that were indispensable in order to secure his win, whether in a bar or with a girl ("Two Gallants," *Dubliners* 53). The superficiality of his contacts and acquaintances allows him to remain a detached and shallow player. Another mimic and an insubordinate character, one whose sacrilegious laughter indicates that he is unperturbed by the labyrinthine quest for *homo totus* and the sacred center, Buck Mulligan, is—like Conrad's harlequin after Kurtz's departure—free-spirited, unbound, a jester and witcracker, an insulting buffoon and a bold trickster clowning around and entertaining both the representative of the colonial power, Haines, and the subaltern, like Stephen.

And how about Boylan's self-assured, leisurely gait? Molly herself knows his approach to life is not very serious: "of course hes right enough in his way to pass the time as a joke sure you might as well be in bed with what with a lion" (*U* 18.1375–7). Bloom considers him to have a "bold hand" (13.843), though one of Boylan's apparent advantages in his games is, as Raleigh notes, "the size of [his] erect member" (167). He certainly is able to silence any pangs of conscience when, after befriending Bloom, he proceeds to sleep with his wife. This player moves smoothly between eyeing the shop assistant's décolletage, "the stalk of the red flower between his smiling teeth" (10.334–35), discussing his horse bet at the Ormond's, and jingling away in his car to meet Molly, offering on his way "to the three ladies" in the cavalcade "the bold admiration of his eyes and the red flower between his lips" (10.1245–46).

Another player, Tom Kernan, is a commercial traveler, overdressed for his social position, the "knight of the road," as he thinks of himself (10.748). Apart from signaling a rather amusing performance of an elevated social status, the phrase is also a title of Percy French's comic opera, whose action is set in post-1798 Ireland and whose hero "is a Robin Hood who bewilders his victims in a variety of disguises" (Gifford 273). Kernan knows that he can play the part of a respectable man by getting quality secondhand overcoats: "Dress does it. Nothing like a dressy appearance. Bowls them over" (10.738–39) and that one must "dress the character for those fellows" (10.748). When he preens himself before a mirror, he compares himself with a British officer just returned from India. This "west Briton" (Gifford 273) trivializes and dismisses Emmet's and other nationalists' struggle for independence with a simple "Well, well. Over and done with" (10.767). In an act of resistance to the past and to an in-depth investigation of the historical and martyrological significance of the spot where Emmet was hanged (in front of St. Catherine's Church), he consciously makes a detour (10.771). When he cannot will his thoughts away from the nationalist struggle, he muses on the 1798 Rebellion again and concludes with an ambiguous subordinate clause lacking its main antecedent: "When you look back on it all now in a kind of retrospective arrangement" (10.783). What should have preceded it? That it is easier to grasp its significance? That it was futile and violent, like "Gaming at Daly's" (10.784), which is a phrase directly following that clause? Completing the sentence would force Kernan into an investigation of historical trauma, an act he carefully avoids in order to remain comfortably on the surface.

Does Molly Bloom find comfort in superficial perception of her environment and noncommitment of episodic games? She reveals her theatrical skills and ability to mimic gestures and attitudes suitable for a variety of occasions, as in "I can do the indifferent" (18.1529), when she thinks about strategies to reconnect with her husband. Cheryl Herr analyzes the theatricality of "Penelope" and Molly's "operatic tour de force," which makes her more of a role than a character. Reminding us that Penelope herself is a role player while she waits for Odysseus, Herr looks at Joyce's counterpart of Odysseus's wife as a performer or the *clou*, the star turn of the book (Herr 130). Molly's performance of gender traits is also the subject of Kimberly Devlin's essay "Pretending in 'Penelope': Masquerade, Mimicry, and Molly Bloom." Devlin notes that Molly is a "weaver and unweaver of identity itself," donning "multiple recognizable masks of womanliness." In her role playing, she "stages herself as Venus in Furs, the indignant and protective spouse, the jealous domestic detective, the professional singer, the professional seductress or femme fatale, the teenage flirt, the teenage naïf, the unrepentant adulteress, the guilt-ridden adulteress, the narcissistic child, the exasperated mother, the pining romantic, the cynical scold, the female seer/fortuneteller" and "the frustrated housewife, the female confidante and adviser, the female misogynist, et cetera, et cetera" (72). Molly is a performer and a player, a skilled manipulator confidently asserting her sexual and material needs. I am therefore inclined to read her final "yes" against the grain, not as the "center" of the text binding all the loose ends together into one courageous affirmation of womanhood, love, and marriage, but as a solipsistic and liberatory proclamation of her independence as a human being capable of shaping her own past and future, making decisions irrespective of outside pressures. It is tempting to give in to a readerly desire for order and closure and to "cosmicize" a text that resists finality and tidy classification. If we follow Joyce's notesheets in the British Museum, we find a description of Molly's "cunt, the Darkest Africa" (494)—a Conradesque phrase which might suggest an uncharted, waiting-to-be-conquered territory. Molly's "yes" could be equally prone to malleability, to an imposition of meaning. But "Darkest Africa" offers richer suggestions dictated by the literary and cultural tradition of the nineteenth- and twentieth-century travel accounts. Let us not forget about other associations the phrase might imply: the wild, the eerie, the dangerous other. Molly, after all, conforms to the myth of *vagina dentata* when she muses: "they ought to be all shot or the cat of nine tails a big brute like that . . . Id cut them off him so I would" (18.996–98). Thus reading her final "yes" as purely conciliatory may be too optimistic and largely speculative. "Yes" is a part of her play. It is an ambiguous and abandoned confirmation, but exactly what it confirms remains in the dark.

Joyce also presents Stephen as a player on at least two levels. In *Portrait*, he performs a part in a Whitsuntide school play at Belvedere College, in which "he found himself on the stage amid the garish gas and the dim scenery, acting before the innumerable faces of the void. It surprised him to see that the play which he had known at rehearsals for a disjointed lifeless thing had suddenly assumed a life of its own. It seemed now to play itself, he and his fellow actors aiding it with their parts" (*Portrait* 96). Performing his part of "a farcical pedagogue" (83), Stephen sees the play as an isolated event and is aware of the artificial nature of this staged performance, even if it acquires "a life of its own." He will play the part of a "pedagogue" once again, in real life, as he teaches his students about Pyrrhus in the second chapter of *Ulysses*. This time the pedagogue is farcical, too; the boys are "aware of [his] lack of rule and of the fees their papas pay" (2.29), and Stephen resorts to asking them unanswerable riddles, knowing (just as Mr Deasy does) that this career is short-lived, like the commitment of Bauman's player figure, who is ultimately unaffected by his episodic games. Stephen engages in a number of short-lived encounters, such as the one in "Scylla and Charybdis," where he elucidates his theory on Shakespeare arguably for the sake of contradicting others, but it would be a mistake to consider the stages of his development as an artist and a man simply as inconsequential games. Even if he denies his allegiance to the nation and church, he remains deeply saturated with their symbolic and real discursive elements.

Joyce tells us in one of his essays that "the relations between drama and life are, and must be of the most vital character" (*Occasional* 23) and that "drama has to do with the underlying laws . . . in all their nakedness and divine severity" (24). He is so fascinated with the form and textual possibilities of the dramatic genre that he crafts an entire chapter in *Ulysses* as a play. "Circe," set in a brothel in Dublin's redlight district, contains innumerable parts (long, short, or mere appearances), gender-switching, real and imaginary actors, and bizarre stage directions and props.[10] For Bloom, it is a culmination of his daylong wandering through the city and psychic filtration of emotions and memories associated with his pilgrimage, but the chapter does form a game that, after all the masochistic, drastic, obscene encounters with other players, will not affect his progress. Like a real player, Bloom will dissociate himself from the events in "Circe," lead Stephen to his own kitchen, and serve him hot cocoa. Joyce himself, however, seemed unable to disengage himself from his part as a creator of "Circe." He complained to Harriet Weaver that Circe was "revenging herself for the unpleasant things" he had "written about her legend" (*Letters* 1: 150) and to Sylvia Beach that "Circe herself is punishing [him] for having written it" (*Letters of James Joyce to Sylvia Beach* 9). The more and more outlandish phantasmagoria of the chapter made Joyce frantic and captivated, and when he finally finished the chapter, the problems with typists refusing to work with such "obscene" material added to his frustration.

But other chapters, such as "Wandering Rocks," for instance, are—if not theatrical—playful and inviting active participation on the part of the reader. I have already mentioned that Joyce seduces us into a sense-making game. The reader-player approaches the text as a riddle to be solved, drawn to assemble the puzzle of metonymical descriptions and to place all these snippets of action in the chapter into a meaningful narrative order. Joyce gives us J. J. O'Molloy's "white careworn face," which "was told that Mr Lambert was in the warehouse" (10.236–37). Who exactly told his face about Mr Lambert? But we get more ghosts and more body parts here: faces (O'Molley's), darkbacked figures (Bloom's), plump arms (Molly's), the shop assistant's "slim fingers" (10.326), the lapidary's "toiling fingers with their vulture nails" (10.803), the "human eyes" of Artifoni (10.356), "Ben Dollard's loose blue cutaway and square hat" (10.901), or John Wyse Nolan's "cold unfriendly eyes" (10.1036). The city itself, with its "unheeding windows" (10.240), is a detached observer. It is up to the reader/player to assemble these fragments into a coherent narrative or to enjoy the puzzle pieces on their own. The readers, not Joyce, choose to be mapmakers.

The episodic nature of Stephen's and Bloom's quests precludes any ordering mythos offering continuity and form. Joyce portrays them as pilgrims who have to pay the price for traveling in the fragmented world toward the empty or ever-shifting center. The modernist pilgrims either have to accept the absence of form and keep pursuing the empty center, or find solutions to make their lives easier, to transform themselves into strollers, vagabonds, tourists, or players, and sometimes all of these figures at once. Although in this unstable world one can often adopt and change identities at will, it is not a strategy effective for shifting power structures and institutionalized agendas. Dedalus and Bloom heroically (or mock-heroically) embark on their quest, but they have a variety of strategies in stock, tactics that make the constant delay of gratification less painful. They display the traits and longings of the archaic pilgrim but do not resort only to the methods known to the premodern hermit. However, they fail in their quest because of their recognition of fissures in seemingly polished, powerful ideologies of turn-of-the-century Dublin. Joyce's pilgrims resist convenient compartmentalization which could provide a sense of belonging and therefore an uncomplicated, but often false, path to self-recognition. Their pilgrimage proves to be incomplete partly because, as *Ulysses* indirectly tells us, achieving telos depends upon binary vision and the ability to subscribe to clearly defined principles and dogmas. Fragmentation and deracination in Ireland torn by sectarian violence and colonial struggle make the already difficult task of finding the true center virtually impossible. Conrad's characters, though, display much less enthusiasm for the task ahead and often dodge it, or rely on others to delimit their quest, thus relinquishing their vestiges of power. But in both authors' delineations of modern pilgrimage, the stroller, the vagabond, the tourist, and the player jointly offer a metaphor for the quest toward, but never reaching, a fully formed identity in contemporary life.

Conclusion

Czesław Miłosz once remarked that an "immigrant will often, for motives of self-defence, cut himself off completely from his land of origin or show toward it a friendly condescension, thereby contrasting his own success to the miseries of those left behind in the old country" (42). Instead of pity and nostalgia, Joseph Conrad and James Joyce expressed mostly critical and accusatory remarks about their nations, possibly in order to present themselves as irreproachable and their immigration as justified. While Conrad admitted that he could not change his "ultra-Slav nature" (*Letters* 2: 230), he sometimes complained about the Poles' bad temper, bigotry, unreliability, and sloth.[1] Joyce pointed to the paralysis, narrow-mindedness, and blind loyalty to religious authorities among the Irish. Ever since he decided to "advance upon Europe with the missionary zeal (though not the piety) of his fellow Celts" (Ellmann, *James Joyce* 111), he thought about his flight from Ireland as a result of his nation's betrayal of his genius. In his letter to Lady Gregory, Joyce confesses that everything is "inconstant except the faith in the soul, which changes all things and fills their inconstancy with light. And although I have been driven out of my country here as a misbeliever I have found no man yet with a faith like mine" (Ellmann 111). Similar bitterness combined with defiance appears in Conrad's response to his compatriots' accusations of disloyalty. He insists that he has "in no way disavowed either [his] nationality or [his] name . . . for the sake of success" (*Letters* 2: 322), and explains: "It does not seem to me that I have been unfaithful to my country by having proved to the English that a gentleman from the Ukraine can be as good a sailor as they, and has something to tell them in their own language" (2: 323). But both authors circumvent the bitterness of rejection and, instead, expose the paralyzing effects of old, colonial grand narratives and the mythical patterns underlying popular description of the margin and the center, a contrived binary used by hegemonic powers to validate their injustice.

They investigate the patterns of movement within and across the confinements of essentialized categories.

In their fiction, political writing, and letters, Conrad and Joyce describe the Congo, Costaguana, Poland, and Ireland always in relation to the artificially and forcefully constructed myth of the center. Although Conrad's criticism seems to be rather selective due to his admitted Anglomania and social conservativism, both writers expose the audacious hypocrisy and sophistry in the strategies the imperial nations adopted to maintain power. Their forecast is rather grim: The subaltern can move in this fragmented milieu, even if their mobility is limited, but they do not seem to get anywhere. Since both the colonizers and the colonized have been positioned in the artificially constructed polarized world, both groups internalize in time the fabricated premises of the hegemonic order. The center is empty, precisely because of the fallacy upon which the entire myth is based: an assumption that the world should and can be successfully divided into spaces of being and non-being. Even if the subaltern were able to reach their destination, perhaps through circular movements gradually narrowing in on the center, they might simply perpetuate the same divisive binary rhetoric and exclusionary practices that previously kept them away from spaces of power. Joyce's citizen and Conrad's Costaguanians are examples of such internalization of violent power grabbing. Their erratic quest whose destination is, quite legitimately, the restoration of power is unfortunately preconditioned by the imperial culture and the paths it has drawn for them. The only characters who understand the pointlessness of this deceitfully independent, imitative progress toward the center of self-recognition, knowledge, and power are either the hate- and resentment-ridden anarchists in *The Secret Agent*, especially the Professor, with his "perfect detonator" capable of blowing the center (London) into pieces, or Leopold Bloom in *Ulysses*, with his call for love, "the opposite of hatred" (*U* 12.1485). Conrad and Joyce, therefore, draw our attention to the internalization of hegemonic practices. Conrad offers in response virtually no hope, no counternarrative that would not be simply a path of destruction. Joyce, however, gives the final word in *Ulysses* to Molly, a subaltern character, disenfranchised because of her gender and ethnicity, expressing vital assertions of life, harmony, love, and sensuality, even if her monologue is a staged performance of sorts.

Similar patterns of pilgrimage, colonization, and the sacred appear in Conrad's *Under Western Eyes*, "Amy Foster," and other tales, and in

Joyce's *Finnegans Wake, Exiles, Stephen Hero,* and the short stories I have mentioned only briefly: "The Sisters," "Araby," "Eveline," "Two Gallants," "Counterparts," "Ivy Day," and, of course, "The Dead." But pilgrimage is one of several ways to approach the sacred; another way of questing for self-identification is the creation of nominal identities. After all, the twentieth century witnessed a debate between the logical positivists, asserting the authorial power and objectivity of language, and poststructuralists, who emphasized incompleteness and deferral of meaning and rejected the idea of ultimate comprehensiveness of language and the Western logocentric bias. Thus the writers' struggles to attain precision and verity in language render a multilayered attempt to represent reality in an effort to approach the sacred center. This endeavor, according to Walter Benjamin, underlies human linguistic capacities and points at yet another controversy, that of the relationship between language and being, and of the postulated primacy of one over the other in the process of creation. Benjamin's essays, especially "On Language as Such and on the Language of Man" in *Illuminations,* and his correspondence with Gershom Scholem and Martin Buber testify to his plea to free language from an instrumental or "bourgeois" function. A renewal of the divine act of Creation through language could be the means of escaping the fallacious and rigidly polarized social, racial, and gender divisions.

Savage Shores

Joyce's Telemachiad ends as Conrad's *Heart of Darkness* begins, with a ship outside a port that was also "one of the dark places of the earth" (*HD* 48).[2] While Marlow imagines Roman conquerors landing on the God-forsaken island to "civilize" it, Stephen muses in "Proteus" on the eighth-century Scandinavian invasions of the Irish shore and the subsequent rule of the island by "Dane vikings" (*U* 3.301), superior to the Irish in their body armor and therefore victorious, "the Lochlanns . . . in quest of prey" with their "bloodbeaked prows" (3.300–301)—a phallic menace to the unspoiled Irish soil. He thinks of the "lost [Spanish] Armada" (3.149) which, defeated in the English Channel in 1588, was wrecked on the coast of Ireland and Scotland (Gifford 51). Add to this Stephen's thoughts on the pollution of the Liffey and Dublin Bay (*U* 3.150–51) and a brief flashback to "a horde of jerkined dwarfs, my people" in a killing frenzy, hacking at the "whalemeat" during the 1331 famine, and we have a picture of a nation ravaged by "Famine, plague and slaughters," savage and defeated. "Their blood is in me, their lusts my waves," notes Stephen, immediately calling himself a "changeling" (3.304) in a schizophrenic maneuver to indicate the difference after asserting the kinship.

Conrad's savage shore of Africa, so much lower on the evolutionary ladder than its British counterpart, is also a witness to slaughter and starvation. While Marlow asserts his kinship—with pride or with disgust—with fellow Europeans, the thought of even remote association with the natives of the Congo, as Achebe famously notes, repels him. The British shore has evolved into a "luminous space" (*HD* 45), an outlet to the venerable Thames, which "after ages of good service done to the race that peopled its banks" (46)—the race to which Marlow claims his belonging with pride in another book[3]—epitomizes military and commercial glory, tranquility, and the progress of Western civilization. Expressing his affinity with this civilized English waterway, he distances himself from its primitive past, its "marshes, forests, savages," its "cold, fog, tempests, disease, exile, and death,—death skulking in the air, in the water, in the bush" (49), just as Stephen cuts himself off from the past (and present) barbarities of the Irish shores. As mentioned in chapter 3, Stephen misquotes a line from Jonathan Swift's "A Letter to the Whole People of Ireland," implying that the goal of the English is to enslave the "primitive" Irish. In the same letter, Swift notably remarks:

> Our neighbours whose understandings are just upon a level with ours (which perhaps are none of the brightest) have a strong contempt for most nations, but especially for Ireland: They look upon us as a sort of savage Irish, whom our ancestors conquered several hundred years ago, and if I should describe the Britons to you as they were in Caesar's time, when they painted their bodies, or clothed themselves with the skins of beasts, I would act full as reasonably as they do: However they are so far to be excused in relation to the present subject, that, hearing only one side of the cause, and having neither opportunity nor curiosity to examine the other, they believe a lie merely for their ease. (Swift 184)

Swift's words must resonate with those who recognize the attempts to define other nations by distancing their own from their "savage" history and embrace reductive Hegelian dialectic as a marker of their own "progress." This dialectic is, says Swift, a convenient lie; Conrad and Joyce recognize the falsified national identity that relies solely on retrospection and narrow definitions of civilization and progress.

The Jesters' Anti-Pilgrimage

Upon the shores of Ireland and the Congo, both *Ulysses* and *Heart of Darkness* give us two characters whose common denominators emerge from an old tradition of the carnivalesque, two tricksters who evade the limitations of the colonial power and the vacillations of the search for the sacred center. While this book has already focused on Marlow's, Stephen's, and Bloom's pilgrimage, there is a striking affinity between two other liminal—though not entirely marginal—characters' quests: those of Conrad's Russian sailor and Joyce's Buck Mulligan. Unlike the Professor, whose nihilism makes him morose and deadly, these two characters pursue no telos, mocking the traditionally established sacred center, clowning their way out of commitment, and filling the spiritual void with meaningless jabber.

Both the harlequin and Buck are hard to classify. Each is a jester at the court of his master,[4] one in front of a Belgian agent-turned-savage-renegade, the other in front of an English enthusiast of the Irish folklore, but it would be erroneous to label them as simply subaltern. Although Joyce introduces Mulligan in a sacrilegious scene mocking the Catholic mass, he never tells his readers whether Buck is a Catholic or a Protestant. True, he might be one of the "Trinity medicals . . . All prick and no pence" (*U* 15.86–87) alluded to by the bawd in "Circe," but Trinity was already open to Catholics in 1904. However, if we consider, for example, Joyce's fondness for patterns, especially those of Trinitarian nature, and if Stephen figures in the text as a Celt and Haines as an Englishman, it is possible that Buck is Anglo-Irish (ergo Protestant by default, although as a materialist, not a "believer"), thus creating a kind of Trinitarian arrangement.[5] Reminiscent of a historically and culturally established figure of an Anglo-Irishman inviting the English to Ireland, he invites Haines to his Martello tower, prompting the Irishman's (Stephen's) departure. Similarly, for Conrad, a Russian character would be implicated in the machinations of an empire, but his Russian is in the Congo—a place under the Belgian control—and he embraces his role of a servant (occupying a liminal position between the colonizer and the native) to such an extent that when his tie with Kurtz is severed, the only thing he can do is disappear into the jungle and become one with the wilderness.

Mulligan appears in "Circe" dressed in "particoloured jester's dress of puce and yellow and clown's cap with curling bell . . . a smoking buttered split scone in his hand" (*U* 15.4166–68), calling himself "Mercurial Malachi" (15.4171). Perhaps it is a mere coincidence that two decades before the publication of *Ulysses* another writer dressed his dancing, jesting character in "parti-colored rags," "brown holland probably, . . . covered with patches all over, with bright patches, blue, red, and yellow" (*HD* 122), colors reminiscent of the map of colonial possessions in Africa. It is also possible that when Joyce called Mulligan a "lubber jester" (*U* 9.1110), he didn't intend the word *lubber* to imply an affinity with Conrad's imbalanced, gesticulating harlequin—one of the two established definitions of the word *lubber* being an unskilled, awkward sailor. (After all, why is the harlequin reading and annotating Towson's *Inquiry*?) Both Conrad and Joyce, however, must have been mindful of the popular cultural archetype, the figure of the harlequin or trickster, while writing these characters into their books.

C. G. Jung compares a traditional trickster with Mercurius, noting "his fondness for sly jokes and malicious pranks, his powers as a shape-shifter, his dual nature . . . his exposure to all kinds of tortures." As a result, Mercurius seems "like a daemonic being resurrected from primitive times" (Jung, *Four Archetypes* 135). He celebrated by singing and dancing, taking part in the "fools' feast" during which "masqueraders with grotesque faces . . . performed their dances, sang indecent songs in the choir, ate their greasy food from the corner of the altar near the priest celebrating mass . . . and hopped about all over the church" (137). This irreverence and apparent lack of direction in the trickster's behavior, when translated into a relatively contemporary colonial setting, prompts a question of loyalty or allegiance. What does the trickster actually do with colonial demarcations, and what is his attitude toward the imperial drive to "cosmicize" the other? While the harlequin's and Buck's insubordination and erratic behavior don't pose any serious threat to the status quo of the Belgian or British empires, or to the power of the Roman Catholic Church, their lack of direction works on the narrative level as an implicitly subversive device.[6]

Both are fools, court jesters, whose props nevertheless indicate a seriousness of purpose in a sinister way, as they include gun cartridges and a razor. They abandon items that the readers may associate with order and code of conduct: Towson's *Inquiry* and medical textbooks. In a world where moral codes make one vulnerable in either colonial progress or anticolonial struggle, these items are obsolete. The Russian sailor does not even understand the moral implications of his association with Kurtz; as Marlow notes, "he was gallantly, thoughtlessly alive, to all appearances indestructible solely by the virtue of his few years and of his unreflecting audacity" (*HD* 126). This thoughtlessness in the face of a real human rights disaster makes him, in a way, not so much indifferent as evil.

Similarly, as Robert H. Bell says in "Mercurial Malachi and Jocoserious Joyce," Buck is more than "a one-dimensional foil for Stephen" (364). This "gifted clown" mocking "Ireland, religion, sex, paternity, and creativity" (365) also appears sinister. Bell notes that "Buck's curtain raiser, the parody of the Mass, almost seems to be assisted by supernatural forces. His 'ungirdled' dressing gown, 'sustained gently behind him on the mild morning air' (1.3–4), suggests a diabolic tail." And as Mulligan "continues his almost uncanny show for Stephen's benefit, it becomes more explicitly a Black Mass, the diabolic priest citing scripture . . . and mocking Christ's words to his disciples at the Last Supper" (365). Stephen possibly "remembers Saint John Chrysostom's insistence, in a sermon on Ephesians 4:32–5:1–2, that 'great evils do dwell in a soul that is given over to jesting'" (365).

But Buck mocks everything and believes in nothing, while the Russian sailor—in his ignorance of the ethical dimension of his attachment to Kurtz—wholeheartedly adores the man who "enlarged [his] mind" (*HD* 125, 140). Moreover, as Bell notices, "if not consistently prophetic, Buck is surely a cogent commentator" throughout *Ulysses* (Bell 369); the harlequin is ignorant, ruptured from the world of reason and ethics by Kurtz's "prophetic" words. Nevertheless, both men's emotional instability and lack of direction, their mimicry and mockery make their progress an anti- or mock-pilgrimage. Note that the word *mock* functions as a verb (to imitate, ridicule, parody) and an adjective (artificial, false, forged). The Russian sailor and Buck ape the traditional movement of the pilgrim and draw the readers' attention to the ineffective and artificial modes of searching for the center. Pilgrimage is based on a broken promise; its telos is sheer forgery.

Mythmaking and the Nation

In a similar mode, Conrad and Joyce play with and mock the teleological nature of the epic novel, a form that traditionally embodies a nation's concept of its history. *Nostromo* and *Ulysses*, with their polymorphous versions of imagined communities, their fragmentations of national identities, and their mock-heroics, present two nations (one invented, one real) either in the midst of upheavals or reliving past upheavals and anticipating future ones, nations at crucial turning points and yet hopelessly paralyzed. This paralysis grows from cycles of revolutions in Costaguana and cycles of spectacular but ineffective insurgencies in occupied Ireland: the 1798 and 1803 uprisings, the blast of Clerkenwell in 1867, the 1882 Phoenix Park murders by the Invincibles (famously misplaced in *Ulysses* to 1881), or the fall of Parnell in 1890–91. Conrad gives us the unsuccessful Blancos' liberator, Bolívar, while Joyce's characters reminisce about their fallen savior, Parnell. Casa Gould and Dublin Castle loom in both novels as seats of colonial or neo-colonial oppression. Holroyd's voraciousness finds its strange parallel in Queen Victoria's thirst for the blood of her unruly subjects.

Indeed, Holroyd's insatiable desire for financial and political influence and his evangelical drive mirror those of Joyce's Queen Victoria, an "old hag with the yellow teeth" (*U* 3.232), "Her Most Excellent Majesty, by grace of God of the United Kingdom of Great Britain and Ireland . . . , defender of the faith, . . . a victress over many peoples" (12.294–97), who believed that England's economic and imperial reign is a result of God-given superiority. In the same vein, Eliose Knapp Hay notes that Holroyd's name might derive from "holy rood" and could also be an anagram for Henry Cabot Lodge, a U.S. senator supporting expansionist policies (Hay, "Nostromo" 86). The symbolic appropriateness of Holroyd's name and Queen Victoria's presence in *Ulysses* allows for a parallel between the early imperial-evangelical drive of the United States and Victorian imperialism inextricable from its missionary foundations and colored by what many considered excessive moral stringency of the queen.

Although national history in *Nostromo* looks like a whirlpool of impersonal forces limiting the possibility of a full political recovery, Conrad blames flesh-and-blood characters and their thirst for power as well as their self-righteous, self-appointed attempts at national salvation for the political collapse in Costaguana. For Conrad, it seems, "imagined" history and "real" history collapse into each other in his fictional accounts of Costaguana's past. This mistrust in the sole culpability of impersonal forces of the past for present disenfranchisement of a nation echoes in Haines's cryptic statement that "it seems history is to blame" (*U* 1.649) for the misery of the Irish and in Stephen's desire to awake from the nightmare of history.

Is Conrad's description of the Montero revolution somehow less "real" than the confused and confusing account of the Invincibles' attack in Phoenix Park in "Eumaeus" and other chapters in *Ulysses*? The veracity of the historical and fictional accounts of the Phoenix Park murders is the subject of James Fairhall's *James Joyce and the Question of History*. Fairhall claims that Joyce "in his fiction, attempted to subvert history, which he saw as both a chronicle of violence and oppression, and as a fixed past that has ousted other possible pasts and thus delimited the present" (xii). In both *Nostromo* and *Ulysses*, semihistorical narratives amount to desperate and stultifying mythmaking feats. Captain Mitchell's compulsion to label every current event as "historic," Don José Avellanos's *Fifty Years of Misrule*, Dawson's and Taylor's speeches, and the nameless narrator's spectacular display of citizen's spiritual kinship with a host of "Irish" heroes in "Cyclops" have many elements in common: a propensity toward gigantism and vacuous rhetoric, an attribution of a sacred mission to national heroes, a selective and sometimes belied memory of past events, and a stubborn belief in the nation's teleological progress toward "salvation." Conrad and Joyce mock these and other "historical" accounts, asking the readers to mistrust those who claim to have unique and objective knowledge of the nation's past and profess the ultimate truth about the nation's future. They both ask us to see the contentiousness and contingency of established historical accounts as well as their privileged perspectives and exclusionary practices. Perhaps this is why both novels lack what readers of traditional fiction would call a final resolution; both have open-ended final chapters that refuse to round up their decentered narratives.

Therefore, I disagree with Miller's assertion in his otherwise enlightening essay "Holroyd's Man" that Conrad fearfully anticipates, through the U.S. globalizing force, "the displacement of historical agency from individual to impersonal forces" (22). Conrad shows us that these "forces" of history are spun by flesh-and-blood individuals often motivated by greed, the pursuit of fame, or a notion that spiritual and economic salvation of a nation is, indeed, in their own hands. Even though the famous Holroyd's speech about the future of the world controlled by the United States seems to suggest some kind of impersonal spirit compelling Americans to take up leadership ("The world cannot help it, neither can we"), the prophesy comes from the mouth of a San Francisco–based financier seeking financial profit and God's favor through his quest to "civilize" Costaguana. Similarly, Joyce identifies the Irish mythmakers and colonial oppressors behind the nightmare of history in *Ulysses* by referring to or including in his narrative Dawson, Taylor, Emmet, Parnell, the Irish clergy, Privates Carr and Compton, Queen Victoria and King Edward, Haines, several figures involved in the Celtic Revival movement, or Michael Cusack modestly disguised as the citizen. Though Conrad's and Joyce's upbringing must have prompted them initially to embrace the concept of the nation as transcendent, inevitable, God-given, and essential to one's individual identity, their fiction shows very strong signs that they eventually rejected this notion and found it a crippling encroachment on one's personal and artistic freedom.

Decoud and Dedalus

Perhaps the most poignant examples of what happens to those upon whom the nation imposes a self-sacrificial duty of devoting their talents to liberatory causes are Martin Decoud's and Stephen Dedalus's struggles to maintain artistic and personal integrity in the face of the pressures of their compatriots' expectations. *Nostromo*'s Decoud—a journalist and boulevardier—"echoes the Romantic nationalism voiced by figures like Johannes Herder, who conceived of the nation as pre-existing its historical being," rhetorically constructing the creation of the new nation as "restoration to a natural state" (Miller 22). His cry "Look at the mountains! Nature itself seems to cry to us 'Separate!'" (*Nostromo* 125), his proclamation of the Republic of Sulaco, and his journalistic work make him the "young apostle of Separation" (331). Stephen Dedalus's secret desire to become an intellectual leader of Ireland, not by issuing public proclamations but by creating a national epic, and to "forge in the smithy of [his] soul the uncreated conscience of [his] race" (*Portrait* 288), echoes Decoud's ambitions. And yet Decoud and Dedalus are writers fantasizing about perfect artistic integrity and independence, about a creation of something meaningful out of the chaos and rubble of insurrections and dogmatism. One, however, embraces political journalism out of his obsession with

Antonia, while the other rejects calls (unlike his creator) to give the Irish "something with a bite in it. Put us all into it, damn its soul" (*U* 7.621). Dedalus explores an avenue different than the one chosen by Decoud—a path for a writer who resists selling his soul to partisan causes and calls for justice. In both cases, however, the artist-skeptic remains unsatisfied, sterile, and solitary.

Let's remember that Decoud's political activism is a sham. Like Stephen, who fears "those big words . . . which make us so unhappy" (2.264), he mistrusts jingoistic rhetoric, outbursts of patriotism, and self-sacrifice in the name of nationalism. Decoud declares to Antonia that even though she made a "Blanco journalist of him, he was no patriot" because the word itself "had no sense for cultured minds, to whom the narrowness of every belief is odious" (126). The detachment and skepticism with which both Decoud and Dedalus observe nationalistic and religious fervor— two sometimes indistinguishable sentiments—mirror their feeling of displacement in Costaguana and Ireland. They try to fly by the nets of doctrinaires, nationalists, colonizers, and representatives of institutionalized religion, finding temporary solace in their self-exile on the boulevards of Paris, suspended in midair, between countries, loyalties, and personal obligations.

They both give in to cynicism and narcissistic navel-gazing and refuse to be drawn into the political turmoil, unless for personal reasons. Decoud masterminds the secession of Sulaco only to be able to leave safely for Europe with Antonia. He looks upon the "tragic farce" of Costaguana's politics with amusement, "in the dry light of his skepticism" (245), and eventually dies "from solitude and want of faith in himself and others" (331). "He resolved not to give himself up to these people in Sulaco, who have beset him, unreal and terrible, like jabbering and obscene spectres" (332). Like Stephen, Martin Decoud "recognised no other virtue than intelligence," and his "sadness was the sadness of the sceptical mind" (333). Father Corbelàn calls him a "sort of Frenchman," neither "the son of his own country nor of any other" and the "victim of this faithless age," who believes "neither in stick nor stone" and whom even a "miracle could not convert" (134).

Stephen enacts what Decoud is unable to accomplish. What would happen if Stephen gave in to the pressure to write for the *Freeman's Journal* or the *Evening Telegraph*, or to use his artistic talent to aid in the nationalistic cause in some other venue? Would he also, like Decoud, become

intellectually sterile? Ludmilla Voitkovska discusses the "intellectual paralysis" through which *Nostromo* "articulates Conrad's mature views on
the writer's role in the preservation of a national identity" and the choice
the writer faces between becoming "a bard for the masters or a scribe for
the slaves"; in both cases, the writer becomes "ethically and intellectually
insignificant" (44). Stephen refuses to choose, as if aware of the dangers of
either option, but while he is not intellectually dead, he certainly remains
unproductive.

As modern and modernist pilgrims, and as artists, Decoud and Dedalus both want to "fly by the nets" of arbitrary political and religious constraints. But Stephen's evasion of these constraints is only partially successful: he is still in Dublin, haunted by his Catholic mother's apparitions
and his guilt, and by the end of *Ulysses* he produces nothing (except a
semiplagiarized poem); the desire to escape arbitrary colonial and doc-
trinal constraints results in silence. Decoud ends up dead after betraying
his ideal of intellectual freedom; he, too, descends into silence, on the
bottom of the gulf, weighed down by four silver ingots. Stephen's pockets
also contain tangible proof of his reliance upon the foreign presence in
his country, Deasy's coins, which—like Costaguana's silver—stand for the
(still) victorious empire, the impersonal efficiency of colonial trade, the
perilous idealism of "material interests," the proof of a successful invasion
of "cosmos" upon "chaos."

Homecoming

For Conrad's and Joyce's cynical, cosmopolitan intellectuals, there is no
closure in homecoming. Home is an empty center, an illusory telos, a
chasm devouring their selves. Decoud and Stephen, like Conrad and Joyce
themselves, find their countries crippled by unsuccessful uprisings, empty
rhetoric, and messianic zeal of nationalists unprepared for combat. As
Voitkovska notes, "Decoud's return to Costaguana dramatizes Conrad's
ambivalence towards the possibility of repatriation and his suspicion that
the desire to return is fed on illusory hopes and doomed to disappointment" (32–33). She links Conrad's "myth of 'home'" with "his fear of the
loss of personal freedom in the reaffirmation of tradition" (33). Conrad,
adds Voitkovska, "stages Decoud's relationship with his parent culture as
ambivalent and volatile, oscillating between emotional acceptance and

unrestrained criticism" (34). Voitkovska also discusses the "right of the expatriate intellectual not to return home where, like Decoud, he or she would have to become a political writer and risk the suicidal consequences of involvement with nationalist liberation movements and a concomitant right to maintain personal intellectual integrity against the massed forces of ethnic nostalgia and metaphysical patriotism" (47). While Decoud gives in to these pressures, sacrificing his self, Dedalus simply says, "Count me out" (*U* 16.1148) and responds to Bloom's remark that "You both belong to Ireland, the brain and the brawn" with this cryptic statement: "You suspect . . . that I must be important because I belong to the *faubourg Saint Patrice* called Ireland. . . . I suspect . . . that Ireland must be important because it belongs to me" (16.1158–65). Here, Dedalus trivializes the patriotic ethos of his compatriots, if it is true that Joyce alludes in these lines to a popular Scottish drinking song.[7] But he also (re)establishes the primacy of an individual over a nation, an ownership reversed, negating imaginary social contracts imposed by the messianic nationalist movement and conditioned by the colonial presence. Although Stephen's behavior links the concepts of "home" and "homecoming" to anti-teleology of repatriation and reminds the reader of his misplacement, it also indicates the irony that Bloom-Odysseus, hardly tolerated in his home country, arrives home at the end of the narrative, having asserted and defended his Irishness in "Cyclops," while Stephen-Telemachus remains itinerant and directionless.

Conrad's Decoud is no Odysseus, either; nor is Verloc, despite Conrad's tongue-in-cheek comparison of Winnie to Penelope. In *The Secret Agent*, where the father figure tricks his uncomprehending ward into an act of suicidal violence, Conrad gives us a grotesque and sinister homecoming scene in which Winnie murders Verloc with a kitchen knife. Marlow returns from his voyages little wiser, it seems, than before his departures, the meaning of his adventures still shrouded in fog, incomprehensible and elusive. Other characters—Jim, Kurtz, Stevie—never reach home, their pilgrimage stalled by death. Similarly, for Joyce's Eveline, Ferguson, and Bloom, home is far from a place of fulfillment, though the first two return because of a sense of obligation, routine, or both, while Bloom rejects a brief thought of divorce and departure and is drawn back to Molly's bed by the "lateness of the hour, rendering procrastinatory: the obscurity of the night, rendering invisible: the uncertainty of thoroughfares, rendering perilous: the necessity for repose, obviating movement: the proximity of an occupied bed, obviating research: the anticipation of warmth (human) tempered with coolness (linen), obviating desire and rendering desirable: the statue of Narcissus, sound without echo, desired desire" (*U* 17.2029–34). That this exposition follows Bloom's mental journey through Ireland and abroad, notably "leaping" over England just as he climbs over the railings to get access to his home, might indicate his semiconscious conflation of the national and the domestic. That the desire is not fulfilled but still "desired" points to Bloom's unending anticipation, suspended climax, and constitutive absence that propels this pilgrim into constant motion toward (self-)acceptance as a husband and an Irishman. It is only one of many examples of Joyce's play throughout *Ulysses* with the double connotations of "home rule," as a political goal and a personal issue. Home Rule is, in both political and domestic senses, still unrealized, but remains a potential. Similarly, in Conrad's *Secret Agent*, the phrase "domestic drama" (222) acquires double meaning: an act of domestic/national terrorism and the tragedy within the Verloc household, both ending with a pointless death, an act of violence that resolves nothing.

Conrad's and Joyce's Heterotopias

Their telos still elusive and ever-shifting, Conrad's and Joyce's modern pilgrims mirror their authors' rather enigmatic—at least at first glance— approach to their own exile and homecoming. To some extent, writing itself could be a way to return to *nostos*.[8] Michel Foucault, in his essay "The Language of Space" reminds us that "Whether or not addressing itself to the past, submitting to the order of chronologies, or applying itself to unraveling them, writing was caught in the fundamental curve of the Homeric return," and that "to write was to make return, it was to return to the origin, to re-capture oneself in the primal moment; it was to be new every morning. From this the mythical function, up until the present, of literature; from this the relation of literature to the ancient; from this the privilege that literature accorded to analogy, to the same, to all the marvels of identity. From this, above all, a structure of repetition that designates its being" ("Language" 161). But in a world of uncertainties and fragmentation, a world dissected by imperial agendas, logos provides only an illusory anchor. Even though Marlow returns from his voyages into the bowels of the earth to tell his stories, his narratives obscure rather than clarify, complicate rather than elucidate. The final dot in "Ithaca" could indicate Bloom's return to the sacred center, to the *omphalos*, a move that completes the narrative curve, however imperfectly. But his place within the house and within Ireland is no clearer than in "Calypso," no matter how positively we understand the final sign in the novel, Molly's concluding but ambiguous "yes."

Conradian and Joycean pilgrimage does not conform to the traditional, simplified pattern of progress from the profane to the sacred. It proves to be ineffective or incomplete partly because their characters live in the world of "non-places," in which, as Marc Augé asserts, culture resists temporal and spatial localization. The deracination of self produced by colonial axioms which are often bound to stultifying binaries of the sacred and the profane makes the already difficult task of finding the center virtually impossible. "Certainly the European, Western 'here' assumes its full meaning in relation to the distant elsewhere—formerly 'colonial,' now 'underdeveloped'" (Augé 10), but the twentieth century witnesses a "discontinuity between the spectator-traveler and the space of the landscape he is contemplating or rushing through" (84). The traveler "engages in the passive joys of identity-loss, and the more active pleasure of role-playing" (103). Since Conrad's and Joyce's characters bemoan their uprootedness and embrace it at the same time, they do not conform to the model of traditional pilgrims seeking and finding order, meaning, and self.

Conrad and Joyce introduce disruptions of the colonial syntax, disturbances that Foucault will later call "heterotopias," spaces of dispersion which "secretly undermine language, because they make it impossible to name this and that, because they shatter and tangle common names, because they destroy 'syntax' in advance, and not only the syntax with which we construct sentences but also that less apparent syntax which causes words and things . . . to 'hold together.'" Heterotopias differ from utopias in that they don't allow for fables and mythically organized, clean binaries of the established discourse. Heterotopias dismantle artificial binaries and arbitrary organizing principles; they "desiccate speech" and "dissolve our myths" (Foucault, *Order* 5). This dissolution of dominant myths marks Conrad and Joyce as nonconformist expatriates, exiles from the neatly charted hierarchies of power and comforting answers provided by principal doctrines of the church and the state.

In the circular flânerie of Nostromo and Bloom, we find two ethnically and socially liminal characters who employ a variety of tactics to facilitate their progress and who return home to contemplate their betrayal, one bitter and defiant, the other choosing to unite with his unfaithful wife, however temporarily, by kissing "the plump mellow yellow smellow melons of her rump" (*U* 17.2241). It seems that both Conrad and Joyce would agree with Theodor Adorno's words about "home," words conditioned by his awareness of far greater atrocities than they were perhaps able to imagine, atrocities of the Holocaust resulting, again, from a nation-state's rigid and destructive adherence to binaries in its drive toward expansion and "purification." Adorno says in *Minima Moralia* about dwelling that "it is now impossible. The traditional residences we grew up in have grown intolerable: each trait of comfort in them is paid for with a betrayal of knowledge; each vestige of shelter with the musty pact of family interests," adding that it is "part of morality not to be at home in one's home" (38). For Conrad and Joyce, to complete one's pilgrimage, to return from exile, to feel home in one's home is to choose to forget. A satisfying return requires a repetitive act of amnesia and self-delusion. Those who refuse to engage in this act of self-deception remain in exile, learning to accept deracination and hybridity; those who return despite their resistance to crippling ideologies and the pain of personal or collective betrayal continue to seek meaningful self-definition, driven forever by "desired desire."

Modernist (Anti-)Teleologies

There is another book to be written on how other modernists, particularly female writers such as Virginia Woolf, Katherine Mansfield, and Dorothy Richardson, do not subscribe to Judeo-Christian teleologies and often challenge traditional turn-of-the-century understanding of order in ethnic and gender relations.[9] Some modernists, such as T. S. Eliot, criticize the concept of an empty, negative God and distinguish between the requisite stripping of one's self in order to approach God through ritual and prayer and the wasteful emptying out of one's soul as a result of a godless pursuit of power. Eliot's "The Hollow Men" (following, of course, *The Waste Land*) envisions a collapse of order provided by Christian theology into chaos and bemoans rejection of God and Christian salvation that result in moral decay and emptiness. The poem begins with two epigraphs, one from *Heart of Darkness* (*Mistah Kurtz—he dead.*) and one evoking poems recited around ceremonial effigies of Guy Fawkes (*A penny for the Old Guy*), both referring to men who tried to explode the sacred center, either by usurping the sacred role themselves or by plotting to blow up the core of the British Empire and its anti-Catholic practices and legislations. In both cases, it seems, Eliot detects a search for meaning gone awry. Conrad himself calls Kurtz a "hollow sham" (*Heart of Darkness* 147) and a man "hollow at the core" (131), filled with an impressive, appealing voice. The last sound he makes, the ambiguous pronouncement of horror, is neither a prayer nor a clear renunciation for salvation. It is the sound of Eliot's "stuffed men," devoid of spirituality, whose "dried voices, when / We whisper together / Are quiet and meaningless" (5–7); men who "*go round the prickly pear*" (68)—a false center—with an infantile chant on their lips; men who cannot turn a potential—"conception," "desire," "potency," "essence"—into completion—"act," "spasm," "existence," "descent"; men for whom "the world ends / Not with a bang but a whimper" (97–98), such as Kurtz's. They resemble Conrad's itinerant anarchists, nihilists, and "pilgrims" in the African interior on their quest for ivory and, to some extent, Joyce's Dubliners, those who embrace contingencies of meaning and are unable to articulate their own meaningful credo independent of outside pressures. Whether the "timid river" (60) in the fourth section of "The Hollow Men" is Conrad's Congo or Dante's Acheron, Eliot's lost men "grope together / And avoid speech" (58–59), calling upon idols, communicating with empty gestures. In *Four Quartets*, especially the "Little Gidding" section, Eliot will show us the path to deliverance, away from spiritual vagrancy and fragmentation of meaning that is "only a shell, a husk" (32): the refining Pentecostal fire of salvation. The "spirit unappeased and peregrine" (123) loitering along London streets after an air raid calls for detachment and humble prayer. Unlike Conrad and Joyce, Eliot translates other modernists' urban, rural, colonial, and gender topographies of power and pursuits of knowledge into a path to metaphysical completion, to salvation through God, and obedience to the sacred center and to the Christian doctrine. This fixed center, the only constant among flux and change, is also the only reality:

We shall not cease from exploration
And the end of all our exploring
Will be to arrive where we started
And know the place for the first time. (241–44)

Movement emanates from and comes back to God. Those floating in chaos acquire meaning inasmuch as they relate to the sacred center. This is the fixity that Conrad both craves and rejects. Joyce mocks and yet perpetuates the pattern of eternal return (if only, to take one of the obvious examples, in the cyclic narrative of *Finnegans Wake*), and many female modernist writers envision it as the product of patriarchal hierarchy and a source not of liberation but of enslavement of the mind, preferring instead a "luminous halo" surrounding each moment, exchange, and gesture.

"Modernist teleology" sounds like an oxymoron, a bizarre marriage of ambiguity and clarity of intention; estrangement and a universal endeavor; dislocation and purpose-driven movement; transgression and progress. Modernist aesthetics and subject matter, especially the theme of late colonial resistance to political and economic hegemony, often disrupt the traditionally established connection between pilgrimage and telos. But there is more at stake in this debate. In order to posit that pilgrimage takes place, one must agree that there is a distinction between the sacred and the profane. In other words, one must acknowledge the existence of the same binaries that modernism tries to abolish, unless one can find a new mode of questing, a model which does not rely on binarisms but transcends them.

One of numerous paradoxes of modernism and its aesthetics is a desire for an unencumbered, subjective search for meaning, on the one hand, and, on the other, fear of a potential ethical vacuum in case the quest for new values fails to replace the old normative practices. Whether we think of modernism as a vast excavation project uncovering the most precise modes of representation of fragmented consciousness or as a directionless, spontaneous drive to replace prefabricated models of understanding and presenting the world with discontinuous and highly reflexive narratives, we need to acknowledge that the modernist search for new forms of expression is always situated within or against a broader and somewhat mundane problem of social and political coercion. Modernist aesthetics and themes respond to socioeconomic change, to threats of capitalism—unification, mechanization, objectification, oppression—and to the ensuing spiritual void. At the same time, however, the reaction against universalism and rationalism and revolutionary anti-normative experimentation are not situated in an ethical vacuum. In the alienating and anti-democratic project of modernist aesthetics, the boundary between performativity and morality is blurred. In *Culture as Praxis*, Zygmunt

Bauman writes of "a misplaced nostalgia for a new, more suitable human-ordering-of-the-world, cast into the illusory realm of individualism by the obfuscating impact of an alienated, ossified, immobile society" (118). The implied danger of this reordering process is that disintegration of one narrative may provide space for another normativizing and equally crippling authority. Conrad and Joyce in particular warn us that disordering foundational narratives and dissolving established norms into chaos and incoherence might create not just emancipatory but also prescriptive space.

Notes

Introduction: Cartographers and Pilgrims

1. It is in *Ulysses* when we see his narcissistic, unsevered attachment to mother Ireland, mother Church, and his biological mother, but *Portrait* gives us a cocky, rebellious character—both qualities requisite in a formation of a fully autonomous self.

2. My translation.

3. Nowaczyński also calls the Irish "Polands [*sic*] of the Western World" ("Teatr irlandzki" 61) and "Poles of the West" (70), embedding these English phrases in his Polish text. He was an expert on Irish theater and literary tradition. John A. Merchant notes that Nowaczyński "clearly viewed the backward state of affairs in Poland and Ireland to be the product of outside interference" (60). Ironically, Nowaczyński, though a sympathizer with the cause of the oppressed Irish, became with time a champion of anti-Semitic comments in the Polish media and hence a proponent of repressive measures against another ethnic group. He notoriously discussed the dangers of "the international Jewish Mafia of the liberal press" in his article "Polska w literaturze angielskiej" in *Sfinks*. Merchant compares Nowaczyński's tone and subject matter to those of D. P. Moran in *The Leader* (57). Joyce himself mentions Moran, a critic of Irish hypocrisy, in "Cyclops" (*U* 267.1239), when the citizen responds, "Raimeis," to Bloom's claim that "Some people . . . can see the mote in others' eyes but they can't see the beam in their own" (267.1237–38). *Raimeis* means "nonsense" in Irish, and according to Gifford, Moran made it a household word for cant.

4. My translations.

5. *Kulturkampf*, the official execution of which began in 1872, was designed by Bismarck, who wanted to consolidate his empire through elimination of ethnic and religious differences. Extremely repressive and cruel measures were preliminary steps in the formation of the Colonization Commission in 1886. Bismarck's anti-Polish propaganda materials resemble anti-Irish posters and cartoons produced in Great Britain.

6. When Norman Davies discusses the partition and colonization of Poland, he admits that in "the British Isles, the only comparable experience was that suffered by the Irish, whose own loss of statehood lasted from 1800 to 1921 and who strove to preserve their own sense of identity from within another rich, confident, and expansive empire" (*God's Playground* 18).

7. The verb *cosmicize*, in the context of this research, refers to the process and reenactments of cosmogony, which will be the focus of the first section. A synonymous phrase for "to cosmicize" could be "to impose (one's own conception of) order."

I use the term *subaltern* to denote the oppressed and the unrepresented/silenced, against Gayatri Spivak's resistance to what she considers a misappropriation of the word (when it is used to name simply those who are disenfranchised). Because the word had been in use before Spivak's famous essay "Can the Subaltern Speak?" and before her dialogue with the Subaltern Group—and was, in fact, adopted by Gramsci as a synonym for the inferior class—I favor the wide definition of "the subaltern," while acknowledging the immense significance of the historiographical study of oppression in South Asian society and the validity of the group's employment of the word in that specific context. Spivak's aversion to the scholars employing this concept beyond the narrowly defined context which she favors indicates, in my opinion, a form of appropriation and control of a term whose etymological relevance to the broader usage justifies its popular definition as "subordinate," "of inferior status, quality, or importance." (All dictionary definitions used in this book, unless otherwise stated, come from the *Oxford English Reference Dictionary*, 1996.)

8. *Manichaeism* is a theological term appropriated by postcolonial theory to denote "the binary structure of imperial ideology" that "polarizes the society, culture, and very being of the colonizer and colonized into the . . . categories of good and evil" (Ashcroft, Griffins, and Tiffin 134).

Chapter 1. Cosmogony and Colonialism: Charting Non-Places

1. The distinction between cosmos and chaos, or the sacred (ordered, consecrated) space and the profane (anarchic, godless) space, also appears in more recent religious systems. Norman Cohn traces the development of this awareness in his book *Cosmos, Chaos, and the World to Come: The Ancient Roots of Apocalyptic Faith* and admits that, developed "by priests and theologians, these world-views were adopted happily enough by those belonging to the upper strata of society: for monarchs and administrators and scribes they served to justify a social order that brought such manifest benefits to the privileged" (3).

2. "Western thought has always thematized the other as a threat to be reduced, as a potential same-to-be, a yet-not-same" (*Heterologies* xiii). In *The Writing of History*, de Certeau's discussion of Jean de Léry's account of the Tupi tribe emphasizes the omnipresent series of oppositions universally upholding the distinction between the "savage" and the "civilized."

3. In her introduction to *Selected Subaltern Studies*, Spivak says that "in vague Hegelian limnings is the anti-humanist and anti-positivist position that it is always the desire for/of (the power of the Other) that produces an image of the self" (11).

4. For a detailed analysis and multiple reprints, see *Apes and Angels: The Irishman in Victorian Caricature* by L. Perry Curtis Jr.

5. Even some scholars born in Dublin (to Protestant parents) who had been transferred to London or other English cities and educated in English schools seemed to

subscribe to the racial differentiation between the Anglo-Saxons and the descendants of the Celts. An example is Sophie Bryant's classification and description of the Irish race in *The Genius of the Gael: A Study in Celtic Psychology and Its Manifestations*, published in London in 1913, in which she compares her task in this study to that of a botanist (45). The author, an educator and suffragist, although apparently enamored with Ireland, acquired and used the essentialist discourse of the colonizers.

6. The Irish themselves sometimes displayed ambiguous attitudes toward the plight of other races. In Irish, the word for Satan is *an fear dubh*, that is, "the black man" (Garner 71–72). Like the rest of European nations, the Irish would not situate themselves on the same level of hierarchy of progress with the population of Africa. It is therefore even more striking that, mainly in order to justify the "civilizing" missions in both places, the English tried to prove strong connections between the Celtic and African races (and, to a lesser extent, the races of North and Latin America). A prolonged contact with either of these "barbaric" cultures was pronounced as dangerous, forcing the "civilized" members of the empire (or "cosmos") to become wild and savage (or to be swallowed by the dark forces of "chaos").

7. Although societies believe myth to be real (and sometimes even the only real occurrence in the world, followed by mere imitations of that real in the profane reality), it is nevertheless told, or retold, by humans who decide to follow its example or teachings. Even if the occurrence of the myth is a result of some kind of theophany, we rely on mortals, not divine beings, to tell about it and to interpret its meaning.

Chapter 2. False Gods of Imperialism in Conrad

1. Even though there is a disagreement among Conrad scholars about the exact location of the imaginary Costaguana, numerous textual details and Conrad's interest in Panama suggest that the republic is somewhere in Central or South America. For an interesting discussion of scholarly attempts to locate Costaguana on the map, see Richard C. Carpenter's "The Geography of Costaguana, or Where 'Is' Sulaco?"

2. Leavis argues in *The Great Tradition* that Conrad's all too eager use of epithets like "inscrutable," "inconceivable," and "unspeakable" is "an interposition, and worse, . . . an intrusion, at times exasperating one. . . . The actual effect is not to magnify but rather to muffle" (202).

3. Significantly, the sketch Marlow admires in Kurtz's hut presents "a woman, draped and blindfolded, carrying a lighted torch" (*Heart of Darkness* 79). Kurtz's image of Astraea-Liberty has often been interpreted by critics as a symbol of a visionless and dysfunctional mission to bring civilization to the dark land.

4. Chinua Achebe comments extensively on the portrayal of the indigenous peoples in *Heart of Darkness*. In *Hopes and Impediments*, Achebe discusses Conrad's "adjectival insistence": "When a writer while pretending to record scenes, incidents and their impact is in reality engaged in inducing hypnotic stupor in his readers through a bombardment of emotive words and other forms of trickery, much more has to be at stake than stylistic felicity. . . . He chose the role of purveyor of comforting myths" (146).

5. To emphasize the identification of the mistress with untamed nature, Conrad adds:

"And in the hush that had fallen suddenly upon the whole sorrowful land, the immense wilderness, the colossal body of the fecund and mysterious life seemed to look at her, pensive, as though it had been looking at the image of its own tenebrous and passionate soul" (99).

6. William R. Mueller says that "the wilderness, viewing Kurtz as a trespasser who must be transformed to be acceptable, took him, 'loved him, embraced him, got into his veins, consumed his flesh, and sealed his soul to its own'" (80), hinting at the voraciousness of the African interior.

7. I will dwell on the myth of *vagina dentata* in greater detail in the next chapter.

8. It is worth noting that in *Heart of Darkness*, Marlow describes Kurtz's writing as "an exotic Immensity ruled by an august Benevolence" (118). Both *Heart of Darkness* and *Nostromo* portray characters who believe themselves to be entitled by their "civilized" milieu to tackle the "immensity" and chaos of the colonized land.

9. Note the similarity to Marlow's impression of Africa: "Paths, paths, everywhere; a stamped-in network of paths spreading over the empty land, through long grass, through burnt grass, through thickets" (*HD* 70).

10. Emphases mine.

11. Hay notes "Conrad's insuppressible antipathy to American politics, institutions, and character" (167).

12. Avellanos himself, as Decoud confesses, has "seen the sheets of 'Fifty Years of Misrule,' which we have begun printing on the presses of the *Porvenir*, littering the Plaza, floating in the gutters, fired out as wads for trabucos loaded with handfuls of type, blown in the wind, trampled in the mud? I have seen pages floating upon the very waters of the harbour" (158–59). See also Conrad's commentary on Avellanos's book in the Author's Note to *Nostromo*.

13. Mrs Gould describes the mine as "feared, hated, wealthy; more soulless than any tyrant, more pitiless and autocratic than the worst Government; ready to crush innumerable lives in the expansion of its greatness" (348).

14. My emphases.

15. My emphases.

Chapter 3. "A free lay church in a free lay state": From the Cosmogonic Discourse to Sacred Secularism in Joyce's Imagined Community

1. Foucault did not review and authorize "Of Other Spaces" ("Des Espace Autres") for publication, though it appeared in *Architecture/Mouvement/Continuité* in 1984. The essay served as the basis for one of Foucault's lectures in 1967.

2. Until the invasion by Scandinavian tribes, says Joyce in "Ireland: Island of Saints and Sages," Ireland had "an uninterrupted record of apostles, missions, and martyrs" (112). He reminds us that the Danes and the Norwegians were called "the black strangers" and "the white strangers" (113). Elizabeth Butler Cullingford says that in this essay, Joyce poses a "genealogical question of who first sanctified Ireland (and with what kind of sanctity)" and that this topic has to be charged ideologically (135).

3. Next to Myles Joyce, there are numerous figures whose fate was decided or

manipulated by the media and other forms of maintaining control, whether by the British political powers or the Roman Catholic Church. Although he was compared to Moses leading the troubled and disorderly people "out of the house of shame to the edge of the Promised Land" ("The Shade of Parnell" 193), Parnell became an immoral adulterer in the eyes of the public and was therefore betrayed. The establishment, through the press and other means, painted Roger Casement as a barbarian after his report on the abominable conditions in the Congo and his general attack on colonial atrocities in Africa (and his rather speculative actions in Germany). In the publicized diaries, now believed to have been forged, Casement appears as a dissatisfied homosexual and therefore as a double other.

4. Douglass, after visiting Ireland, said in one of his speeches: "I see much here to remind me of my former condition. . . . He who really and truly feels for the American slave, cannot steel his heart to the woes of others; and he who thinks himself an abolitionist, yet cannot enter into the wrongs of others, has yet to find a true foundation for his anti-slavery faith" (qtd in Bornstein 371).

5. *Rigorism, the Number of the Chosen, and the Doctrine of Salvation* (Brussels, 1899).

6. Christine van Boheemen's "Molly's Heavenly Body" is an interesting reading of Molly as a "confessing vagina" (267) and chapter 18 itself as "the *locus* of the invention of what we now call 'gender,' the understanding of sexual difference as inscription and style, rather than an ontological essence" (268).

7. Although Chester Anderson (in his Explanatory Notes to the critical edition of *Portrait*) mentions *The Count of Monte Cristo*, especially the Count's remark: "Oh, man, man! race of crocodiles!" as a possible source for Stephen's statement, and although "the race of clodhoppers" could also refer to the English, since the exclamation follows Stephen's recollection of the Irish mourners of Gladstone, I find the relation to Joyce's compatriots the most convincing. A juxtaposition of Joyce's remarks on the nature of the Irish (expressed in his letters, essays, and fiction) and the definition of the word *clodhopper* leads me to believe that Joyce refers to the Irish here.

8. Anderson traces the transition from a religious, universal, transnational language (that renders the concept of a nation insignificant and expendable) to the secular languages that sprouted after the collapse of the sacred imperia of premodern times and to changing concepts of time and space. Nationalism, he says, is a systematizing principle replacing religion as an organizing tool. The fading power of the sacred, all-encompassing language (e.g., Latin) understood only by the elite marked the emergence of profane, more democratic languages that, in turn, engendered the idea of a secular state.

9. The first similar remark is uttered in Bloom's presence: "Those are nice things, says the citizen, coming over here to Ireland filling the country with bugs" (12.1441–42).

10. "Joyce," Ellmann writes, "needed exile as a reproach to others and a justification of himself. His feeling of ostracism from Dublin lacked, as he was well aware, the moral decisiveness of his hero Dante's exile from Florence, in that he kept the keys to the gate" (*James Joyce* 113). Ellmann adds that "whenever his relations with his native land were in danger of improving, he was to find a new incident to solidify his intransigence and to reaffirm the rightness of his voluntary absence" (113).

11. In his letter to Griffith, Joyce said: "I quite see, of course, that the Church is still, as it was in the time of Adrian IV, the enemy of Ireland" (Ellmann, *Selected Letters* 246).

Chapter 4. Tenuous Itineraries

1. Darlene M. Juschka calls Turner a "map-maker in ritual studies" (1) before discrediting his theories of anti-structure and communitas. The attack on Turner's sacred "cartography" is explained in this chapter.

2. This anti-structural and egalitarian quality of communitas has been the basis for attack by contemporary anthropological researchers who stress immense diversity within the culture of initiation rites as well as pilgrimages. These scholars accuse both Eliade and Turner of wide generalizations and negligence of contrasting data which indicate that pilgrimage is often a realm of competing discourses, "a religious void, a ritual space capable of accommodating diverse meanings and practices" (Eade and Sallnow 15). What is at stake in the debates between the opponents (e.g., Eade, Sallnow, Morinis) and supporters (e.g., Platvoet, van der Torn) of Turner and Eliade is often a question of power. Both Turner and Eliade had actively pursued the subject of pilgrimage in particular, and the categories of the sacred and the profane in general, before postcolonial discourse became popular (or simply possible) and before questions of race, ethnicity, or gender entered the academic conversation about power allocation with the full force. While accusations about Turner's understanding of pilgrimage solely as a sacred journey and ignoring "the economic base structure of tourism that figures in its structures" (Juschka 2) seem to be refutable—after all, Turner's scope of research was necessarily limited to his area of expertise, which did not include financial systems, nor Marxist dialogue on base, superstructure, and economic gains—some attacks are well grounded. Turner seems to be more concerned with so-called primitive cultures than the institutionalized and highly organized pilgrimage of the modern period. Juschka rightly observes what Turner only mentions in passing: "Pilgrimage is about social power and not the absence of social power" (3). "Liminality and communitas," adds Juschka, "may be useful categories only insofar as the analysis of power is fully engaged in connection with them" (3).

3. By George Yeats's account, W. B. Yeats wrote "The Second Coming" in 1919 (as Ellmann asserts in *The Identity of Yeats*). The poem was first published in *The Dial* in 1920.

4. There seems to be a connection here with the ludic behavior within rites of passage in archaic societies.

5. As Bauman admits, "the 'aestheticized' world is the world inhabited by tourists" ("From Pilgrim" 30).

6. Accordingly, Bauman says that identity, "though ostensibly a noun, behaves like a verb, albeit a strange one to be sure: it appears only in the future tense." He adds that "identity has the ontological status of a project and a postulate" ("From Pilgrim" 19). Identity itself seems to have embarked on a constant, tireless pilgrimage.

7. It is perhaps best realized in Virginia Woolf's "moment" or "a luminous halo," or the empty chapel in T. S. Eliot's *The Waste Land*.

Chapter 5. "Circles, circles, circles": Conrad's Pilgrimage

1. "The Romance of Travel" was published in the magazine *Countries of the World* in February 1924.

2. Other characters make sincere attempts to communicate. Mr Verloc wants to communicate with Winnie at least twice in the novel—a quiet plea which his wife rejects, in her insistence that "things do not stand much looking into" (*Secret Agent* 177). Winnie herself, in the end, unsuccessfully seeks understanding and help in Ossipon. Michaelis, although leading a hermit's existence in prison and later in his cottage, nevertheless attends the famous parties of his lady patroness, who lends an ear to his utopian stories of the future society, even if others treat him condescendingly.

3. Jung, on his influential trip to Africa (to Mombasa, Masai, Bugishu, and other places), also apparently participated in tribal dances inducing trance and stupor, though probably not cannibalism. As Gloria L. Young notes in "Quest and Discovery: Joseph Conrad's and Carl Jung's African Journeys," "Marlow longed to go ashore for a howl and a dance, and Jung did go, dancing and swinging his rhinoceros whip wildly" (583). In *Heart of Darkness*, Marlow recollects that "Mr Kurtz lacked restraint in the gratification of his various lusts" and "that there was something wanting in him. . . . I think the knowledge came to him at last—only at the very last. But the wilderness had found him out early, and had taken on him a terrible vengeance for the fantastic invasion. I think it had whispered to him things about himself which he did not know, things of which he had no conception till he took counsel with this great solitude—and the whisper had proved irresistibly fascinating" (131).

4. Most people know him simply as Jim, although he "had, of course, another name, but he was anxious that it should not be pronounced" (2), and the Malays call him Tuan Jim. Marlow identifies him once, as he thinks of writing a letter on Jim's behalf, as "Mr James So-and-so" (110). We learn, however, that "he did after a time become perfectly known, and even notorious, within the circle of his wanderings (which had a diameter of, say, three thousand miles), in the same way as an eccentric is known to a whole countryside" (143).

5. Amidst the "hazy splendour" (3) of the "bewitching" (7) sea offering "the gift of endless dreams" (7), Jim "would forget himself, and beforehand live in his mind the sea-life of light literature" (3).

6. Marlow thus relates his impressions after meeting Jim: "The views he let me have of himself . . . fed one's curiosity without satisfying it; they were no good for purposes of orientation. Upon the whole he was misleading" (55). "I cannot say," admits the sailor, "I had ever seen him distinctly" (162).

7. "The Future of the Proletariat" is a secret society whose leaflets display the logo of "a hammer, pen, and torch crossed" (26). A similar symbolic representation appears in Kurtz's oil sketch, "representing a woman, draped and blindfolded, carrying a lighted torch" (*Heart of Darkness* 79) on a black background. Kurtz apparently recognized the irony of the crusading colonizers' zeal to "civilize" the natives and its danger, as "the effect of the torch-light on the face was sinister" (79). Conrad never suggests that Verloc is capable of drawing such conclusions and discovering covert motives.

8. Stevie was, moreover, highly unsuccessful as an errand boy: "He forgot his messages; he was easily diverted from the straight path of duty by the attractions of stray cats and dogs, . . . by the comedies of the streets which he contemplated open-mouthed, . . . or by the dramas of fallen horses" (8–9). Claire Rosenfield claims that "Stevie's appearance suggests a perversion of divinity consistent with the tone of the entire novel" (104) because, among other things, "Stevie's actions, though ritualized, do manifest irrationality" (104).

9. It is also impossible to determine Kurtz's profession. Marlow wonders "whether he ever had any—which was the greatest of his talents" (*Heart of Darkness* 153). He takes him "for a painter who wrote for the papers, or else for a journalist who could paint" (154), and even Kurtz's cousin is unable to explain his vocation.

10. Rather ironically, although Conrad used the epithet "Apollo-like" to describe Ossipon, this character does not display any characteristics that would liken him to this god of truth and art. This "Apollonian" character relies on deception for his survival and takes advantage of unsuspecting ladies. He is, moreover, not even remotely interested in art. He puts his trust only in science. Joyce also uses the figure of Apollo in his description of a "pilgrimaging" character (see the next chapter).

11. The Professor himself calls his adverse relationship with Heat "the game!" (94). Heat answers him: "It may yet be necessary to make people believe that some of you ought to be shot at sight like mad dogs. Then that will be the game. But I'll be damned if I know what yours is. I don't believe you know yourselves. You'll never get anything by it" (94–95).

12. After Heat finds the fabric with Stevie's address on it and realizes that the investigation will jeopardize his informant, Verloc, he "no longer [considers] it eminently desirable all round to establish publicly the identity of the man who had blown himself up that morning with such horrible completeness" (90).

13. Since he received the sedentary job of the Assistant Commissioner of the London police (due to his wife's aversion to the colonial climate), his only excitement is a "daily whist party at his club" (102) and an occasional reception at the lady patroness's.

14. Heat "had his own crusading instincts. This affair, which, in one way or another, disgusted Chief Inspector Heat, seemed to him a providentially given starting-point for a crusade. He had it much at heart to begin" (222).

Chapter 6. Teleology without a Telos? Constitutive Absence in Joyce's Pilgrimage

1. The other, as Gifford notes, is "Nothing too much (or in excess)" (254).

2. The subject of Father Conmee's theology and Victorian efficiency came up during one of the fruitful discussions at the National Endowment for the Humanities seminar in Dublin, which I attended in the summer of 2007. My thanks for this idea go to all the seminar participants and to Kevin Dettmar, our moderator.

3. "To ourselves" seems to refer to the Irish "Sinn Fein" ("We ourselves"). Gifford explains new paganism as a "slogan associated with the avant-garde 'younger generation' of the 1890s," proclaiming that "'the religion of our forefathers' has ceased to be a vital

force and that 'a new epoch is about to be inaugurated,'" in which "'literature dominated by the various sources of sexual emotion should prevail.'" He adds that the proponents of new paganism qualify "'sexual emotion' as only 'one among the many motive forces of life'" (17).

4. For an interesting discussion of *Ulysses* and the Ordnance Survey of Ireland, see Jon Hegglund's "*Ulysses* and the Rhetoric of Cartography."

5. Senn notes that when Penelope's suitors see Odysseus in disguise and abuse him, they call him *plankte*, "someone wandering," implying that he does not belong to the place, but also that he is "wandering in mind," "distraught" (156).

6. This assertion is, significantly, followed by Haines's anti-Semitic remark, the first element in *Ulysses* that foreshadows Bloom's alienation in twentieth-century Dublin. His enthusiasm for Irish literature and tradition triggers some derogatory remarks among the islanders. John Eglinton says that the "peatsmoke is going to his [Haines's] head" (9.100), and Stephen calls him a "penitent thief" (9.101). The narrator mocks Haines in "Oxen of the Sun," when he describes the Englishman's appearance in the maternity ward, "a portfolio full of Celtic literature in one hand, in the other a phial marked *Poison*. Surprise, horror, loathing were depicted on all faces while he eyed them with a ghostly grin. I anticipated some such reception, he began with an eldritch laugh, for which, it seems, history is to blame" (14.1011–16).

7. The Reverend Hugh C. Love of Sallins, a man with a "refined accent" (10.406), who spends his time in Dublin writing a book on the Fitzgeralds, is also a tourist interested in the intellectual potential of the city.

8. Although Murphy may differ from Marlow as a storyteller, Joyce himself comes closer to Conrad's style in this chapter when he describes Skin-the-Goat's face as "inscrutable," "a work of art, a perfect study in itself" (16.598).

9. The sailor's tales also induce Bloom's reverie of "the homecoming to the mariner's roadside shieling. . . . Across the world for a wife" (16.423–24) and his evocation of "Enoch Arden and Rip van Winkle" (16.425–26). He also muses on "uptodate tourist traveling . . . as yet merely in its infancy, so to speak, and the accommodation left much to be desired" (16.564–65).

10. For an interesting analysis of a connection between theater and brothel in "Circe," see Austin Briggs's "Whorehouse/Playhouse."

Conclusion

1. In his letter to Cunninghame Graham, Conrad admits: "Yes. We Poles are poor specimens. The strain of national worry has weakened the moral fibre—and no wonder when You think of it. It is not a fault; it is a misfortune. Forgive my jeremiads. I don't repine at the nature of my inheritance but now and then it is too heavy not to let out a groan" (March 5, 1898, *Letters* 2: 44). He also says that "Poles are lazy" (January 20, 1894, 1: 145) in his correspondence with Marguerite Poradowska and that he has "scarcely any confidence in [his] compatriots" (August 16, 1894, 1: 168).

2. I would like to thank Sebastian Knowles for this suggestion and for encouraging me to look at parallels between Mulligan and the harlequin.

3. In *Lord Jim*, Marlow uses an exclusionist phrase "one of us" (56) to delineate the boundaries of his race.

4. Although it is Stephen who calls himself a "jester at the court of his master, indulged and disesteemed, winning a clement master's praise" (*U* 2.44–45), Buck Mulligan's clowning about in the presence of Haines (and Stephen) places him in the same category with Dedalus, "their land [an Englishman's] pawnshop" (2.47).

5. I am grateful to Thomas Rice for suggesting this idea to me.

6. Both also carry the innuendo of homosexuality. That their sexual orientation is buried in excessive words and gestures and only implicitly suggested in the texts points to yet another "circularity" of these characters' behavior.

7. Gifford quotes from the song in his Ulysses *Annotated*: "I belong to Glasgow, / Good old Glasgow town, / But what's the matter with Glasgow / For it's going round and round? / I'm only a common old working chap, / As anyone here can see, / But when I've had a couple of drinks of a Saturday, / Glasgow belongs to me" (550).

8. As Adorno maintains, for "a man who no longer has a homeland, writing becomes a place to live" (87), however illusory and impermanent.

9. While Katherine Mansfield, Virginia Woolf, and Dorothy Richardson were all fascinated with a state of exile—literal and metaphorical—only Mansfield came to Europe from a British colony. Their investigation of a variety of cultural practices, performance of masculinity within the empire, transnationalism and insularity, liminality, and urban identity led to further captivating questions about the relationship between modernist aesthetics and thematic choices, between the public and the private, the center and the margin, form and anti-form.

Bibliography

Achebe, Chinua. *Hopes and Impediments: Selected Essays, 1965–1987*. London: Heinemann, 1988.

Adams, David. *Colonial Odysseys: Empire and Epic in the Modernist Novel*. Ithaca: Cornell University Press, 2003.

Adorno, Theodor. *Minima Moralia: Reflections from Damaged Life*. London: New Left Books, 1951.

Anderson, Benedict. *Imagined Communities: Reflections on the Origin and Spread of Nationalism*. London: Verso Books, 1991.

Anderson, Chester G. Explanatory Notes. *A Portrait of the Artist as a Young Man*. By James Joyce. Viking Critical Library. Harmondsworth: Penguin Books, 1977. 481–550.

Andrews, J. H. *Shapes of Ireland: Maps and Their Makers, 1564–1839*. Dublin: Geography Publications, 1997.

Arendt, Hannah. *The Origins of Totalitarianism*. New York: Harcourt, Brace & World, 1966.

Ashcroft, Bill, Gareth Griffiths, and Helen Tiffin. *Post-Colonial Studies: The Key Concepts*. London: Routledge, 2000.

Augé, Marc. *Non-Places: Introduction to an Anthropology of Supermodernity*. London: Verso, 2000.

Bachelard, Gaston. *The Poetics of Space*. Trans. Maria Jolas. Boston: Beacon Press, 1964.

Bakhtin, M. M. *The Dialogic Imaginations*. Trans. Caryl Emerson and Michael Holquist. Ed. Michael Holquist. Austin: University of Texas Press, 2002.

Barns, T. Alexander. *The Wonderland of the Eastern Congo: The Region of the Snow-Crowned Volcanoes, the Pygmies, the Giant Gorilla, and the Okapi*. London: Putnam, 1922.

Bauman, Zygmunt. *Culture as Praxis*. London: Routledge, 1973.

———. "From Pilgrim to Tourist—or a Short History of Identity." *Questions of Cultural Identity*. Ed. Stuart Hall and Paul du Gay. London: SAGE, 1996. 18–36.

———. *Modernity and Ambivalence*. Ithaca: Cornell University Press, 1991.

———. *Wieloznaczność nowoczesna: Nowoczesność wieloznaczna*. Warsaw: PWN, 1993.

Bell, Robert H. "Mercurial Malachi and Jocoserious Joyce." *Modern Language Quarterly* 48.4 (1987): 364–77.

Benjamin, Walter. *Illuminations*. Trans. Harry Zohn. New York: Schocken Books, 1968.

Bhabha, Homi K. *The Location of Culture*. London: Routledge, 1998.

Blamires, Harry. *The Bloomsday Book*. London: Routledge, 1991.

Boheemen, Christine van. "Molly's Heavenly Body and the Economy of the Sign: The Invention of Gender in 'Penelope.'" *Ulysses En-gendered Perspectives*. Ed. Kimberly J. Devlin and Marilyn Reizbaum. Columbia: University of South Carolina Press, 1999.

Boland, Eavan. "That the Science of Cartography Is Limited." *In a Time of Violence*. New York: Norton, 1995.

Bornstein, George. "The Colors of Zion: Black, Jewish, and Irish Nationalisms at the Turn of the Century." *Modernism/modernity* 12.3 (2005): 369–84.

Bowen, Zack. "Joyce, Minstrels, and Mimes." *James Joyce Quarterly* 39.4 (2002): 813–19.

Brantlinger, Patrick. "Victorians and Africans: The Genealogy of the Myth of the Dark Continent." *Critical Inquiry* 12.1 (1985): 166–203.

Briggs, Austin. "Whorehouse/Playhouse: The Brothel as Theater in the 'Circe' Chapter of *Ulysses*." *Journal of Modern Literature* 26.1 (2002): 42–57.

Brown, Richard. "Everything in 'Circe.'" *Reading Joyce's "Circe."* Ed. Andrew Gibson. European Joyce Studies 3. Amsterdam: Rodopi, 1994.

———. "Time, Space, and the City in 'Wandering Rocks.'" *Joyce's "Wandering Rocks."* Ed. Andrew Gibson and Steven Morrison. European Joyce Studies 12. Amsterdam: Rodopi, 2002.

Bryant, Sophie. *The Genius of the Gael: A Study in Celtic Psychology and Its Manifestations*. London: T. Fisher Unwin, 1913.

Budgen, Frank. *James Joyce and the Making of* Ulysses. Bloomington: Indiana University Press, 1960.

Burton, W.F.P. *How They Live in Congoland: An Account of the Character and Customs of This Most Interesting Race and Efforts to Win Them for Christ*. London: Pickering & Inglis, n.d.

Carpenter, Richard C. "The Geography of Costaguana, or Where 'Is' Sulaco?" *Journal of Modern Literature* 5.2 (1976): 321–26.

Castelein, A. *Le rigorisme, le nombre des élus, et la doctrine du Salut*. Brussels, 1899.

Certeau, Michel de. *Heterologies: Discourse on the Other*. Trans. Brian Massumi. Theory and History of Literature Series 17. Minneapolis: University of Minnesota Press, 2000.

———. *The Mystic Fable*. Vol. 1. Trans. Michael B. Smith. Chicago: University of Chicago Press, 1995.

———. *The Practice of Everyday Life*. Trans. Steven Rendall. Berkeley: University of California Press, 1988.

———. *The Writing of History*. Trans. Tom Conley. New York: Columbia University Press, 1988.

Cheng, Vincent J. *Joyce, Race, and Empire*. Cambridge: Cambridge University Press, 1995.

Chow, Rey. "Where Have All the Natives Gone?" *Displacements: Cultural Identities in Question*. Ed. Angelica Bammer. Bloomington: Indiana University Press, 1994.

Cohn, Norman. *Cosmos, Chaos, and the World to Come: The Ancient Roots of Apocalyptic Faith*. New Haven: Yale University Press, 1993.

Coleridge, Samuel Taylor. "The Rime of the Ancient Mariner." *The Norton Anthology of English Literature.* 7th ed. Vol. 2. New York: Norton, 1999.

Conrad, Joseph. *The Collected Letters of Joseph Conrad.* 5 vols. Ed. Karl R. Frederick. Cambridge: Cambridge University Press, 1983–96.

———. *Heart of Darkness.* London: Dent, 1948.

———. *Last Essays.* London: Dent, 1926.

———. *Lord Jim.* New York: Doubleday, 1920.

———. *Nostromo.* Chatham: Wordsworth Classics, 1996.

———. "An Outpost of Progress." *Selected Short Stories.* Ware: Wordsworth Classics, 1997. 3–23.

———. *A Personal Record.* London: Dent, 1919.

———. *The Secret Agent.* London: Dent, 1947.

———. *Under Western Eyes.* New York: Doubleday, 1924.

Cullingford, Elizabeth Butler. *Ireland's Others: Gender and Ethnicity in Irish Literature and Popular Culture.* Critical Conditions: Field Day Essays and Monographs 10. Cork: Cork University Press, 2001.

Curtin, Nancy J. "'A Nation of Abortive Men': Gendered Citizenship and Early Irish Republicanism." *Reclaiming Gender: Transgressive Identities in Modern Ireland.* Ed. Marilyn Cohen and Nancy J. Curtin. New York: St. Martin's, 1995. 33–52.

Curtis, L. Perry, Jr. *Apes and Angels: The Irishman in Victorian Caricature.* Rev. ed. Washington: Smithsonian Institution Press, 1997.

Davies, Norman. *God's Playground: A History of Poland.* Vol. 1. New York: Columbia University Press, 1982.

———. *Heart of Europe: The Past in Poland's Present.* New York: Oxford University Press, 2001.

Derrida, Jacques. "Ulysses Gramophone: Hear Say Yes in Joyce." *A Derrida Reader: Between the Blinds.* Ed. Peggy Kamuf. New York: Columbia University Press, 1991.

Devlin, Kimberly J. "Pretending in 'Penelope': Masquerade, Mimicry, and Molly Bloom." *Novel* 25 (1991): 71–89.

Doyle, A. Conan. *The Crime of the Congo.* New York: Doubleday, Page, 1909.

Duffy, Enda. *The Subaltern* Ulysses. Minneapolis: University of Minnesota Press, 1994.

Eade, John, and Michael J. Sallnow, eds. *Contesting the Sacred: The Anthropology of Christian Pilgrimage.* London: Routledge, 1991.

Egan, Rory. "Nelson's Pillar." *Irish Independent* 12 March 2006.

Eliade, Mircea. *Images and Symbols: Studies in Religious Symbolism.* Trans. Philip Mairet. Princeton: Princeton University Press, 1991.

———. *The Myth of the Eternal Return; or, Cosmos and History.* Trans. Willard R. Trask. Bollingen Series 46. Princeton: Princeton University Press, 1954.

———. *Myths, Dreams, and Mysteries: The Encounter between Contemporary Faiths and Archaic Realities.* Trans. Philip Mairet. New York: Harper Torchbooks, 1967.

———. *Patterns in Comparative Religion: A Study of the Element of the Sacred in the History of Religious Phenomena.* Cleveland: Meridian Books, 1963.

———. *The Sacred and the Profane.* Trans. Willard R. Trask. New York: Harper Torchbooks, 1959.

Eliot, T. S. *Four Quartets*. San Diego: Harcourt, 1971.

———. "The Hollow Men." *The Norton Anthology of English Literature*. 7th ed. Vol. 2. New York: Norton, 1999.

———. *The Waste Land*. *The Norton Anthology of English Literature*. 7th ed. Vol. 2. New York: Norton, 1999.

Ellmann, Richard. *The Identity of Yeats*. New York: Oxford University Press, 1964.

———. *James Joyce*. Oxford: Oxford University Press, 1972.

———, ed. *Selected Letters of James Joyce*. London: Faber, 1975.

Fairhall, James. *James Joyce and the Question of History*. Cambridge: Cambridge University Press, 1995.

Fanon, Frantz. *Black Skin, White Masks*. Trans. Charles Lam Markmann. New York: Grove Press, 1967.

———. *The Wretched of the Earth*. New York: Grove Press, 1963.

Firchow, Peter Edgerly. *Envisioning Africa: Racism and Imperialism in Conrad's* Heart of Darkness. Lexington: University Press of Kentucky, 2000.

Forbath, Peter. *The River Congo: The Discovery, Exploration, and Exploitation of the World's Most Dramatic River*. New York: Harper & Row, 1977.

Foucault, Michel. "The Language of Space." Trans. Gerald Moore. *Space, Knowledge, and Power: Foucault and Geography*. Ed. Jeremy W. Crampton and Stuart Elden. Burlington: Ashgate, 2007.

———. "Of Other Spaces." *The Visual Culture Reader*. Ed. Nicholas Mirzoeff. London: Routledge, 2002.

———. *The Order of Things: An Archaeology of the Human Sciences*. London: Vintage, 1994.

Garner, Steve. *Racism in the Irish Experience*. London: Pluto Press, 2004.

Gibson, Andrew. "'Strangers in My House, Bad Manners to Them!' England in 'Circe.'" *Reading Joyce's "Circe."* Ed. Andrew Gibson. European Joyce Studies 3. Amsterdam: Rodopi, 1994. 179–221.

Gifford, Don. Ulysses *Annotated: Notes for James Joyce's* Ulysses. Rev. ed. Berkeley: University of California Press, 1989.

Guérard, Albert J. *Conrad the Novelist*. Cambridge: Harvard University Press, 1958.

Habinek, Thomas. *Ancient Rhetoric and Oratory*. Malden, Mass.: Blackwell, 2005.

Hamilton, Edith. *Mythology: Timeless Tales of Gods and Heroes*. New York: Mentor, 1942.

Hardt, Michael, and Antonio Negri. *Empire*. Cambridge: Harvard University Press, 2000.

Hay, Eloise Knapp. "Nostromo." *The Cambridge Companion to Joseph Conrad*. Ed. J. H. Stape. Cambridge: Cambridge University Press, 1996.

———. *The Political Novels of Joseph Conrad*. Chicago: University of Chicago Press, 1963.

Hegglund, Jon. "*Ulysses* and the Rhetoric of Cartography." *Twentieth-Century Literature* 49.2 (2003): 164–92.

Herr, Cheryl. "'Penelope' as Period Piece." *Novel* 22 (1989): 130–42.

Herring, Philip, ed. *Joyce's* Ulysses: *Notesheets in the British Museum.* Charlottesville: University Press of Virginia, 1972.

Holloway, Bolton Julia. "*Semus Sumus*: Joyce and Pilgrimage." *Thought* 56.221 (1981): 212–25.

Howe, Irving. *Politics and the Novel.* Cleveland: Meridian Books, 1957.

Hyland, Caroline. "Równoległe Biografie." *Wokół Jamesa Joyce'a.* Kraków: Universitas, n.d.

Johnston, H. H. *The River Congo: From Its Mouth to Bólóbó.* 4th ed. London: Sampson Low, Marston, 1895.

Joyce, James. *Dubliners.* Harmondsworth: Penguin Books, 1996.

———. *Exiles.* Harmondsworth: Penguin Books, 1973.

———. *Finnegans Wake.* Harmondsworth: Penguin Books, 1992.

———. "Ireland at the Bar." *Occasional, Critical, and Political Writing.* Ed. Kevin Barry. Oxford: Oxford University Press, 2000. 145–51.

———. "Ireland: Island of Saints and Sages." *Occasional, Critical, and Political Writing.* Ed. Kevin Barry. Oxford: Oxford University Press, 2000. 108–26.

———. *James Joyce's Letters to Sylvia Beach, 1921–1940.* Ed. Melissa Banta and Oscar A. Silverman. Bloomington: Indiana University Press, 1987.

———. *Letters of James Joyce*, Vol. 1. Ed. Stuart Gilbert, 1957; rev. Richard Ellmann, 1966. New York: Viking Press, 1966. Vols. 2 and 3. Ed. Richard Ellmann. New York: Viking Press, 1966.

———. *A Portrait of the Artist as a Young Man.* Harmondsworth: Penguin Books, 1996.

———. *Selected Letters of James Joyce.* Ed. Richard Ellmann. New York: Viking Press, 1975.

———. "The Shade of Parnell." *Occasional, Critical, and Political Writing.* Ed. Kevin Barry. Oxford: Oxford University Press, 2000. 191–96.

———. *Stephen Hero.* New York: New Directions Books, 1963.

———. *Ulysses.* Gabler Edition. New York: Vintage Books, 1993.

Jung, Carl G. *Four Archetypes: Mother, Rebirth, Spirit, Trickster.* Trans. R.F.C. Hull. Princeton: Princeton University Press, 1973.

Juschka, Darlene M. "Whose Turn Is It to Cook? Communitas and Pilgrimage Questioned." *Mosaic* 36.4 (2003): 189–204.

Kingsley, Charles. *Charles Kingsley: His Letters and Memories of His Life.* Vol. 2. Ed. Frances Kingsley. London: Henry S. King, 1877.

Kipling, Rudyard. "The White Man's Burden." *The Broadview Anthology of Victorian Poetry and Poetic Theory.* Ed. Thomas J. Collins and Vivienne J. Rundle. Ontario: Broadview Press, 1999.

Krajka, Wiesław. "Conrad and Poland: Under the Eyes of My Generation." *Contexts for Conrad.* Ed. Keith Carabine, Owen Knowles, and Wiesław Krajka. Boulder: East European Monographs, 1993.

Lampert, Eugene. "Modernism in Russia, 1893–1917." *Modernism: A Guide to European Literature.* Ed. Malcolm Bradbury and James McFarlane. Harmondsworth: Penguin Books, 1991.

Leavis, F. R. *The Great Tradition.* London: Chatto and Windus, 1948.

Lindqvist, Sven. *Exterminate All the Brutes*. Trans. Joan Tate. New York: New Press, 1996.

Lovin, Robin W., and Frank E. Reynolds, eds. *Cosmogony and Ethical Order: New Studies in Comparative Ethics*. Chicago: University of Chicago Press, 1985.

Lyotard, Francois. *Peregrinations: Law, Form, Event*. Trans. Cecile Lindsay. New York: Columbia University Press, 1988.

Mansfield, Katherine. *Stories*. New York: Vintage Classics, 1991.

———. "The Woman at the Store." *Katherine Mansfield's Selected Stories*. Ed. Vincent O'Sullivan. Norton Critical Edition. New York: Norton, 2006.

McCance, Dawne. "Crossings: An Interview with Erin Moure." *Mosaic* 36.4 (2003): 1–16.

McKibben, Sarah. "*The Poor Mouth*: A Parody of (Post)Colonial Irish Manhood." *Research in African Literatures* 34.4 (2003): 96–114.

Merchant, John A. "The Impact of Irish Ireland on Young Poland, 1890–1918." *New Hibernia Review* 5.3 (2001): 42–65.

Miller, C. Brook. "Holroyd's Man: Tradition, Fetishization, and the United States in *Nostromo*." *Nostromo: Centennial Essays*. Ed. Allan Simmons and J. H. Stape. Amsterdam: Rodopi, 2004. 14–30.

Miłosz, Czesław. "Joseph Conrad in Polish Eyes." *The Art of Joseph Conrad: A Critical Symposium*. Ed. R. W. Stallman. East Lansing: Michigan State University Press, 1980. 35–44.

Morgan, James. "Harlequin in Hell: Marlow and the Russian Sailor in Conrad's *Heart of Darkness*." *Conradiana* 33.1 (2001): 40–48.

Morris, Colin, and Peter Roberts, eds. *Pilgrimage: The English Experience from Becket to Bunyan*. Cambridge: Cambridge University Press, 2002.

Morrison, Steven. Introduction. *Joyce's "Wandering Rocks."* Ed. Andrew Gibson and Steven Morrison. European Joyce Studies 12. Amsterdam: Rodopi, 2002. 1–16.

Moseley, Virginia. *Joyce and the Bible*. De Kalb: Northern Illinois University Press, 1967.

Mueller, William R. "*Nostromo* and the Orders of Creation: An Ontological Argument." *Celebration of Life: Studies in Modern Fiction*. New York: Sheed & Word, 1972. 77–97.

Nairn, Tom. *The Break-up of Britain: Crisis and Neonationalism*. London: NLB and Verso, 1981.

Najder, Zdzisław. *Życie Conrada-Korzeniowskiego*. Vols. 1 and 2. Warsaw: PWN, 1980.

Nietzsche, Friedrich. *Will to Power*. New York: Vintage, 1968.

Nowaczyński, Adolf. "Odrodzenie Erynu." *Dodatek do Świat* 9–10 (1907): 2.

———. "Polska w literaturze angielskiej." *Sfinks*, 1915. 60.

———. "Teatr irlandzki." *Szkice literackie*. Poznań: Ostoja, 1918. 61–70.

O'Malley, Patrick. *Catholicism, Sexual Deviance, and Victorian Gothic Culture*. Cambridge: Cambridge University Press, 2006.

Orr, John. "Joyce: The Lineaments of Desire." *The Making of the Twentieth-Century Novel*. London: Macmillan, 1987. 44–59.

O'Sullivan, Aidan. "Crannogs: Places of Resistance in the Contested Landscapes of Early Modern Ireland." *Contested Landscapes: Movement, Exile, and Place.* Ed. Barbara Bender and Margot Winer. Oxford: Berg, 2001. 87–102.

Otero, Solimar. "'Fearing Our Mothers': An Overview of the Psychoanalytic Theories Concerning the Vagina Dentata." *American Journal of Psychoanalysis* 56.3 (1996): 269–88.

Oxford English Reference Dictionary. 2nd ed. Ed. Judy Pearsall and Bill Trumble. Oxford: Oxford University Press, 1996.

Parins, James W., Robert J. Dilligan, and Todd K. Bender, eds. *A Concordance to Conrad's Nostromo.* New York: Garland, 1984.

Peake, C. H. *James Joyce: The Citizen and the Artist.* London: Edward Arnold, 1977.

Prażmowska, Anita J. *A History of Poland.* Palgrave Essential Histories. New York: Palgrave Macmillan, 2004.

Raleigh, John Henry. *The Chronicle of Leopold and Molly Bloom: Ulysses as Narrative.* Berkeley: University of California Press, 1977.

Rella, Franco. *The Myth of the Other: Lacan, Deluze, Foucault, Bataille.* Trans. Nelson Moe. Postmodern Positions 7. Washington, D.C.: Maisonneuve Press, 1994.

Rice, Thomas Jackson. *Cannibal Joyce.* Florida James Joyce Series. Gainesville: University Press of Florida, 2008.

———. "Condoms, Conrad, and Joyce." *Twenty-first Joyce.* Ed. Ellen Carol Jones and Morris Beja. Gainesville: University Press of Florida, 2004. 219–38.

———. *Joyce, Chaos, and Complexity.* Urbana: University of Illinois Press, 1997.

Rignall, John. *Realist Fiction and the Strolling Spectator.* London: Routledge, 1992.

Rolleston, T. W. *Celtic Myths and Legends.* New York: Dover, 1990.

———. *Ireland and Poland: A Comparison.* London: T. Fisher Unwin, 1917.

Rosenfield, Claire. *Paradise of Snakes: An Archetypal Analysis of Conrad's Political Novels.* Chicago: University of Chicago Press, 1967.

Rushdie, Salman. *Imaginary Homelands: Essays and Criticism, 1981–1991.* London: Granta Books, 1992.

Said, Edward. *Culture and Imperialism.* New York: Vintage Books, 1993.

———. *Orientalism.* New York: Vintage Books, 1994.

———. *Reflections on Exile and Other Essays.* Cambridge: Harvard University Press, 2002.

Sartre, Jean-Paul. *Colonialism and Neocolonialism.* Trans. Azzedine Haddour et al. London: Routledge, 2001.

Senn, Fritz. "Charting Elsewhereness: Erratic Interlocations." *Joyce's "Wandering Rocks."* Ed. Andrew Gibson and Steven Morrison. European Joyce Studies 12. Amsterdam: Rodopi, 2002. 155–86.

Shaffer, Brian W. "'The Commerce of Shady Wares': Politics and Pornography in Conrad's *The Secret Agent." ELH* 62.2 (1995): 443–66.

Spivak, Gayatri Chakravorty. "Subaltern Studies: Deconstructing Historiography." *Selected Subaltern Studies.* Oxford: Oxford University Press, 1988.

Swift, Jonathan. "Letter IV: A Letter to the Whole People of Ireland." *Drapier's Letters. The Works of Jonathan Swift: Tracts Relative to Ireland.* Vol. 6. London: Bickers and Son, 1883. 409–30.

wa Thiong'o, Ngũgĩ. *Moving the Centre: The Struggle for Cultural Freedoms*. London: James Currey, 1993.

Tindall, William York. *Forces in Modern British Literature, 1885–1946*. New York: Knopf, 1947.

Torrance, Robert M. *The Spiritual Quest: Transcendence in Myth, Religion, and Science*. Berkeley: University of California Press, 1994.

Turner, Victor. *Image and Pilgrimage in Christian Culture: Anthropological Perspectives*. New York: Columbia University Press, 1978.

———. *Process, Performance, and Pilgrimage: A Study in Comparative Symbology*. Ranchi Anthropology Series 1. New Delhi: Concept, 1979.

Voitkovska, Ludmilla. "Homecoming in *Nostromo*." *Nostromo: Centennial Essays*. Ed. Allan Simmons and J. H. Stape. Amsterdam: Rodopi, 2004. 31–48.

Watt, Ian. *Joseph Conrad: Nostromo*. Cambridge: Cambridge University Press, 1988.

Yeats, W. B. "The Second Coming." "The Song of Wandering Aengus." *The Collected Poems of W. B. Yeats*. Rev. 2nd ed. Ed. Richard J. Finneran. New York: Scribner Paperback Poetry, 1996.

Young, Gloria. "Quest and Discovery: Joseph Conrad's and Carl Jung's African Journeys." *Modern Fiction Studies* 28.4 (1982): 583–89.

Young, Robert J. C. "Sartre: The 'African Philosopher.'" *Colonialism and Neocolonialism*. By Jean-Paul Sartre. London: Routledge, 2001. vii–xxiv.

Index

and dangerous sexual practices, 65; as vagabond, 92

"An Outpost of Progress," 30; dream-like perceptions of, 31; ethnocentric discourse, 33

Outside and inside, dialectics of, 27

Pacifism, conflict over, 8

Parnell, 156, 173n3

Patriarchy, myths and imperialism, 17

Peake, C. H., 123

Peasant consciousness, 21

Penelope: Conrad and Joyce as combined figure, ix; Molly and, 144–45; Winnie compared, 108

Peregrinus, 96

Periphery, Ireland as, 59

Personal Record (Conrad), 9, 11

Phoenix Park murders, 157

Pilgrim: as a stranger, 96; Conmee as, 125; Conrad and Joyce as pathfinders, 2; derivation of term, 95–96; driving force, 91; Holloway on, 119; of modern era, 89; modernist, 147; modern versions, 116; as orderly, 134; origins of word, 128; *The Secret Agent* characters, 105–11; Stephen as, 127; subaltern pilgrim, 95–97

Pilgrimage: as absence from desire, 94; anti-pilgrimage, 153–55; approach to sacred, 151; archaic, 90; archaic passage toward center, 94; archaic quest for meaning, 91; attempt at self-discovery, 91; avoiding binaries, 5; challenge of, 121; changes to environment, 133; as competing discourses, 174n2; Conrad's personal, 98; Conrad's works, 150; control over space, 5; de Certeau on, 94; Delphi as destination, 122; desert, 120; incomplete, 148, 163; ineffective or incomplete, 163; issues summarized, 95; of Jews, 129–30; Jim, 100; Jim's, toward redemption, 104; Joyce's works, 150; liminal space, 100; margin towards center, 13; mock-pilgrimage, 155; modernity and, 87; modern lack of center, 94; nature of Bloom's, 135; nature of modernist, 94;

nature of progress, 131; negotiating realm of profane, 4; new forms, 90–91; power relations related, 97; primary nature, 94; as process of identity formation, 94; quest for self-recognition, 88; redefined, 111–17; redemption theme, 132; religious void in, 95; route to the sacred, 5; sacred and profane, 5, 166; as social power, 174n2; solely as sacred journey, 174n2; stages of, 89; telos and, 166; theory of, 88–89; "Third Space," 96; traditional, 88–90; *Ulysses* characters, 119

Player figure: Bauman on, 93; Bloom as, 146; Boylan as, 143–44; Heat as, 115–16; Joyce, 143; Kernan as, 144; Molly as, 145; *Secret Agent* characters, 115; Stephen as, 145–46

Pluralism, decenteredness related, 120

The Poetics of Space (Bachelard), 27

Pokorny, Julius, 137

Poland: affinities with Ireland, 7–8; Conrad's early experience, 29; Davies on, 169n6; as easy target, 10–11; Prussian views, 10; religion compared, 10; as unstable environment, 7–8

Polish, Conrad on, 149, 177n1

Polish nationalism: four elements, 11; Krajka on, 8; myth and literature, 79; Nowaczyński comparison, 9–10

Political journalism, 158–59

Postcolonial consciousness, 75–76

Postcolonial struggles, 54, 64, 69–71, 96

Postcolonial theory, Manichaeism, 170n8

Poststructuralists, 151

Power: in profane world of London, 117; theories of pilgrimage, 174n2

Power, location of: Conrad's delineations, 44; gender relations, 49; skin color and, 39–40; travel accounts, 33

Powerful, arbitrary divisions, 57

Power/knowledge mechanisms, 51

Power relations, 5; pilgrimage related, 97

The Practice of Everyday Life (de Certeau), 20, 72

Predestination, 44; Joyce on white man's, 57

Prescriptive space, 167

Agata Szczeszak-Brewer is associate professor of English at Wabash College and a recipient of the Bruce Harkness Young Conrad Scholar Award.

Wake Rites: The Ancient Irish Rituals of Finnegans Wake, by George Cinclair Gibson (2005)

Ulysses *in Critical Perspective*, edited by Michael Patrick Gillespie and A. Nicholas Fargnoli (2006)

Joyce and the Narrative Structure of Incest, by Jen Shelton (2006)

Joyce, Ireland, Britain, edited by Andrew Gibson and Len Platt (2006)

Joyce in Trieste: An Album of Risky Readings, edited by Sebastian D. G. Knowles, Geert Lernout, and John McCourt (2007)

Joyce's Rare View: The Nature of Things in Finnegans Wake, by Richard Beckman (2007)

Joyce's Misbelief, by Roy Gottfried (2007)

James Joyce's Painful Case, by Cóilín Owens (2008)

Cannibal Joyce, by Thomas Jackson Rice (2008)

Manuscript Genetics, Joyce's Know-How, Beckett's Nohow, by Dirk Van Hulle (2008)

Catholic Nostalgia in Joyce and Company, by Mary Lowe-Evans (2008)

A Guide through Finnegans Wake, by Edmund Lloyd Epstein (2009)

Bloomsday 100: Essays on Ulysses, edited by Morris Beja and Anne Fogarty (2009)

Joyce, Medicine, and Modernity, by Vike Martina Plock (2010; first paperback edition, 2012)

Who's Afraid of James Joyce?, by Karen R. Lawrence (2010; first paperback edition, 2012)

Ulysses *in Focus: Genetic, Textual, and Personal Views*, by Michael Groden (2010; first paperback edition, 2012)

Foundational Essays in James Joyce Studies, edited by Michael Patrick Gillespie (2011)

Empire and Pilgrimage in Conrad and Joyce, by Agata Szczeszak-Brewer (2011; first paperback edition, 2017)

The Poetry of James Joyce Reconsidered, edited by Marc C. Conner (2012; first paperback edition, 2015)

The German Joyce, by Robert K. Weninger (2012; first paperback edition 2016)

Joyce and Militarism, by Greg Winston (2012; first paperback edition, 2015)

Renascent Joyce, edited by Daniel Ferrer, Sam Slote, and André Topia (2013; first paperback edition, 2014)

Before Daybreak: "After the Race" and the Origins of Joyce's Art, by Cóilín Owens (2013; first paperback edition, 2014)

Modernists at Odds: Reconsidering Joyce and Lawrence, edited by Matthew J. Kochis and Heather L. Lusty (2015)

James Joyce and the Exilic Imagination, by Michael Patrick Gillespie (2015)

The Ecology of Finnegans Wake, by Alison Lacivita (2015)

Joyce's Allmaziful Plurabilities: Polyvocal Explorations of Finnegans Wake, edited by Kimberly J. Devlin and Christine Smedley (2015)

Exiles: A Critical Edition, by James Joyce, edited by A. Nicholas Fargnoli and Michael Patrick Gillespie (2016)

Up to Maughty London: Joyce's Cultural Capital in the Imperial Metropolis, by Eleni Loukopoulou (2017)

Joyce and the Law, edited by Jonathan Goldman (2017)